BIOGRAPHY

OF

THE LATE

MARGARET MILLER DAVIDSON.

BIOGRAPHY

AND

POETICAL REMAINS

OF THE LATE

MARGARET MILLER DAVIDSON.

BY WASHINGTON IRVING.

Thou wert unfit to dwell with clay,
For sin too pure, for earth too bright!
And Death, who call'd thee hence away,
Plac'd on his brow a gem of light!

MARGARET TO HER SISTER.

A New Edition, revised.

PHILADELPHIA:
LEA AND BLANCHARD.
1843.

Entered, according to the Act of Congress, in the year one thousand eight hundred and forty-one, by Washington Irving, in the Clerk's Office of the District Court of the United States for the Southern District of New York.

J. FAGAN, STEREOTYPER.

T. K. AND P. G. COLLINS, PRINTERS.

(12)

CONTENTS.

BIOGRAPHY

OF

MISS MARGARET DAVIDSON.

THE reading world has long set a cherishing value on the name of Lucretia Davidson, a lovely American girl, who, after giving early promise of rare poetic excellence, was snatched from existence in the seventeenth year of her age. An interesting biography of her by President Morse of the American Society of Arts, was published shortly after her death; another has since appeared from the classic pen of Miss Sedgwick, and her name has derived additional celebrity in Great Britain from an able article by Robert Southey, inserted some years since in the London Quarterly Review.

An intimate acquaintance in early life with some of the relatives of Miss Davidson had caused me, while in Europe, to read with great interest every thing concerning her; when, therefore, in 1833, about a year after my return to the United States, I was told, while in New York, that Mrs. Davidson, the mother of the deceased, was in the city and desirous of consulting me about a new edition of her daughter's works, I lost no time in waiting upon her. Her appearance corresponded with the interesting idea given of her in her daughter's biography; she was feeble and emaciated, and supported by pillows in an easy chair, but there were the lingerings of grace and beauty in her form and features, and her eye still gleamed with intelligence and sensibility.

While conversing with her on the subject of her daughter's works, I observed a young girl, apparently not more than eleven years of age, moving quietly about her; occasionally arranging a pillow, and at the same time listening earnestly to our conversation. There was an intellectual beauty about this child that struck me; and that was heightened by a blushing diffidence when Mrs. Davidson presented her to me as her daughter Margaret. Shortly afterwards, on her leaving the room, her mother, seeing that she had attracted my attention, spoke of her as having evinced the same early poetical talent that had distinguished her sister, and as evidence, showed me several copies of verses remarkable for such a child. On further inquiry I found that she had very nearly the same moral and physical constitution, and was prone to the same feverish excitement of the mind, and kindling of the imagination that had acted so powerfully on the fragile frame of her sister Lucretia. I cautioned the mother, therefore, against fostering her poetic vein, and advised such studies and pursuits as would tend to strengthen her judgment, calm and regulate the sensibilities, and enlarge that common sense which is the only safe foundation for all intellectual superstructure.

I found Mrs. Davidson fully aware of the importance of such a course of treatment, and disposed to pursue it, but saw at the same time that she would have difficulty to carry it into effect; having to contend with the additional excitement produced in the mind of this sensitive little being by the example of her sister, and the intense enthusiasm she evinced concerning her.

Three years elapsed before I again saw the subject of this memoir. She was then residing with her mother at a rural retreat in the neighbourhood of New York. The interval that had elapsed had rapidly developed the powers of her mind, and heightened the loveliness of her person, but my apprehensions had been verified. The soul was wearing out the body. Preparations were making to take her on a tour for the benefit of her health, and her mother appeared to flatter herself that it might prove efficacious; but when I noticed the fragile delicacy of her form, the hectic bloom of her cheek, and the almost unearthly lustre of her eye, I felt convinced that she was not long for this world; in truth, she already appeared more spiritual than mortal. We parted, and I never saw her more. Within three years afterwards, a number of manuscripts were placed in my hands, as all that was left of her. They were accompanied by copious memoranda concerning her, furnished by her mother at my request. From these I have digested and arranged the following particulars, adopting in many places the original manuscript, without alteration. In fact, the narrative will be found almost as illustrative of the character of the mother as of the child; they were singularly identified in taste, feelings, and pursuits; tenderly entwined together by maternal and filial affection; they reflected an inexpressibly touching grace and interest upon each other by this holy relationship, and, to my mind, it would be marring one of the most beautiful and affecting groups in the history of modern literature, to sunder them.

Margaret Miller Davidson, the youngest daughter of Dr. Oliver and Mrs. Margaret Davidson, was born at the family residence on Lake Champlain, in the village of Plattsburgh, on the 26th of March, 1823. She evinced fragility of constitution from her very birth. Her sister Lucretia, whose brief poetical career has been so celebrated in literary history, was her early and fond attendant, and some of her most popular lays were composed with the infant sporting in her arms. She used to gaze upon her little sister with intense delight, and, remarking the uncommon brightness and beauty of her eyes, would exclaim, "She must, she will be a poet!" The exclamation was natural enough in an enthusiastic girl who regarded every thing through the medium of her ruling passion; but it was treasured up by her mother, and considered almost prophetic. Lucretia did not live to see her prediction verified. Her brief sojourn upon earth was over before Margaret was quite two years and a half old; yet to use her mother's fond expressions, "On ascending to the skies, it seemed as if her poetic mantle fell like a robe of light on her infant sister."

Margaret, from the first dawnings of intellect, gave evidence of being no common child: her ideas and expressions were not like those of other children, and often startled by their precocity. Her sister's death had made a strong impression on her, and, though so extremely young, she already understood and appreciated Lucretia's character. An evidence of this, and of the singular precocity of thought and expression just noticed, occurred but a few months afterwards. As Mrs. Davidson was seated, at twilight, conversing with a female friend, Margaret entered the room with a light elastic step, for which she was remarked.

"That child never walks," said the lady; then turning to her, "Margaret, where are you flying now?" said she.

"To heaven!" replied she, pointing up with her finger, "to meet my sister Lucretia, when I get my new wings."

"Your new wings! When will you get them?"

"Oh soon, very soon; and then I shall fly!"

"She loved," says her mother, "to sit hour after hour on a cushion at my feet, her little arms resting upon my lap, and her full dark eyes fixed upon mine, listening to anecdotes of her sister's life and details of the events which preceded her death, often exclaiming, while her face beamed with mingled emotions, 'Oh mamma, I will try to fill her place! Oh teach me to be like her!'"

Much of Mrs. Davidson's time was now devoted to her daily instruction; noticing, however, her lively sensibility, the rapid developement of her mind, and her eagerness for knowledge, her lessons were entirely oral, for she feared for the present to teach her to read, lest by too early and severe application, she should injure her delicate frame. She had nearly attained her fourth year before she was taught to spell. Ill health then obliged Mrs. Davidson, for the space of a year, to entrust her tuition to a lady in Canada, a valued friend, who had other young girls under her care. When she returned home she could read fluently, and had commenced lessons in writing. It was now decided that she should not be placed in any public seminary, but that her education should be conducted by her mother. The task was rendered delightful by the docility of the pupil; by her affectionate feelings, and quick kindling sensibilities. This maternal instruction, while it kept her apart from the world, and fostered a singular purity and innocence of thought, contributed greatly to enhance her imaginative powers, for the mother partook largely of the poetical temperament of the child; it was, in fact, one poetical spirit ministering to another.

Among the earliest indications of the poetical character in this child were her perceptions of the beauty of natural scenery. Her home was in a picturesque neighbourhood, calculated to awaken and foster such perceptions. The following description of it is taken from one of her own writings: "There stood on the banks of the Saranac a small neat cottage, which peeped forth from the surrounding foliage, the image of rural quiet and contentment. An old-fashioned piazza extended along the front, shaded with vines and honeysuckles; the turf on the bank of the river was of the richest and brightest emerald; and the wild rose and sweet briar, which twined over the neat enclosure, seemed to bloom with more delicate freshness and perfume within the bounds of this earthly paradise. The scenery around was wildly yet beautifully romantic; the clear blue river glancing and sparkling at its feet, seemed only as a preparation for another and more magnificent view, when the stream, gliding on to the west, was buried in the broad white bosom of Champlain, which stretched back wave after wave in the distance, until lost in faint blue mists that veiled the sides of its guardian mountains, seeming more lovely from their indistinctness."

Such were the natural scenes which presented themselves to her dawning perceptions, and she is said to have evinced from her earliest childhood, a remarkable sensibility to their charms. A beautiful tree, or shrub, or flower, would fill her with delight; she would note with surprising discrimination the various effects of the weather upon the surrounding landscape; the mountains wrapped in clouds; the torrents roaring down their sides in times of tempest; the "bright warm sunshine," the "cooling showers," the "pale cold moon," for such was already her poetical phraseology. A bright starlight night, also, would seem to awaken a mysterious rapture in her infant bosom, and one of her early expressions in speaking of the stars was, that they "shone like the eyes of angels."

One of the most beautiful parts of the maternal instruction was in guiding these kindling perceptions from nature up to nature's God.

"I cannot say," observes her mother, "at what age her religious impressions were imbibed. They seemed to be interwoven with her existence. From the very first exercise of reason she evinced strong devotional feelings, and although she loved play, she would at any time prefer seating herself beside me, and, with every faculty absorbed in the subject, listen while I attempted to recount the wonders of Providence, and point out the wisdom and benevolence of God, as manifested in the works of creation. Her young heart would swell with rapture, and the tear would tremble in her eye, when I explained to her, that he who clothed the trees with verdure, and gave the rose its bloom, had also created her with capacities to enjoy their beauties: that the same power which clothed the mountains with sublimity, made her happiness his daily care. Thus a sentiment of gratitude and affection towards the Creator entered into all her emotions of delight at the wonders and beauties of creation."

There is nothing more truly poetical than religion when properly inculcated, and it will be found that this early piety, thus amiably instilled, had the happiest effect upon her throughout life; elevating and ennobling her genius; lifting her above every thing gross and sordid; attuning her thoughts to pure and lofty themes; heightening rather than impairing her enjoyments, and at all times giving an ethereal lightness to her spirit. To use her mother's words, "she was like a bird on the wing, her fairy-form scarcely seemed to touch the earth as she passed." She was at times in a kind of ecstasy from the excitement of her imagination and the exuberance of her pleasurable sensations. In such moods every object of natural beauty inspired a degree of rapture, always mingled with a feeling of gratitude to the Being "who had made so many beautiful things for her." In such moods too her little heart would overflow with love to all around; indeed, adds her mother, to love and be beloved was necessary to her existence. Private prayer became a habit with her at a very early age; it was almost a spontaneous expression of her feelings, the breathings of an affectionate and delighted heart.

"By the time she was six years old," says Mrs. Davidson, "her language assumed an elevated tone, and her mind seemed filled with poetic imagery, blended with veins of religious thought. At this period I was chiefly confined to my room by debility. She was my companion and friend, and, as the greater part of my time was devoted to her instruction, she advanced rapidly in her studies. She read not only well, but elegantly. Her love of reading amounted almost to a passion, and her intelligence surpassed belief. Strangers viewed with astonishment a child little more than six years old reading with enthusiastic delight Thomson's Seasons, the Pleasures of Hope, Cowper's Task, the writings of Milton, Byron, and Scott, and marking, with taste and discrimination, the passages which struck her. The sacred writings were her daily studies; with her little Bible on her lap, she usually seated herself near me, and there read a chapter from the holy volume. This was a duty which she was taught not to perform lightly, and we have frequently spent two hours in reading and remarking upon the contents of a chapter."

A tendency to "lisp in numbers," was observed in her about this time. She frequently made little impromptus in rhyme, without seeming to be conscious that there was any thing peculiar in the habit. On one occasion, while standing by a window at which her mother was seated, and looking out upon a lovely landscape, she exclaimed—

"See those lofty, those grand trees;
Their high tops waving in the breeze;
They cast their shadows on the ground,
And spread their fragrance all around."

Her mother, who had several times been struck by little rhyming ejaculations of the kind, now handed her writing implements, and requested her to write down what she had just uttered. She appeared surprised at the request, but complied; writing it down as if it had been prose, without arranging it in a stanza, or commencing the lines with capitals; not seeming aware that she had rhymed. The notice attracted to this impromptu, however, had its effect, whether for good or for evil. From that time she wrote some scraps of poetry, or rather rhyme, every day, which would be treasured up with delight by her mother, who watched with trembling, yet almost fascinated anxiety, these premature blossomings of poetic fancy.

On another occasion, towards sunset, as Mrs. Davidson was seated by the window of her bed-room, little Margaret ran in, greatly excited, exclaiming that there was an awful thundergust rising, and that the clouds were black as midnight.

"I gently drew her to my bosom," says Mrs. Davidson, "and after I had soothed her agitation, she seated herself at my feet, laid her head in my lap, and gazed at the rising storm. As the thunder rolled, she clung closer to my knees, and when the tempest burst in all its fury, I felt her tremble. I passed my arms round her, but soon found it was not fear that agitated her. Her eyes kindled as she watched the warring elements, until, extending her hand, she exclaimed,

"The lightning plays along the sky,
The thunder rolls and bursts from high!
Jehovah's voice amid the storm
I heard—methinks I see his form,
As riding on the clouds of even,
He spreads his glory o'er the heaven.

This likewise her mother made her write down at the instant; thus giving additional impulse to this growing inclination.

I shall select one more instance of this early facility at numbers, especially as it involves a case of conscience, creditable to her early powers of self-examination. She had been reproved by her mother for some trifling act of disobedience, but aggravated her fault by attempting to justify it; she was, therefore, banished to her bed-room until she should become sensible of her error. Two hours elapsed, without her evincing any disposition to yield: on the contrary, she persisted in vindicating her conduct, and accused her mother of injustice.

Mrs. Davidson mildly reasoned with her; entreated her to examine the spirit by which she was actuated; placed before her the example of our Saviour in submitting to the will of his parents; and, exhorting her to pray to God to assist her, and to give her meekness and humility, left her again to her reflections.

"An hour or two afterwards," says Mrs. Davidson, "she desired I would admit her. I sent word that, when she was in a proper frame of mind I would be glad to see her. The little creature came in, bathed in tears, threw her arms round my neck, and sobbing violently, put into my hands the following verses:

"Forgiven by my Saviour dear,
For all the wrongs I 've done,
What other wish could I have here?
Alas there yet is one.

I know my God has pardon'd me,
I know he loves me still;
I wish forgiven I may be,
By her I 've used so ill.

Good resolutions I have made,
And thought I loved my Lord;
But ah! I trusted in myself,
And broke my foolish word.

But give me strength, oh Lord, to trust
For help alone in thee;
Thou know'st my inmost feelings best,
Oh teach me to obey."

We have spoken of the buoyancy of Margaret's feelings, and the vivid pleasure she received from external objects; she entered, however, but little into the amusements of the few children with whom she associated, nor did she take much delight in their society; she was conscious of a difference between them and herself, but scarce knew in what it consisted. Their sports seemed to divert for a while, but soon wearied her, and she would fly to a book, or seek the conversation of persons of maturer age and mind. Her highest pleasures were intellectual. She seemed to live in a world of her own creation, surrounded by the images of her own fancy. Her own childish amusements had originality and freshness, and called into action the mental powers, so as to render them interesting to persons of all ages. If at play with her little dog or kitten, she would carry on imaginary dialogues between them; always ingenious, and sometimes even brilliant. If her doll happened to be the plaything of the moment, it was invested with a character exhibiting knowledge of history, and all the powers of memory which a child can be supposed to exercise. Whether it was Mary Queen of Scots, or her rival, Elizabeth, or the simple cottage maiden, each character was maintained with propriety. In telling stories, (an amusement all children are fond of,) hers were always original, and of a kind calculated to elevate the minds of the children present, giving them exalted views of truth, honour, and integrity; and the sacrifice of all selfish feelings to the happiness of others was illustrated in the heroine of her story.

This talent for extemporaneous story-telling increased with exercise, until she would carry on a narrative for hours together; and in nothing was the precocity of her inventive powers more apparent than in the discrimination and individuality of her fictitious characters; the consistency with which they were sustained; the graphic force of her descriptions; the elevation of her sentiments, and the poetic beauty of her imagery.

This early gift caused her to be sought by some of the neighbours; who would lead her unconsciously into an exertion of her powers. Nothing was done by her from vanity or a disposition to "show off," but she would become excited by their attention and the pleasure they seemed to derive from her narration. When thus excited, a whole evening would be occupied by one of her stories; and when the servant came to take her home, she would observe, in the phraseology of the magazines, "the story to be continued in our next."

Between the age of six and seven she entered upon a course of English grammar, geography, history, and rhetoric, still under the direction and superintendence of her mother; but such was her ardour and application, that it was necessary to keep her in check, lest a too intense pursuit of knowledge should impair her delicate constitution. She was not required to commit her lessons to memory, but to give the substance of them in her own language, and to explain their purport; thus she learnt nothing by rote, but every thing understandingly, and soon acquired a knowledge of the rudiments of English education. The morning lessons completed, the rest of the day was devoted to recreation; occasionally sporting and gathering wild flowers on the banks of the Saranac; though the extreme delicacy of her constitution prevented her taking as much exercise as her mother could have wished.

In 1830 an English gentleman, who had been strongly interested and affected by the perusal of the biography and writings of Lucretia Davidson, visited Plattsburgh, in the course of a journey from Quebec to New York, to see the place where she was born and had been buried. While there, he sought an interview with Mrs. Davidson, and his appearance and deportment were such as at once to inspire respect and confidence. He had much to ask about the object of his literary pilgrimage, but his inquiries were managed with the most considerate delicacy. While he was thus conversing with Mrs. Davidson, the little Margaret, then about seven years of age, came tripping into the room, with a book in one hand and a pencil in the other. He was charmed with her bright intellectual countenance, but still more with finding that the volume in her hand was a copy of Thomson's Seasons, in which she had been marking with a pencil the passages which most pleased her. He drew her to him; his frank, winning manner soon banished her timidity; he engaged her in conversation, and found, to his astonishment, a counterpart of Lucretia Davidson before him. His visit was necessarily brief; but his manners, appearance, and conversation, and, above all, the extraordinary interest with which he had regarded her, sank deep in the affectionate heart of the child, and inspired a friendship that remained one of her strongest attachments through the residue of her transient existence.

The delicate state of her health this summer rendered it advisable to take her to the Saratoga Springs, the waters of which appeared to have a beneficial effect. After remaining here some time, she accompanied her parents to New York. It was her first visit to the city, and of course, fruitful of wonder and excitement; a new world seemed to open before her; new scenes, new friends, new occupations, new sources of instruction and enjoyment; her young heart was overflowing, and her head giddy with delight. To complete her happiness, she again met with her English friend, whom she greeted with as much eagerness and joy as if he had been a companion of her own age. He manifested the same interest in her that he had shown at Plattsburgh, and took great pleasure in accompanying her to many of the exhibitions and places of intellectual gratification of the metropolis, and marking their effects upon her fresh, unhackneyed feelings and intelligent mind. In company with him, she, for the first and only time in her life, visited the theatre. It was a scene of magic to her, or rather, as she said, like a "brilliant dream." She often recurred to it with vivid recollection, and the effect of it upon her imagination was subsequently apparent in the dramatic nature of some of her writings.

One of her greatest subjects of regret on leaving New York, was the parting with her intellectual English friend; but she was consoled by his promising to pay Plattsburgh another visit, and to pass a few days there previous to his departure for England. Soon after returning to Plattsburgh, however, Mrs. Davidson received a letter from him saying that he was unexpectedly summoned home, and would have to defer his promised visit until his return to the United States.

It was a severe disappointment to Margaret, who had conceived for him an enthusiastic friendship remarkable in such a child. His letter was accompanied by presents of books and various tasteful remembrances, but the sight of them only augmented her affliction. She wrapped them all carefully in paper, and treasured them up in a particular drawer, where they were daily visited, and many a tear shed over them.

The excursions to Saratoga and New York had improved her health, and given a fresh impulse to her mind. She resumed her studies with great eagerness; her spirits rose with mental exercise; she soon was in one of her veins of intellectual excitement. She read, she wrote, she danced, she sang, and was for the time the happiest of the happy. In the freshness of early morning, and towards sunset, when the heat of the day was over, she would stroll on the banks of the Saranac, following its course to where it pours itself into the beautiful Bay of Cumberland in Lake Champlain. There the rich variety of scenery which bursts upon the eye; the islands, scattered, like so many gems, on the broad bosom of the lake; the Green Mountains of Vermont beyond, clothed in the atmospherical charms of our magnificent climate; all these would inspire a degree of poetic rapture in her mind, mingled with a sacred melancholy; for these were scenes which had often awakened the enthusiasm of her deceased sister Lucretia.

Her mother, in her memoranda, gives a picture of her in one of those excited moods.

"After an evening's stroll along the river bank, we seated ourselves by a window to observe the effect of the full moon rising over the waters. A holy calm seemed to pervade all nature. With her head resting on my bosom, and her eyes fixed on the firmament, she pointed to a particularly bright star, and said:

"'Behold that bright and sparkling star
Which setteth as a queen afar:
Over the blue and spangled heaven
It sheds its glory in the even!

"'Our Jesus made that sparkling star
Which shines and twinkles from afar.
Oh! 't was that bright and glorious gem
Which shone o'er ancient Bethlehem!'"

"The summer passed swiftly away," continues her mother, "yet her intellectual advances seemed to outstrip the wings of time. As the autumn approached, however, I could plainly perceive that her health was again declining. The chilly winds from the lake were too keen for her weak lungs. My own health, too, was failing; it was determined, therefore, that we should pass the winter with my eldest daughter, Mrs. T——, who resided in Canada, in the same latitude it is true, but in an inland situation. This arrangement was very gratifying to Margaret; and, had my health improved by the change, as her own did, she would have been perfectly happy. During this period she attended to a regular course of study, under my direction; for, though confined wholly to my bed, and suffering extremely from pain and debility, Heaven in mercy preserved my mental faculties from the wreck that disease had made of my physical powers." The same plan as heretofore was pursued. Nothing was learnt by rote, and the lessons were varied to prevent fatigue and distaste, though study was always with her a pleasing duty rather than an arduous task. After she had studied her lessons by herself, she would discuss them in conversation with her mother. Her reading was under the same guidance. "I selected her books," says Mrs. Davidson, "with much care, and to my surprise found that, notwithstanding her poetical temperament, she had a high relish for history, and that she would read with as much apparent interest an abstruse treatise that called forth the reflecting powers, as she did poetry or works of the imagination. In polite literature Addison was her favourite author, but Shakspeare she dwelt upon with enthusiasm. She was restricted, however, to certain marked portions of this inimitable writer; and having been told that it was not proper for her to read the whole, such was her innate delicacy and her sense of duty, that she never overstepped the prescribed boundaries."

In the intervals of study she amused herself with drawing, for which she had a natural talent, and soon began to sketch with considerable skill. As her health had improved since her removal to Canada, she frequently partook of the favourite winter recreation of a drive in a traineau or sleigh, in company with her sister and her brother-in-law, and completely enveloped in furs and buffalo-robes; and nothing put her in a finer flow of spirits, than thus skimming along, in bright January weather, on the sparkling snow, to the merry music of the jingling sleigh-bells. The winter passed away without any improvement in the health of Mrs. Davidson; indeed she continued a helpless invalid, confined to her bed, for eighteen months; during all which time little Margaret was her almost constant companion and attendant.

"Her tender solicitude," writes Mrs. Davidson, "endeared her to me beyond any other earthly thing; although under the roof of a beloved and affectionate daughter, and having constantly with me an experienced and judicious nurse, yet the soft and gentle voice of my little darling, was more than medicine to my worn-out frame. If her delicate hand smoothed my pillow, it was soft to my aching temples, and her sweet smile would cheer me in the lowest depths of despondency. She would draw for me—read to me—and often, when writing at her little table, would surprise me by some tribute of love, which never failed to operate as a cordial to my heart. At a time when my life was despaired of, she wrote the following lines while sitting at my bed—

"'I'll to thy arms in rapture fly,
And wipe the tear that dims thine eye;
Thy pleasure will be my delight,
Till thy pure spirit takes its flight.

"'When left alone—when thou art gone,
Yet still I will not feel alone;
Thy spirit still will hover near,
And guard thy orphan daughter dear!'"

In this trying moment, when Mrs. Davidson herself had given up all hope of recovery, one of the most touching sights was to see this affectionate and sensitive child tasking herself to achieve a likeness of her mother, that it might remain with her as a memento. " How often would she sit by my bed," says Mrs. Davidson, "striving to sketch features that had been vainly attempted by more than one finished artist; and when she found that she had failed, and that the likeness could not be recognised, she would put her arms around my neck and weep, and say, 'Oh dear mamma, I shall lose you, and not even a sketch of your features will be left me! and if I live to be a woman, perhaps I shall even forget how you looked!' This idea gave her great distress, sweet lamb! I then little thought this bosom would have been her dying pillow!"

After being reduced to the very verge of the grave, Mrs. Davidson began slowly to recover, but a long time elapsed before she was restored to her usual degree of health. Margaret in the meantime increased in strength and stature; she still looked fragile and delicate, but she was always cheerful and buoyant. To relieve the monotony of her life, which had been passed too much in a sick chamber, and to preserve her spirits fresh and elastic, little excursions were devised for her about the country, to Missique Bay, St. Johns, Alburgh, Champlain, &c. The following lines, addressed to her mother on one of these occasional separations, will serve as a specimen of her compositions in this the eighth year of her age, and of the affectionate current of her feelings.

" Farewell, dear mother! for a while
I must resign thy plaintive smile;
May angels watch thy couch of woe,
And joys unceasing round thee flow.

" May the Almighty Father spread
His sheltering wings above thy head;
It is not long that we must part,
Then cheer thy downcast, drooping heart.

" Remember, oh remember me,
Unceasing is my love for thee;
When death shall sever earthly ties,
When thy loved form all senseless lies.

" Oh that my soul with thine could flee,
And roam through wide eternity;
Could tread with thee the courts of heaven,
And count the brilliant stars of even!

"Farewell, dear mother! for a while
I must resign thy plaintive smile;
May angels watch thy couch of woe,
And joys unceasing round thee flow."

In the month of January, 1833, while still in Canada, she was brought very low by an attack of scarlet fever, under which she lingered many weeks, but had so far recovered by the middle of April as to take the air in a carriage. Her mother, too, having regained sufficient strength to travel, it was thought advisable, for both their healths, to try the effect of a journey to New York. They accordingly departed about the beginning of May, accompanied by a family party. Of this journey, and a sojourn of several months in New York, she kept a journal, which evinces considerable habits of observation, but still more that kindling of the imagination which, in the poetic mind, gives to commonplace realities the witchery of romance. She was deeply interested by visits to the "School for the Blind," and the "Deaf and Dumb Asylum;" and makes a minute of a visit of a very different nature—to Black Hawk and his fellow-chiefs, prisoners of war, who, by command of government, were taken about through various of our cities, that they might carry back to their brethren in the wilderness, a cautionary idea of the overwhelming power of the white man.

"On the 25th June I saw and shook hands with the famous Black Hawk, the Indian chief, the enemy of our nation, who has massacred our patriots, murdered our women and helpless children! Why is he treated with so much attention by those whom he has injured? It cannot surely arise from benevolence. It must be *policy*. Be it what it may, I cannot understand it. His son, the Prophet, and others who accompanied him, interested *me* more than the chief himself. His son is no doubt a fine specimen of Indian beauty. He has a high brow, piercing black eyes, long black hair, which hangs down his back, and, upon the whole, is well suited to captivate an Indian maiden. The Prophet we found surveying himself in a looking-glass, undoubtedly wishing to show himself off to the best advantage in the fair assembly before him. The rest were dozing on a sofa, but they were awakened sufficiently to shake hands with us, and others who had the courage to approach so near them. I remember I dreamed of them the following night."

During this visit to New York, she was the life and delight

of the relatives with whom she resided, and they still retain a lively recollection of the intellectual nature of her sports among her youthful companions, and of the surprising aptness and fertile invention displayed by her in contriving new sources of amusement. She had a number of playmates, nearly of her own age, and one of her projects was to get up a dramatic entertainment for the gratification of themselves and their friends. The proposal was readily agreed to, provided she would write the play. This she readily undertook, and indeed devised and directed the whole arrangements, though she had never been but once to a theatre, and that on her previous visit to New York. Her little companions were now all busily employed, under her direction, preparing dresses and equipments; robes with trains were fitted out for the female characters, and quantities of paper and tinsel were consumed in making caps, helmets, spears, and sandals.

After four or five days had been spent in these preparations, Margaret was called upon to produce the play. "Oh!" she replied, "I have not written it yet."—"But how is this! Do you make the dresses first, and then write the play to suit them?"—"Oh!" replied she gaily, "the writing of the play is the easiest part of the preparation; it will be ready before the dresses." And, in fact, in two days she produced her drama, "The Tragedy of Alethia." It was not very voluminous, to be sure, but it contained within it sufficient of high character and astounding and bloody incident to furnish out a drama of five times its size. A king and queen of England resolutely bent upon marrying their daughter, the Princess Alethia, to the Duke of Ormond. The princess most perversely and dolorously in love with a mysterious cavalier, who figures at her father's court under the name of Sir Percy Lennox, but who, in private truth, is the Spanish king, Rodrigo, thus obliged to maintain an incognito on account of certain hostilities between Spain and England. The odious nuptials of the princess with the Duke of Ormond proceed: she is led, a submissive victim, to the altar; is on the point of pledging her irrevocable word; when the priest throws off his sacred robe, discovers himself to be Rodrigo, and plunges a dagger into the bosom of the king. Alethia instantly plucks the dagger from her father's bosom, throws herself into Rodrigo's arms, and kills herself. Rodrigo flies to a cavern, renounces England, Spain, and his royal throne, and devotes himself to eternal remorse. The queen ends the play by a passionate apostrophe to the spirit of her daughter, and sinks dead on the floor.

The little drama lies before us, a curious specimen of the prompt talent of this most ingenious child, and by no means more incongruous in its incidents than many current dramas by veteran and experienced playwrights.

The parts were now distributed and soon learnt; Margaret drew out a play-bill, in theatrical style, containing a list of the dramatis personæ, and issued regular tickets of admission. The piece went off with universal applause: Margaret figuring, in a long train, as the princess, and killing herself in a style that would not have disgraced an experienced stage heroine.

In these, and similar amusements, her time passed happily in New York, for it was the study of the intelligent and amiable relatives with whom she sojourned, to render her residence among them as agreeable and profitable as possible. Her visit, however, was protracted much beyond what was originally intended. As the summer advanced, the heat and restraint of the city became oppressive; her heart yearned after her native home on the Saranac; and the following lines, written at the time, express the state of her feelings—

HOME.

I would fly from the city, would fly from its care,
To my own native plants and my flow'rets so fair;
To the cool grassy shade, and the rivulet bright,
Which reflects the pale moon on its bosom of light.
Again would I view the old mansion so dear,
Where I sported, a babe, without sorrow or fear;
I would leave this great city, so brilliant and gay,
For a peep at my home on this fine summer day.
I have friends whom I love and would leave with regret,
But the love of my home, oh, 't is tenderer yet!
There a sister reposes unconscious in death—
'T was there she first drew and there yielded her breath—
A father I love is away from me now—
Oh could I but print a sweet kiss on his brow,
Or smooth the grey locks, to my fond heart so dear,
How quickly would vanish each trace of a tear!
Attentive I listen to pleasure's gay call,
But my own darling home, it is dearer than all.

At length, late in the month of October, the travellers turned their faces homewards; but it was not the "darling home" for which Margaret had been longing: her native cottage on the beautiful banks of the Saranac. The wintry winds from Lake Champlain had been pronounced too severe for her constitution, and the family residence had been reluctantly changed to the village of Ballston. Margaret felt this change most deeply. We have already shown the tender as well as poetical associations that linked her heart to the beautiful home of her childhood; a presentiment seemed to come over her mind that she would never see it more; a presentiment unfortunately prophetic. She was now accustomed to give prompt utterance to her emotions in rhyme, and the following lines, written at the time, remain a touching record of her feelings—

MY NATIVE LAKE.

Thy verdant banks, thy lucid stream,
Lit by the sun's resplendent beam,
Reflect each bending tree so light
Upon thy bounding bosom bright,
Could I but see thee once again,
My own, my beautiful Champlain!

The little isles that deck thy breast,
And calmly on thy bosom rest,
How often, in my childish glee,
I've sported round them, bright and free!
Could I but see thee once again,
My own, my beautiful Champlain!

How oft I've watch'd the fresh'ning shower
Bending the summer tree and flower,
And felt my little heart beat high
As the bright rainbow graced the sky.
Could I but see thee once again,
My own, my beautiful Champlain!

And shall I never see thee more,
My native lake, my much-loved shore?
And must I bid a long adieu,
My dear, my infant home, to you?
Shall I not see thee once again,
My own, my beautiful Champlain?

Still, though disappointed at not returning to the Saranac, she soon made herself contented at Ballston. She was at home, in the bosom of her own family, and reunited to her two youngest brothers, from whom she had long been separated. A thousand little plans were devised by her, and some few of them put in execution, for their mutual pleasure and improvement. One of the most characteristic of these was a "weekly paper," issued by her in manuscript, and entitled "The Juvenile Aspirant." All their domestic occupations and amusements were of an intellectual kind. Their mornings were spent in study; the evenings enlivened by conversation, or by the work of some favourite author, read aloud for the benefit of the family circle.

As the powers of this excitable and imaginative little being developed themselves, Mrs. Davidson felt more and more conscious of the responsibility of undertaking to cultivate and direct them; yet to whom could she confide her that would so well understand her character and constitution? To place her in a boarding-school would subject her to increased excitement, caused by emulation, and her mind was already too excitable for her fragile frame. Her peculiar temperament required peculiar culture; it must neither be stimulated nor checked; and while her imagination was left to its free soarings, care must be taken to strengthen her judgment, improve her mind, establish her principles, and inculcate habits of self-examination and self-control. All this, it was thought, might best be accomplished under a mother's eye; it was resolved, therefore, that her education should, as before, be conducted entirely at home. "Thus she continued," to use her mother's words, "to live in the bosom of affection, where every thought and feeling was reciprocated. I strove to draw out the powers of her mind by conversation and familiar remarks upon subjects of daily study and reflection, and taught her the necessity of bringing all her thoughts, desires and feelings under the dominion of reason; to understand the importance of self-control, when she found her inclinations were at war with its dictates. To fulfil all her duties from a conviction of right, because they were duties; and to find her happiness in the consciousness of her own integrity, and the approbation of God. How delightful was the task of instructing a mind like hers! She seized with avidity upon every new idea, for the instruction proceeded from lips of love. Often would she exclaim, 'Oh mamma! how glad I am that you are not too ill to teach me! Surely I am the happiest girl in the world!' She had read much for a child of little more than ten years of age. She was well versed in both ancient and modern history, (that is to say, in the courses generally prescribed for the use of schools,) Blair, Kaimes, and Paley had formed part of her studies. She was familiar with most of the British poets. Her command of the English language was remarkable, both in conversation and writing. She had learned the rudiments of French, and was anxious to become perfect in the language; but I had so neglected my duty in this respect after I left school, that I was not qualified to instruct her. A friend, however, who understood French, called occasionally and gave her lessons for his own amusement; she soon translated well, and such was her talent for the acquisition of languages, and such her desire to read every thing in the original, that every obstacle vanished before her perseverance. She made some advances in Latin, also, in company with her brother, who was attended by a private teacher; and they were engaged upon the early books of Virgil, when her health again gave way, and she was confined to her room by severe illness. These frequent attacks upon a frame so delicate awakened all our fears. Her illness spread a gloom throughout our habitation, for fears were entertained that it would end in a pulmonary consumption." After a confinement of two months, however, she regained her usual, though at all times fragile, state of health. In the following spring, when she had just entered upon the eleventh year of her age, intelligence arrived of the death of her sister, Mrs. T., who had been resident in Canada. The blow had been apprehended from previous accounts of her extreme illness, but it was a severe shock. She had looked up to this sister as to a second mother, and as to one who, from the precarious health of her natural parent, might be called upon to fulfil that tender office. She was one also calculated to inspire affection; lovely in person, refined and intelligent in mind, still young in years; and with all this, her only remaining sister! In the following lines, poured out in the fulness of her grief, she touchingly alludes to the previous loss of her sister Lucretia, so often the subject of her poetic regrets, and of the consolation she had always felt in still having a sister to love and cherish her.

ON THE DEATH OF MY SISTER ANNA ELIZA.

While weeping o'er our sister's tomb,
And heaving many a heartfelt sigh,
And while in youth's bewitching bloom,
I thought not that thou too couldst die.

When gazing on that little mound,
Spread o'er with turf, and flowers, and mould,
I thought not that thy lovely form
Could be as motionless and cold.

When her light, airy form was lost
To fond affection's weeping eye,
I thought not we should mourn for thee,
I thought not that thou too couldst die.

Yes, sparkling gem! when thou wert here,
From death's encircling mantle free,
Our mourning parents wiped each tear,
And cried, "Why weep? we still have thee."

Each tender thought on thee they turn'd,
Each hope of joy to thee was given,
And, dwelling on each matchless charm,
They half forgot the saint in heaven.

But thou art gone, for ever gone!
Sweet wanderer in a world of woe!
Now, unrestrained our grief must pour;
Uncheck'd our mourning tears must flow.

How oft I've pressed my glowing lip
In rapture to thy snowy brow,
And gazed upon that angel eye,
Closed in death's chilling slumber now!

While tottering on the verge of life,
Thine every nerve with pain unstrung,
That beaming eye was raised to heaven,
That heart to God for safety clung.

And when the awful moment came,
Replete with trembling hope and fear,
Though anguish shook thy slender frame,
Thy thoughts were in a brighter sphere.

The wreath of light which round thee play'd,
Bore thy pure spirit to the skies;
With thee we lost our brightest gem,
But heaven has gained a glorious prize.

Oh may the bud of promise left,
Follow the brilliant path she trod,
And of her fostering care bereft,
Still seek and find his mother's God.

But he, the partner of her life,
Who shared her joy and soothed her woe,
How can I heal his broken heart?
How bid his sorrow cease to flow?

It's only time these wounds can heal;
Time, from whose piercing pangs alone
The poignancy of grief can steal,
And hush the heart's convulsive moan.

To parry the effect of this most afflicting blow, Margaret was sent on a visit to New York, where she passed a couple of months in the society of affectionate and intelligent friends, and returned home in June, recruited in health and spirits. The sight of her mother, however, though habituated to sorrow and suffering, yet bowed down by her recent bereavement, called forth her tenderest sympathies; and we consider it as illustrating the progress of the intellect and the history of the heart of this most interesting child, to insert another effusion called forth by this domestic calamity:

TO MY MOTHER OPPRESSED WITH SORROW.

Weep, oh my mother! I will bid thee weep!
For grief like thine requires the aid of tears;
But oh, I would not see thy bosom thus
Bow'd down to earth, with anguish so severe!
I would not see thine ardent feelings crush'd,
Deaden'd to all save sorrow's thrilling tone,
Like the pale flower, which hangs its drooping head
Beneath the chilling blasts of stern Æolus!
Oh I have seen that brow with pleasure flush'd,
The lightning smile around it brightly playing,
And the dark eyelids trembling with delight—
But now how changed!—thy downcast eye is bent,
With heavy, thoughtful glances, on the ground,
And oh how quickly starts the tear-drop there!
It is not age which dims its wonted fire,
Or plants his lilies on thy pallid cheek,
But sorrow, keenest, darkest, biting sorrow!
When love would seek to lead thy heart from grief,
And fondly pleads one cheering look to view,
A sad, a faint sad smile one instant gleams
Athwart the brow where sorrow sits enshrined,
Brooding o'er ruins of what once was fair;
But like departing sunset, as it throws
One farewell shadow o'er the sleeping earth,
(So soon in sombre twilight to be wrapt,)
Thus, thus it fades! and sorrow more profound
Dwells on each feature where a smile, so cold,
It scarcely might be called the mockery
Of cheerful peace, but just before had been.
Long years of suffering, brightened not by joy,
Death and disease, fell harbinger of woe,
Must leave their impress on the human face,
And dim the fire of youth, the glow of pride;
But oh my mother! mourn not thus for *her*,
The rose, just blown, transplanted to its home,
Nor weep that her angelic soul has found
A resting-place with God.
Oh let the eye of heaven-born faith disperse
The dark'ning mists of earthly grief, and pierce
The clouds which shadow dull mortality!
Gaze on the heaven of glory crown'd with light,
Where rests thine own sweet child with radiant brow,
In the same voice which charm'd her father's halls,
Chanting sweet anthems to her Maker's praise;
And watching with delight the gentle buds
Which she had lived to mourn; watching thine own,
My mother! the soft unfolding blossoms,
Which, ere the breath of earthly sin could taint,
Departed to their Saviour; there to wait
For thy fond spirit in the home of bliss!
The angel babes have found a second mother;
But when thy soul shall pass from earth away,

The little cherubs then shall cling to thee,
And their sweet guardian welcome thee with joy,
Protector of their helpless infancy,
Who taught them how to reach that happy home.
Oh think of this, and let one heartfelt smile
Illume the face so long estranged from joy;
But may it rest not on thy brow alone,
But shed a cheering influence o'er thy heart,
Too sweet to be forgotten! Though thy loved
And beautiful are fled from earth away,
Still there are those who love thee—who would live
With thee alone—who weeps or smiles with thee.
Think of thy noble sons, and think of her
Who prays thee to be happy in the hope
Of meeting those in heaven who loved thee here,
And training those on earth that they may live
A band of saints with thee in Paradise.

The regular studies of Margaret were now resumed, and her mother found, in attending to her instruction, a relief from the poignancy of her afflictions. Margaret always enjoyed the country, and in fine weather indulged in long rambles in the woods, accompanied by some friend, or attended by a faithful servant woman. When in the house, the versatility of her talents, her constitutional vivacity, and an aptness at coining occupation and amusement out of the most trifling incident, perpetually relieved the monotony of domestic life; while the faint gleam of health that occasionally flitted across her cheek, beguiled the anxious foreboding that had been indulged concerning her. "A strong hope was rising in my heart," says her mother, "that our frail, delicate blossom would continue to flourish, and that it was possible I might live to behold the perfection of its beauty! Alas! how uncertain is every earthly prospect! Even then the canker was concealed within the bright bud, which was eventually to destroy its loveliness! About the last of December she was again seized with a liver complaint, which, by sympathy, affected her lungs, and again awakened all our fears. She was confined to her bed, and it was not until March that she was able to sit up and walk about her room. The confinement then became irksome, but her kind and skilful physician had declared that she must not be permitted to venture out until mild weather in April." During this fit of illness her mind had remained in an unusual state of inactivity; but with the opening of spring, and the faint return of health, it broke forth with a brilliancy and a restless excitability that astonished and alarmed. "In conversation," says her mother, "her sallies of wit were dazzling. She composed and wrote incessantly, or rather would have done so, had I not interposed my authority to prevent this unceasing tax upon both her mental and physical strength. Fugitive pieces were produced every day, such as, 'The Shunamite,' 'Belshazzar's Feast,' 'The Nature of Mind,' 'Boabdil el Chico,' &c. She seemed to exist only in the regions of poetry." We cannot help thinking that these moments of intense poetical exaltation sometimes approached to delirium, for we are told by her mother that "the image of her departed sister Lucretia mingled in all her aspirations; the holy elevation of Lucretia's character had taken deep hold of her imagination, and in her moments of enthusiasm she felt that she held close and intimate communion with her beatified spirit."

This intense mental excitement continued after she was permitted to leave her room, and her application to her books and papers was so eager and almost impassioned, that it was found expedient again to send her on an excursion. A visit to some relatives, and a sojourn among the beautiful scenery on the Mohawk river, had a salutary effect; but on returning home she was again attacked with alarming indisposition, which confined her to her bed.

"The struggle between nature and disease," says her mother, "was for a time doubtful; she was, however, at length restored to us. With returning health, her mental labours were resumed. I reasoned and entreated, but at last became convinced that my only way was to let matters take their course. If restrained in her favourite pursuits she was unhappy. To acquire useful knowledge was a motive sufficient to induce her to surmount all obstacles. I could only select for her a course of calm and quiet reading, which, while it furnished real food for the mind, would compose rather than excite the imagination. She read much, and wrote a great deal. As for myself, I lived in a state of constant anxiety lest these labours should prematurely destroy this delicate bud."

In the autumn of 1835, Dr. Davidson made arrangements to remove his family to a rural residence near New York, pleasantly situated on the banks of the Sound, or East River, as it is commonly called. The following extract of a letter from Margaret to Moss Kent, Esq.,* will show her anticipations and plans on this occasion.

* This gentleman was an early and valued friend of the Davidson family, and is honourably mentioned by Mr. Morse for the interest he

September 20, 1835.

"We shall soon leave Ballston for New York. We are to reside in a beautiful spot, upon the East River, near the Shot Tower, four miles from town, romantically called Ruremont. Will it not be delightful! Reunited to father and brothers, we must, we will be happy! We shall keep a horse and a little pleasure-wagon, to transport us to and from town. But I intend my time shall be constantly employed in my studies, which I hope I shall continue to pursue at home. I wish (and mamma concurs in the opinion that it is best) to devote this winter to the study of the Latin and French languages, while music and dancing will unbend my mind after close application to those studies, and give me that recreation which mother deems requisite for me. If father can procure private teachers for me, I shall be saved the dreadful alternative of a boarding-school. Mother could never endure the thought of one for me, and my own aversion is equally strong. Oh! my dear uncle, you must come and see us. Come soon and stay long. Try to be with us at Christmas. Mother's health is not as good as when you were here. I hope she will be benefited by a residence in her native city—in the neighbourhood of those friends she best loves. The state of her mind has an astonishing effect upon her health."

---

took in the education of Lucretia. The notice of Mr. Morse, however, leaves it to be supposed that Mr. Kent's acquaintance with Dr. and Mrs. Davidson was brought about by his admiration of their daughter's talents, and commenced with overtures for her instruction. The following extract of a letter from Mrs. Davidson will place this matter in a proper light, and show that these offers on the part of Mr. Kent, and the partial acceptance of them by Dr. and Mrs. Davidson, were warranted by the terms of intimacy which before existed between them. "I had the pleasure," says Mrs. Davidson, "to know Mr. Kent before my marriage, after which he frequently called at our house when visiting his sister, with whom I was on terms of intimacy. On one of these occasions he saw Lucretia. He had often seen her when a child, but she had changed much. Her uncommon personal beauty, graceful manners, and superior intellectual endowments made a strong impression on him. He conversed with her, and examined her on the different branches which she was studying, and pronounced her a good English scholar. He also found her well read, and possessing a fund of general information. He warmly expressed his admiration of her talents, and urged me to consent that he should adopt her as his daughter, and complete her education on the most liberal plan. I so far acceded to his proposition as to permit him to place her with Mrs. Willard, and assured him I would take his generous offer into consideration. Had she lived, we should have complied with his wishes, and Lucretia would have been the child of his adoption. The pure and disinterested friendship of this excellent man continued until the day of his death. For Margaret he manifested the affection of a father, and the attachment was returned by her with all the warmth of a young and grateful heart. She always addressed him as her dear uncle Kent."

The following letter to the same gentleman, is dated October 18, 1835:

"We are now at Ruremont, and a more delightful place I never saw. The house is large, pleasant, and commodious. and the old-fashioned style of every thing around it transports the mind to days long gone by, and my imagination is constantly upon the rack to burden the past with scenes transacted on this very spot. In the rear of the mansion a lawn, spangled with beautiful flowers, and shaded by spreading trees, slopes gently down to the river side, where vessels of every description are constantly spreading their white sails to the wind. In front, a long shady avenue leads to the door, and a large extent of beautiful undulating ground is spread with fruit-trees of every description. In and about the house there are so many little nooks and by-places, that sometimes I fancy it has been the resort of smugglers; and who knows but I shall yet find their hidden treasures somewhere? Do come and see us, my dear uncle; but you must come soon, if you would enjoy any of the beauties of the place. The trees have already doffed their robe of green, and assumed the red and yellow of autumn, and the paths are strewed with fallen leaves. But there is loveliness even in the decay of nature. But do, do come soon, or the branches will be leafless, and the cold winds will prevent the pleasant rambles we now enjoy. Dear mother has twice accompanied me a short distance about the grounds, and indeed I think her health has improved since we removed to New York, though she is still very feeble. Her mind is much relieved, having her little family gathered once more around her. You well know how great an effect her spirits have upon her health. Oh! if my dear mother is only in comfortable health, and you will come, I think I shall spend a delightful winter prosecuting my studies at home."

"For a short time," writes Mrs. Davidson, "she seemed to luxuriate upon the beauties of this lovely place. She selected her own room, and adjusted all her little tasteful ornaments. Her books and drawing implements were transported to this chosen spot. Still she hovered around me like my shadow. Mother's room was still her resting-place; mother's bosom her sanctuary. She sketched a plan for one or two poems which were never finished. But her enjoyment was soon interrupted. She was again attacked by her old enemy, and though her confinement to her room was of short duration, she did not get rid of the cough. A change now came over her mind. Hitherto she had always delighted in serious conversation on heaven; the pure and elevated occupations of saints and angels in a future state had proved a delightful source of contemplation; and she would become so animated that it seemed sometimes as if she would fly to realize her hopes and joys!—Now her young heart appeared to cling to life and its enjoyments, and more closely than I had ever known it. 'She was never ill.'—When asked the question, 'Margaret, how are you?" 'Well, quite well,' was her reply, when it was obvious to me, who watched her every look, that she had scarcely strength to sustain her weak frame. She saw herself the last daughter of her idolizing parents—the only sister of her devoted brothers! Life had acquired new charms; though she had always been a happy, light-hearted child."

The following lines, written about this time, show the elasticity of her spirit, and the bounding vivacity of her imagination, that seemed to escape, as in a dream, from the frail tenement of clay in which they were encased:

STANZAS.

Oh for the pinions of a bird,
To bear me far away,
Where songs of other lands are heard,
And other waters play!

For some aerial car, to fly
On through the realms of light,
To regions rife with poesy,
And teeming with delight.

O'er many a wild and classic stream
In ecstasy I'd bend,
And hail each ivy-cover'd tower,
As though it were a friend.

O'er piles where many a wintry blast
Is swept in mournful tones,
And fraught with scenes long glided past,
It shrieks, and sighs, and moans.

Through many a shadowy grove, and round
Full many a cloister'd hall,
And corridors, where every step
With echoing peal doth fall.

Enchanted with the dreariness,
And awe-struck with the gloom,
I would wander, like a spectre,
'Mid the regions of the tomb.

And Memory her enchanting veil
  Around my soul should twine,
And Superstition, wildly pale,
  Should woo me to her shrine;

I'd cherish still her witching gloom,
  Half shrinking in my dread,
But, powerless to dissolve the spell,
  Pursue her fearful tread.

Oh what unmingled pleasure then
  My youthful heart would feel,
As o'er its thrilling cords each thought
  Of former days would steal!

Of centuries in oblivion wrapt,
  Of forms which long were cold,
And all of terror, all of woe,
  That history's page has told.

How fondly in my bosom
  Would its monarch, Fancy, reign,
And spurn earth's meaner offices
  With glorious disdain!

Amid the scenes of past delight,
  Or misery, I'd roam,
Where ruthless tyrants sway'd in might,
  Where princes found a home.

Where heroes have enwreathed their brows
  With chivalric renown,
Where beauty's hand, as valour's meed,
  Hath twined the laurel crown.

I'd stand where proudest kings have stood,
  Or kneel where slaves have knelt,
Till wrapt in magic solitude,
  I feel what they have felt.

Oh for the pinions of a bird,
  To waft me far away,
Where songs of other lands are heard,
  And other waters play!

About this time Mrs. Davidson received a letter from the English gentleman for whom Margaret, when quite a child, had conceived such a friendship, her dear elder brother, as she used to call him. The letter bore testimony to his undiminished regard. He was in good health; married to a very estimable and lovely woman; was the father of a fine little girl, and was at Havana with his family, where he kindly entreated Mrs. Davidson and Margaret to join them; being sure that a winter passed in that mild climate would have the happiest effect upon their healths. His doors, his heart, he added, were open to receive them, and his amiable consort impatient to bid them welcome. "Margaret," says Mrs. Davidson, "was overcome by the perusal of this letter. She laughed and wept alternately;—one moment urged me to go, 'she was herself well, but she was sure it would cure me;' the next moment felt as though she could not leave the friends to whom she had so recently been reunited. Oh! had I gone at that time, perhaps my child might still have lived to bless me!"

During the first weeks of Margaret's residence at Ruremont, the character and situation of the place seized powerfully upon her imagination. "The curious structure of this old-fashioned house," says Mrs. Davidson, "its picturesque appearance, the varied and beautiful grounds which surrounded it, called up a thousand poetic images and romantic ideas. A long gallery, a winding staircase, a dark, narrow passage, a trap-door, large apartments with massive doors, and heavy iron bars and bolts, all set her mind teeming with recollections of what she had read and imagined of old castles, banditti, smugglers, &c. She roamed over the place in perfect ecstasy, peopling every part with images of her own imagination, and fancying it the scene of some foregone event of dark and thrilling interest." There was, in fact, some palpable material for all this spinning and weaving of the fancy. The writer of this memoir visited Ruremont at the time it was occupied by the Davidson family. It was a spacious, and somewhat crazy and poetical-looking mansion, with large waste apartments. The grounds were rather wild and overgrown, but so much the more picturesque. It stood on the banks of the Sound, the waters of which rushed, with whirling and impetuous tides, below, hurrying on to the dangerous strait of Hell Gate. Nor was this neighbourhood without its legendary tales. These wild and lonely shores had, in former times, been the resort of smugglers and pirates. Hard by this very place stood the country retreat of Ready-Money Prevost, of dubious and smuggling memory, with his haunted tomb, in which he was said to conceal his contraband riches; and scarce a secret spot about these shores but had some tradition connected with it of Kidd the pirate and his buried treasures. All these circumstances were enough to breed thick-coming fancies in so imaginative a brain; and the result was a drama in six acts, entitled "The Smuggler," the scene of which was laid at Ruremont in the old time of the province. The play was written with great rapidity, and,

4

considering she was little more than twelve years of age, and had never visited a theatre but once in her life, evinced great aptness and dramatic talent. It was to form a domestic entertainment for Christmas holidays; the spacious back parlour was to be fitted up for the theatre. In planning and making arrangements for the performance, she seemed perfectly happy, and her step resumed its wonted elasticity, though her anxious mother often detected a suppressed cough, and remarked a hectic flush upon her cheek. "We now found," says Mrs. Davidson, "that private teachers were not to be procured at Ruremont, and I feared to have her enter upon a course of study which had been talked of, before we came to this place. I thought she was too feeble for close mental application, while *she* was striving, by the energies of her mind and bodily exertion, (which only increased the morbid excitement of her system,) to overcome disease, that she feared was about to fasten itself upon her. She was the more anxious, therefore, to enter upon her studies; and when she saw solicitude in my countenance and manner, she would fix her sweet sad eyes upon my face, as if she would read my very soul, yet dreaded to know what she might find written there. I knew and could understand her feelings; she also understood mine; and there seemed to be a tacit compact between us that this subject, *at present*, was forbidden ground. Her father and brothers were lulled into security by her cheerful manner and constant assertion that she was well, and considered her cough the effect of recent cold. My opinion to the contrary was regarded as the result of extreme maternal anxiety."

She accordingly went to town three times a week, to take lessons in French, music, and dancing. Her progress in French was rapid, and the correctness and elegance of her translations surprised her teachers. Her friends in the city, seeing her look so well and appear so sprightly, encouraged her to believe that air and exercise would prove more beneficial than confinement to the house. She went to town in the morning and returned in the evening in an open carriage, with her father and one of her elder brothers, each of whom was confined to his respective office until night. In this way she was exposed to the rigours of an unusually cold season; yet she heeded them not, but returned home full of animation to join her little brothers in preparations for their holiday fête. Their anticipations of a joyous Christmas were doomed to sad disappointment. As the time approached, two of her brothers were taken ill. One of these, a beautiful boy about nine years of age, had been the favourite companion of her recreations, and she had taken great interest in his mental improvement. "Towards the close of 1835," says her mother, "he began to droop; his cheek grew pale, his step languid, and his bright eye heavy. Instead of rolling the hoop, and bounding across the lawn to meet his sister on her return from the city, he drooped by the side of his feeble mother, and could not bear to be parted from her; at length he was taken to his bed, and, after lingering four months, he died. This was Margaret's first acquaintance with death. She witnessed his gradual decay almost unconsciously, but still persuaded herself 'he will, he must get well!' She saw her sweet little playfellow reclining upon my bosom during his last agonies; she witnessed the bright glow which flashed upon his long-faded cheek; she beheld the unearthly light of his beautiful eye, as he pressed his dying lips to mine, and exclaimed, 'Mother! dear mother! the last hour has come!' Oh! it was indeed an hour of anguish never to be forgotten. Its effect upon her youthful mind was as lasting as her life. The sudden change from life and animation to the still unconsciousness of death, for the time almost paralysed her. She shed no tear, but stood like a statue upon the scene of death. But when her eldest brother tenderly led her from the room, her tears gushed forth—it was near midnight, and the first thing that aroused her to a sense of what was going on around her, was the thought of my bereavement, and a conviction that it was her province to console me."

We subjoin a record, from her own pen, of her feelings on this lamentable occasion.

ON THE CORPSE OF MY LITTLE BROTHER KENT.

Beauteous form of soulless clay!
  Image of what once was life!
Hush'd is thy pulse's feeble play,
  And ceased the pangs of mortal strife.

Oh! I have heard thy dying groan,
  Have seen thy last of earthly pain;
And while I weep that thou art gone,
  I cannot wish thee here again.

For ah! the calm and peaceful smile
  Upon that clay-cold brow of thine,
Speaks of a spirit freed from sin,
  A spirit joyful and divine.

But thou art gone! and this cold clay
Is all that now remains of thee;
For thy freed soul hath wing'd its way
To blessed immortality.

That dying smile, that dying groan,
I never, never can forget,
Till death's cold hand hath clasp'd my own,
His impress on my brow has set.

Those low, and sweet, and plaintive tones,
Which o'er my heart like music swept,
And the deep, deathlike, chilling moans,
Which from thy heaving bosom crept.

Oh! thou wert beautiful and fair,
Our loveliest and our dearest one!
No more thy pains or joys we share,
No more—my brother, thou art gone.

Thou 'rt gone! What agony, what woe
In that brief sentence is express'd!
Oh that the burning tears could flow,
And draw this mountain from my breast!

The anguish of the mother was still more intense, as she saw her bright and beautiful but perishable offspring thus, one by one, snatched away from her. "My own weak frame," says she, "was unable longer to sustain the effects of long watching and deep grief. I had not only lost my lovely boy, but I felt a strong conviction that I must soon resign my Margaret; or rather, that she would soon follow me to a premature grave. Although she still persisted in the belief that she was well, the irritating cough, the hectic flush, (so often mistaken for the bloom of health,) the hurried beating of the heart, and the drenching night perspirations confirmed me in this belief, and I sank under this accumulated load of affliction. For three weeks I hovered upon the borders of the grave, and when I arose from this bed of pain—so feeble that I could not sustain my own weight, it was to witness the rupture of a blood-vessel in her lungs, caused by exertions to suppress a cough. Oh! it was agony to see her thus! I was compelled to conceal every appearance of alarm, lest the agitation of her mind should produce fatal consequences. As I seated myself by her, she raised her speaking eyes to mine with a mournful, inquiring gaze, and as she read the anguish which I could not conceal, she turned away with a look of despair. She spoke not a word, but silence, still, deathlike silence, pervaded the apartment." The best of medical aid was called in, but the physicians gave no hope; they considered it a deep-seated case of pulmonary consumption. All that could be done was to alleviate the symptoms, and protract life as long as possible by lessening the excitement of the system. When Mrs. Davidson returned to the bedside, after an interview with the physicians, she was regarded with an anxious, searching look, by the lovely little sufferer, but not a question was made. Margaret seemed fearful of receiving a discouraging reply, and "lay, all pale and still, (except when agitated by the cough,) striving to calm the tumult of her thoughts," while her mother seated herself by her pillow, trembling with weakness and sorrow. Long and anxious were the days and nights spent in watching over her. Every sudden movement or emotion excited the hemorrhage. "Not a murmur escaped her lips," says her mother, "during her protracted sufferings. 'How are you, love? how have you rested during the night?' 'Well, dear mamma; I have slept sweetly.' I have been night after night beside her restless couch, wiped the cold dew from her brow, and kissed her faded cheek in all the agony of grief, while she unconsciously slept on; or if she did awake, her calm sweet smile, which seemed to emanate from heaven, has, spite of my *reason*, lighted my heart with hope. Except when very ill, she was ever a bright dreamer. Her visions were usually of an unearthly cast: about heaven and angels. She was wandering among the stars; her sainted sisters were her pioneers; her cherub brother walked hand in hand with her through the gardens of paradise! I was always an early riser, but after Margaret began to decline I never disturbed her until time to rise for breakfast, a season of social intercourse in which she delighted to unite, and from which she was never willing to be absent. Often when I have spoken to her she would exclaim, 'Mother, you have disturbed the brightest visions that ever mortal was blessed with! I was in the midst of such scenes of delight! Cannot I have time to finish my dream?' And when I told her how long it was until breakfast, 'It will do,' she would say, and again lose herself in her bright imaginings; for I considered these as moments of inspiration rather than sleep. She told me it was not sleep. I never knew but one, except Margaret, who enjoyed this delightful and mysterious source of happiness: that one was her departed sister Lucretia. When awaking from these reveries, an almost ethereal light played about her eye, which seemed to irradiate her whole face. A holy calm pervaded her manner, and in truth she looked more like an angel who had been communing with kindred spirits in the world of light, than any thing of a grosser nature."

How truly does this correspond with Milton's exquisite description of the heavenly influences that minister to virgin innocence—

"A thousand liv'ried angels lackey her,
Driving far off each thing of sin and guilt;
And in clear dream and solemn vision,
Tell her of things that no gross ear can hear:
Till oft converse with heavenly habitants
Begin to cast a beam on the outward shape,
The unpolluted temple of the mind,
And turn it by degrees to the soul's essence,
Till all be made immortal."

Of the images and speculations that floated in her mind during these half dreams, half reveries, we may form an idea from the following lines, written on one occasion after what her mother used to term her "descent into the world of reality."

THE JOYS OF HEAVEN.

Oh who can tell the joy and peace
Which souls redeem'd shall know,
When all their earthly sorrows cease,
Their pride, and pain, and woe!
Who may describe the matchless love
Which reigneth with the saints above?

What earthly tongue can ever tell
The pure, unclouded joy
Which in each gentle soul doth swell,
Unmingled with alloy,
As, bending to the Lord Most High,
They sound his praises through the sky?

Through the high regions of the air,
On angels' wings, they glide.
And gaze in wondering silence there
On scenes to us denied:
Their minds expanding every hour,
And opening like the summer flower.

Though not like them to fade away,
To die, and bloom no more;
Beyond the reach of fell decay,
They stand in light and power;
But pure, eternal, free from care,
They join in endless praises there!

When first they leave this world of woe
For fair, immortal scenes of light,
Angels attend them from below,
And upward wing their joyful flight;
Where, fired with heavenly rapture's flame,
They raise on high Jehovah's name.

O'er the broad arch of heaven it peals,
While shouts of praise unnumbered flow;
The full, sweet notes sublimely swell,
And prostrate angels humbly bow;
Each heart is tuned to joy above,
Its theme, a Saviour's matchless love.

The dulcet voice, which here below
Charm'd with delight each listening ear,
Mix'd with no lingering tone of woe,
Swelling harmonious, soft and clear,
Will sweetly fill the courts above,
In strains of heavenly peace and love.

The brilliant genius, which on earth
Is struggling with disease and pain,
Will there unfold in power and light,
Nought its bright current to restrain;
And as each brilliant day rolls on,
'T will find some grace, till then unknown.

And as the countless years flit by,
Their minds progressing still,
The more they know, these saints on high
Praise more His sovereign will;
No breath from sorrow's whirlwind blast
Around their footsteps cast.

From their high throne they gaze abroad
On vast creation's wondrous plan,
And own the power, the might of God,
In each resplendent work they scan;
Though sun and moon to nought return,
Like stars these souls redeem'd shall burn.

Oh! who could wish to stay below,
If sure of such a home as this,
Where streams of love serenely flow,
And every heart is filled with bliss?
They praise, and worship, and adore
The Lord of heaven for ever more.

During this dangerous illness she became acquainted with Miss Sedgwick. The first visit of that most excellent and justly distinguished person, was when Margaret was in a state of extreme debility. It laid the foundation of an attachment on the part of the latter, which continued until her death. The visit was repeated; a correspondence afterwards took place, and the friendship of Miss Sedgwick became to the little enthusiast a source of the worthiest pride and purest enjoyment throughout the remainder of her brief existence.

At length the violence of her malady gave way to skilful remedies and the most tender and unremitting assiduity. When enabled to leave her chamber, she rallied her spirits, made great exertions to be cheerful, and strove to persuade herself that all might yet be well with her. Even her parents, with that singular self-delusion inseparable from this cruelly flattering malady, began to indulge a trembling hope that she might still be spared to them.

In the month of July, her health being sufficiently re-established to bear the fatigues of travelling, she was taken by her mother and eldest brother on a tour to Dutchess County and the western part of New York. On leaving home, she wrote the following lines, expressive of the feelings called forth by the events of the few preceding months, and of a foreboding that she should never return:

FAREWELL TO RUREMONT.

Oh! sadly I gaze on this beautiful landscape,
And silent and slow do the big tear-drops swell;
And I haste to my task, while the deep sigh is breaking,
To bid thee, sweet Ruremont, a lasting farewell.

Oh! soft are the breezes which play round the valley,
And warm are the sunbeams which gild thee with light,
All clear and serenely the deep waves are rolling,
The sky in its radiance is dazzlingly bright.

Oh! gaily the birds 'mid thy dark vines are sporting,
And, heaven-taught, pouring their gladness in song;
While the rose and the lily their fair heads are bending
To hear the soft anthems float gently along.

Full many an hour have I bent o'er thy waters,
Or watch'd the light clouds with a joy-beaming eye,
Till, delighted, I long'd for the eagle's swift pinions,
To pierce the full depths of that beautiful sky.

Though wild were the fancies which dwelt in my bosom,
Though endless the visions which swept o'er my soul,
Indulging those dreams was my dearest enjoyment—
Enjoyment unmingled, unchained by control!

But each garden of earth has a something of sorrow,
A thorn in its rose, or a blight in its breeze,
Though blooming as Eden, a shadow hangs o'er thee,
The spirit of darkness, of pain, of disease!

Yes, Ruremont! thy brow, in its loveliness deck'd,
Is entwined with a fatal but beautiful wreath,
For thy green leaves have shrunk at the mourner's cold touch,
And thy pale flowers have wept in the presence of death.

Yon violets, which bloom in their delicate freshness,
Were strew'd o'er the grave of our fairest and best;
Yon roses, which charm by their richness and fragrance,
Have wither'd and died on his icy-cold breast.

The soft voice of spring had just breathed o'er the valley,
  The sweet birds just caroll'd their song in her bower,
When the angel of death in his terror swept o'er us,
  And placed in his bosom our fragile young flower.

Thus, Ruremont, we mourn not thy beauties alone,
  Thy flowers in their freshness, thy stream in its pride,
But we leave the loved scene of our mourning and tears,
  We leave the dear spot where our cherish'd one died.

The mantle of beauty thrown gracefully o'er thee,
  Must touch a soft chord in each delicate heart;
But the tie is more sacred which bids us deplore thee,
  Endear'd by affliction 't is harder to part.

The scene of enjoyment is ever most lovely,
  Where blissful young spirits dance mirthful and glad;
But when sorrow has mingled her tears with our pleasure,
  Our love is more tender, our parting more sad.

How mild is the wing of this delicate zephyr,
  Which fans in its coolness my feverish brow!
But that light wing is laden with breezes that wither,
  And check the warm current of life in its flow.

Why blight such an Eden, oh spirit of terror!
  Which sweepest thy thousands each hour to the tomb?
Why, why shouldst thou roam o'er this beautiful valley,
  And mingle thy breath with the rose's perfume?

The sun rises bright o'er the clear dancing waters,
  And tinges with gold every light waving tree,
And the young birds are singing their welcome to morning—
  Alas! they will sing it no longer for me!

The young buds of summer their soft eyes are opening,
  The wild flowers are bending the pure ripples o'er;
But I bid them farewell, and my heart is nigh breaking
  To think I shall see them and tend them no more.

I mark yonder path, where so often I 've wander'd,
  Yon moss-covered rock, with its sheltering tree,
And a sigh of deep sadness bursts forth to remember
  That no more its soft verdure shall blossom for me.

How often my thoughts, to these loved scenes returning,
  Shall brood o'er the past with its joy and its pain:
Till waking at last from the long, pleasing slumber,
  I sigh to behold thee, thus blooming, again.

The little party was absent on its western tour about two months. "Margaret," says her mother, "appeared to enjoy the scenery, and every thing during the journey interested her. But there was a sadness in her countenance, a pensiveness in her manner, unless excited by external circumstances, which deeply affected me. She watched every variation in my countenance; marked every little attention directed to herself, such as an alteration in her diet, dress, exposure to the changes of weather, yet still discovered an unwillingness to speak of her declining health, and laboured to conceal every unfavourable symptom or change for the worse. This, of course, imposed upon me the most painful restraint. How heart-breaking to find that she considered my tongue as the herald of mournful tidings, and my face as the mirror of evil to come! How true that self-deception seems to be almost an invariable sympton attending this dreadful complaint! Margaret, all unconscious of the rapid strides of the destroyer, taught herself to believe that the alarming symptoms of her case existed only in the imagination of her too anxious mother. Yet knowing my experience in these matters, she still doubted and trembled, and feared to ask, lest a confirmation of her vague apprehensions should be the result. She avoided the slightest allusion to the subject of her disease in any way; and in the morbid excitement of her mind it appeared to her almost like accusing her of something wrong to say that she was not well."

The following letter was written by her to Miss Sedgwick, after her arrival in Dutchess County.

"Lithgow, Dutchess County.

"Happy as I am, my dear madam, in the privilege of writing to you, I cannot permit another day to pass ere I inform you of our safe arrival at one of the most lovely spots in this beautiful and healthy country. Our passage up the river was rather tedious, being debarred the pleasure of remaining upon deck, but this privation was counterbalanced by the pleasure of a few moments' conversation with my dear brother, who was permitted to meet us when the boat stopped at West Point. Arrived at Poughkeepsie, brother M. procured a private carriage, which was to convey us to the end of our journey, a distance of twenty miles. The drive was delightful! The scenery ever changing, ever beautiful! We arrived at Lithgow without much fatigue, where a hearty welcome, that sweetest of cordials, was awaiting us. Oh! it is a lovely spot! I thought Ruremont the perfection of beauty! but here I find the flowers are as blooming, the birds as gay, the air as sweet, and the prospect far more varied and extensive; 't is true we have lost the beautiful East River, with its crowd of vessels sweeping gracefully along, but here are hills crowned with the richest foliage, valleys sprinkled with flowers, and watered with winding rivulets; and here, what we prize more than all, a mild, salubrious air, which seems, in the words of the divine poet, "to bear healing in its wings." Dear mother bore the fatigue of our journey better than we anticipated; and although I do not think she is permanently better, she certainly breathes more freely, and seems altogether more comfortable than when in the city. Oh! how sincerely I hope that a change of air and scene may raise her spirits and renovate her strength. She is now in the midst of friends whom she has known and loved for many years; and surrounded by scenes connected with many of her earliest remembrances. Farewell, my dear madam! Please give my love to your dear little nieces; and should you have the leisure and inclination to answer this, believe me your letter will be a source of much gratification to your

Highly obliged little friend,

M. M. Davidson.

Miss Catherine Sedgwick.

August, 1836."

The travellers returned to Ruremont in September. The tour had been of service to Margaret, and she endeavoured to persuade herself that she was quite well. If asked about her health, her reply was, that "if her friends did not tell her she was ill, she should not, from her own feelings, suspect it." That she was, notwithstanding, dubious on this subject, was evident from her avoiding to speak about it, and from the uneasiness she manifested when it was alluded to. It was still more evident from the change that took place in her habits and pursuits; she tacitly adopted the course of conduct that had repeatedly and anxiously, but too often vainly, been urged by her mother, as calculated to allay the morbid irritability of her system. She gave up her studies, rarely indulged in writing or drawing, and contented herself with light reading, with playing a few simple airs on the piano, and with any other trivial mode of passing away the time. The want of her favourite occupations, however, soon made the hours move heavily with her. Above all things, she missed the exciting exercise of the pen, against which she had been especially warned. Her mother observed the listlessness and melancholy that were stealing over her, and hoped a change of scene might banish them. The airs from the river, too, had been pronounced unfavourable to her health; the family, therefore, removed to town. The change of residence, however, did not produce the desired effect. She became more and more dissatisfied with herself, and with the life of idleness, as she considered it, that she was leading; but still she had resolved to give the prescribed system a thorough trial. A new source of solicitude was now awakened in the bosom of her anxious mother, who read in her mournfully quiet manner and submissive silence, the painful effects of compliance with her advice. There was not a murmur, however, from the lips of Margaret, to give rise to this solicitude; on the contrary, whenever she caught her mother's eye fixed anxiously and inquiringly on her, she would turn away and assume an air of cheerfulness.

Six months had passed in this inactive manner. "She was seated one day by my side," says Mrs. Davidson, "weary and restless, and scarcely knowing what to do with herself, when, marking the traces of grief upon my face, she threw her arms about my neck, and kissing me, exclaimed, 'My dear, dear mother!' 'What is it affects you now, my child?' 'Oh! I know you are longing for something from my pen!' I saw the secret craving of the spirit that gave rise to the suggestion. 'I do indeed, my dear, delight in the effusions from your pen, but the exertion will injure you.' 'Mamma, I *must write!* I can hold out no longer! I will return to my pen, my pencil, and my books, and shall again be happy!' I pressed her to my bosom, and cautioned her to remember she was feeble. 'Mother,' exclaimed she, 'I am well! I wish you were only as well as I am!'"

The heart of the mother was not proof against these appeals: indeed she had almost as much need of self-denial on this subject as her child, so much did she delight in these early blossomings of her talent. Margaret was again left to her own impulses. All the frivolous expedients for what is usually termed *killing time* were discarded by her with contempt; her studies were resumed; in the sacred writings and in the pages of history she sought fitting aliment for her mind, half famished by its long abstinence; her poetical vein again burst forth, and the following lines, written at the time, show the excitement and elevation of her feelings:

EARTH.

Earth! thou hast nought to satisfy
  The cravings of immortal mind!
Earth! thou hast nothing pure and high,
  The soaring, struggling soul to bind.

Impatient of its long delay,
  The pinion'd spirit fain would roam,
And leave this crumbling house of clay,
  To seek above its own bright home!

The spirit, 'tis a spark of light
  Struck from our God's eternal throne,
Which pierces through these clouds of night,
  And longs to shine where once it shone!

Earth! there will come an awful day,
  When thou shalt crumble into nought;
When thou shalt melt beneath that ray
  From whence thy splendours first were caught.

Quench'd in the glories of its God,
  Yon burning lamp shall then expire;
And flames, from heaven's own altar sent,
  Shall light the great funereal pyre.

Yes, thou must die! and yon pure depths
  Back from thy darken'd brow shall roll;
But never can the tyrant death
  Arrest this feeble, trusting soul.

When that great voice, which form'd thee first,
  Shall tell, surrounding world, thy doom,
Then the pure soul, enchain'd by thee,
  Shall rise triumphant o'er thy tomb.

Then on, still on, the unfetter'd mind
  Through realms of endless space shall fly;
No earth to dim, no chain to bind,
  Too pure to sin, too great to die.

Earth! thou hast nought to satisfy
  The cravings of immortal mind!
Earth! thou hast nothing pure and high,
  The soaring, struggling soul to bind.

Yet is this never-dying ray
  Caught in thy cold, delusive snares,
Cased in a cell of mouldering clay,
  And bow'd by woes, and pain, and cares!

Oh! how mysterious is the bond
  Which blends the earthly with the pure,
And mingles that which death may blight
  With that which ever must endure!

Arise, my soul, from all below,
  And gaze upon thy destined home,
The heaven of heavens, the throne of God,
  Where sin and care can never come.

Prepare thee for a state of bliss,
  Unclouded by this mortal veil,
Where thou shalt see thy Maker's face,
  And dews from heaven's own air inhale.

How sadly do the sins of earth
  Deface thy purity and light,
That thus, while gazing at thyself,
  Thou shrink'st in horror at the sight!

Compound of weakness and of strength,
  Mighty, yet ignorant of thy power!
Loftier than earth, or air, or sea,
  Yet meaner than the lowliest flower!

Soaring towards heaven, yet clinging still
  To earth, by many a tender tie!
Longing to breathe a purer air,
  Yet fearing, trembling thus to die!

She was soon all cheerfulness and enjoyment. Her pen and her pencil were frequently in her hand; she occupied herself also with her needle in embroidery on canvass, and other fancy work. Hope brightened with the exhilaration of her spirits. "I now walk and ride, eat and sleep as usual," she observes in a letter to a young friend, "and although not well, have strong hopes that the opening spring, which renovates the flowers, and fields, and streams, will revive my enfeebled frame, and restore me to my wonted health." In these moods she was the life of the domestic circle, and these moods were frequent and long. And here we should observe, that though these memoirs, which are furnished principally from the recollections of an afflicted mother, may too often represent this gifted little being as a feeble invalid struggling with mortality, yet in truth her life, though a brief, was a bright and happy one. At times she was full of playful and innocent gaiety; at others of intense mental exaltation; and it was the very intensity of her enjoyment that made her so often indulge in those poetic paroxysms, if we may be allowed the expression, which filled her mother with alarm. A few weeks of this intellectual excitement was followed by another rupture of a blood-vessel in the lungs, and a long interval of extreme debility. The succeeding winter was one of vicissitude. She had several attacks of bleeding at the lungs, which evidently alarmed her at the time, though she said nothing, and endeavoured to repress all manifestation of her feelings. If taken suddenly, she instantly resorted to the sofa, and, by a strong effort, strove to suppress every emotion. With her eyes closed, her lips compressed, and her thin pale hand resting in that of her anxious mother, she seemed to be waiting the issue. Not a murmur would escape her lips, nor did she ever complain of pain. She would often say, by way of consolation to her mother, "Mamma, I am highly favoured. I hardly know what is meant by pain. I am sure I never, to my recollection, have felt it." The moment she was able to sit up, after one of these alarming attacks, every vestige of a sick chamber must be removed. No medicine, no cap, no bed-gown, no loose wrapper must be in sight. Her beautiful dark hair must be parted on her broad, high forehead, her dress arranged with the same care and neatness as when in perfect health; indeed she studied to banish from her appearance all that might remind her friends that her health was impaired, and, if possible, to drive the idea from her own thoughts. Her reply to every inquiry about her health was, "Well, quite well; or at least *I* feel so, though mother continues to treat me as an invalid. True I have a cold, attended by a cough, that is not willing to leave me; but when the spring returns, with its mild air and sweet blossoms, I think this cough, which alarms mother so much, will leave me."

She had, indeed, a strong desire to live; and the cause of that desire is indicative of her character. With all her retiring modesty, she had an ardent desire for literary distinction. The example of her sister Lucretia was incessantly before her; she was her leading star, and her whole soul was but to emulate her soarings into the pure regions of poetry. Her apprehensions were that she might be cut off in the immaturity of her powers. A simple, but most touching ejaculation, betrayed this feeling, as, when lying on a sofa, in one of those alarming paroxysms of her malady, she turned her eyes, full of mournful sweetness, upon her mother, and, in a low, subdued voice, exclaimed, "Oh! my dear, dear mother! *I am so young!*"

We have said that the example of her sister Lucretia was incessantly before her, and no better proof can be given of it than in the following lines, written at this time, which breathe the heavenly aspirations of her pure young spirit, in strains, to us, quite unearthly. We may have read poetry more artificially perfect in its structure, but never any more truly divine in its inspiration.

TO MY SISTER LUCRETIA.

My sister! With that thrilling word
   What thoughts unnumber'd wildly spring!
What echoes in my heart are stirr'd,
   While thus I touch the trembling string!

My sister! ere this youthful mind
   Could feel the value of thine own;
Ere this infantine heart could bind,
   In its deep cell, one look, one tone.

To glide along on memory's stream,
  And bring back thrilling thoughts of thee
Ere I knew aught but childhood's dream,
  Thy soul had struggled and was free!

My sister! with this mortal eye,
  I ne'er shall see thy form again;
And never shall this mortal ear
  Drink in the sweetness of thy strain!

Yet fancy wild, and glowing love,
  Reveal thee to my spirit's view,
Enwreath'd with graces from above,
  And deck'd in heaven's own fadeless hue.

Thy glance of pure seraphic light
  Sheds o'er my heart its soft'ning ray;
Thy pinions guard my couch by night,
  And hover o'er my path by day.

I cannot weep that thou art fled,—
  For ever blends my soul with thine;
Each thought, by purer impulse led,
  Is soaring on to realms divine.

Thy glance unfolds my heart of hearts,
  And lays its inmost recess bare;
Thy voice a heavenly calm imparts,
  And soothes each wilder passion there.

I hear thee in the summer breeze,
  See thee in all that 's pure or fair;
Thy whisper in the murmuring trees,
  Thy breath, thy spirit everywhere.

Thine eyes, which watch when mortals sleep,
  Cast o'er my dreams a radiant hue;
Thy tears, "such tears as angels weep,"
  Fall nightly with the glistening dew.

Thy fingers wake my youthful lyre,
  And teach its softer strains to flow;
Thy spirit checks each vain desire,
  And gilds the low'ring brow of woe.

When fancy wings her upward flight
  On through the viewless realms of air,
Clothed in its robe of matchless light,
  I view thy ransom'd spirit there!

Far from her wild delusive dreams,
  It leads my raptured soul away,
Where the pure fount of glory streams,
  And saints live on through endless day.

When the dim lamp of future years
  Sheds o'er my path its glimmering faint,
First in the view thy form appears,
  My sister, and my guardian saint!

Thou gem of light! my leading star!
What thou hast been, I strive to be;
When from the path I wander far,
Oh turn thy guiding beam on me.

Teach me to fill thy place below,
That I may dwell with thee above;
To soothe, like thee, a mother's woe,
And prove, like thine, a sister's love.

Thou wert unfit to dwell with clay,
For sin too pure, for earth too bright!
And death, who call'd thee hence away,
Placed on his brow a gem of light!

A gem, whose brilliant glow is shed
Beyond the ocean's swelling wave,
Which gilds the memory of the dead,
And pours its radiance on thy grave.

When day hath left his glowing car,
And evening spreads her robe of love;
When worlds, like travellers from afar,
Meet in the azure fields above;

When all is still, and fancy's realm
Is opening to the eager view,
Mine eye full oft, in search of thee,
Roams o'er that vast expanse of blue.

I know that here thy harp is mute,
And quench'd the bright poetic fire,
Yet still I bend my ear, to catch
The hymnings of thy seraph lyre.

Oh! if this partial converse now
So joyous to my heart can be,
How must the streams of rapture flow
When both are chainless, both are free!

When borne from earth for evermore,
Our souls in sacred joy unite,
At God's almighty throne adore,
And bathe in beams of endless light!

Away, away, ecstatic dream!
I must not, dare not dwell on thee;
My soul, immersed in life's dark stream,
Is far too earthly to be free.

Though heaven's bright portal were unclosed,
And angels wooed me from on high,
Too much I fear my shrinking soul
Would cast on earth its longing eye.

Teach me to fill thy place below,
That I may dwell with thee above;
To soothe, like thee, a mother's woe,
And prove, like thine, a sister's love.

It was probably this trembling solicitude about the duration of her existence, that made her so anxious, about this time, to employ every interval of her precarious health in the cultivation of her mental powers. Certain it is, during the winter, chequered as it was with repeated fits of indisposition, she applied herself to historical and other studies with an ardour that often made her mother tremble for the consequences.

The following letters to a young female friend were written during one of these intervals.

"New York, February 26, 1837.

"Notwithstanding all the dangers which might have befallen your letter, my dear Henrietta, it arrived safely at its resting-place, and is now lying open before me, as I am quietly sitting, this chill February morning, to inform you of its safe arrival. I find I was not mistaken in believing you too kind to be displeased at my remissness; and I now hope that through our continued intercourse neither will have cause to complain of the other's negligence.

"For my own part, I am always willing to assign every reason but that of forgetfulness for a friend's silence. Knowing how often I am obliged to claim this indulgence for myself, and how often ill health prevents me from writing to those I love, I am the more ready to frame apologies for others; indeed I think this spirit of *charity* (if so I may call it) is necessary to the happiness of correspondents, and as I am sure you possess it, I trust we shall both glide quietly along without any of those little *jars* which so often interrupt the purest friendships. And now that my dissertation on letter-writing is at an end, I must proceed to inform you of what I fear will be a disappointment, as it breaks away all those sweet anticipations expressed in your affectionate letter. Father has concluded that we shall not return to Plattsburgh next spring, as he had once intended; he fears the effects of the cold winds of Lake Champlain upon mother and myself, who are both delicate; and as we have so many dear friends in and about the city, a nearer location would be pleasanter to us and to them. We now think seriously of returning to Ballston, that beautiful little village where we have already spent two delightful years; and though in this case I must relinquish the idea of visiting my dear '*old home*' and my dear *young friend*, hope points to the hour when *you* may become *my* guest, and where the charms of novelty will in some degree repay us for the delightful associations and remembrances we had hoped to enjoy. But I cannot help now and then casting a backward glance upon the beautiful scenes you describe, and wishing myself with you. A philosopher would say, 'Since you cannot enjoy what you desire, turn to the pleasures you may possess, and seek in them consolation for what you have lost;' but I am no philosopher.

* * * * * * *

"I will endeavour to answer your question about Mrs. Hemans. I have read several lives of this distinguished poetess, by different authors, and in all of them find something new to admire in her character and venerate in her genius! She was a woman of deep feeling, lively fancy, and acute sensibilities; so acute, indeed, as to have formed her chief unhappiness through life. She mingles her own feelings with her poems so well, that in reading *them* you read *her* character. But there is one thing I have often remarked: the mind soon wearies in perusing many of her pieces at *once*. She expresses those sweet sentiments so often, and introduces the same stream of beautiful ideas so constantly, that they sometimes degenerate into monotony. I know of no higher treat than to read a few of her best productions, and comment upon and feel their beauties; but perusing her *volume* is to me like listening to a strain of sweet music repeated over and over again, until it becomes so familiar to the ear, that it loses the charm of variety.

"Now, dear H., is not this presumption in me, to criticise so exquisite an author? But you desired my opinion, and I have given it to you without reserve.

"You desire me to send you an *original poem* for yourself. Now, my dear Hetty, this is something I am not at present able to do for any of my friends, writing being supposed quite injurious to persons with weak lungs. And I have still another reason. You say the effect of conveying feelings from the heart and recording them upon paper, seems to deprive them of half their warmth and ardour! Now, my dear friend, would not the effect of forming them into verse seem to render them still *less* sincere! Is not plain prose, as it slides rapidly from the pen, more apt to speak the feelings of the heart, than when an hour or two is spent in giving them rhyme and measure, and all the attributes of poetry!" * * * * * * *

TO THE SAME.

"New York, April 2d, 1837.

"About an hour since, my dear Henrietta, I received your token of remembrance, and commence my answer with an act of obedience to your sovereign will; but I fear you will repent when too late, and while nodding over the closely written sheet, and peering impatiently into each crowded corner, you will secretly wish you had allowed my pen to commence its operations at a more respectful distance from the top of the page. However, the request was your own: I obey like an obedient friend, and you must abide the consequences of your rash demand. Should the first glance at my well-filled sheet be followed by a *yawn*, or its last word be welcomed with a smile, you must blame your own imprudence in bringing down upon your luckless head the accumulated nothings of a scribbler like myself. It is indeed true that we shall not return to Plattsburgh; and much as I long to revisit the home of my infancy, and the friends of my earliest remembrance, I shall be obliged to relinquish the pleasure in reality, though fancy, unshackled by earth, shall direct her pinions to the north, and linger, delighted, on the beautiful banks of the Champlain! Methinks I hear you exclaim, with impatience, '*Fancy!* what is it? I long for something more substantial.'. So do I, *ma chere*, but since I cannot hope to behold my dear native village and its dear inhabitants with *other* eyes than those of fancy, I will e'en employ them to the best of my ability. You may be sure we do not prefer the confined and murky atmosphere of the city to the pure and health-giving breezes of the country; far from it—we are already preparing to remove, as soon as the mild influence of spring has prevailed over the chilling blasts which we still hear whistling around us; and gladly shall we welcome the day that will release us from our bondage. But there is some drawback to every pleasure—some bitter drop in almost every cup of enjoyment; and we shall taste this most keenly when we bid farewell to the delightful circle of friends who have cheered us during the solitude and confinement of this dreary winter. The New York air, so far from agreeing with us, has deprived us of every enjoyment beyond the boundaries of our own walls, and it will be hard to leave those friends who have taught us to forget the privations of ill health in the pleasure of their society. We have chosen Ballston for our temporary home, from the hope of seeing them oftener *there* than we could in a secluded town, and because pure air, medicinal waters, and good society have all combined to render it a delightful country residence; yet with all these advantages, it can never possess half the charms of my dear old home!

"That dear old home, where pass'd my childish years,
When fond affection wiped my infant tears!
Where first I learn'd from whence my blessings came,
And lisp'd in faltering tones, a *mother's* name!

"That *dear* old *home*, where memory fondly clings,
Where eager fancy spreads her soaring wings;
Around whose scenes my thoughts delight to stray,
And pass the hours in pleasing dreams away!

"Oh, shall I ne'er behold thy waves again,
My native lake, my beautiful Champlain?
Shall I no more above thy ripples bend
In sweet communion with my childhood's friend?

"Shall I no more behold thy rolling wave,
The patriot's cradle and the warrior's grave?
Thy mountains, tinged with daylight's parting glow?
Thy islets, mirror'd in the stream below?

"Back! back!—thou *present!* robed in shadows lie,
And rise, thou *past*, before my raptured eye!
Fancy shall gild the frowning lapse between,
And memory's hand shall paint the glowing scene!

"Lo! how the view beneath her pencil grows!
The flow'ret blooms, the winding streamlet flows;
With former friends I trace my footsteps o'er,
And muse, delighted, on my own green shore!

"Alas it fades—the fairy dream is past!
Dissolved the veil by sportive fancy cast.
Oh why should thus our brightest dreams depart,
And scenes illusive cheat the longing heart?

"Where'er through future life my steps may roam,
I ne'er shall find a spot like thee, my home;
With all my joys the thought of *thee* shall blend,
And joined with *thee*, shall rise my childhood's friend.

"Mother is most truly alive to all these feelings. During our first year in New York, we were living a few miles from the city, at one of the loveliest situations in the world! I think I have seldom seen a sweeter spot; but all its beauties could not divert her thoughts from our own dear *home*, and despite the superior advantages we there enjoyed, she wept to enjoy it again. But enough of this; if I suffer my fancy to dwell longer upon these loved scenes, I shall scribble over my whole sheet, and, leaving out what I most wish to say, fill it with nothing but 'Home, home, sweet, sweet home!' as the song goes.

June, 1837.

"Now for the mighty theme upon which I scarcely dare to dwell: my visit to Plattsburgh! Yes, my dear H., I do think, or rather I do *hope*, that such a time may come when I may spend at least a week with you. I dare not hope for a longer time, for I know I shall be disappointed. About the middle of this month brother graduates, and will leave West Point for home. He intends to visit Plattsburgh, and it will take much to wean me from my favourite plan of accompanying him. However, all is uncertain—I must not think of it too much—but if I do come, it will be with the hope of gaining a still greater pleasure. We are now delightfully situated. Can you not return with me, and make me a visit? What joy is like the joy of anticipation? What pleasure like those we look forward to, through a long lapse of time, and dwell upon as some bright land that we shall inhabit when the *present* shall have become the *past?* I have heard it observed that it was foolish to anticipate—that it was only increasing the pangs of disappointment. Not so: do we not, in our most sanguine hopes, acknowledge to ourselves a fear, a doubt, an expectation of disappointment? Shall we lose the enjoyment of the present, because evil may come in future? No, no—if anticipation was not meant for a solace, an alleviation of the sorrows of life, would it have been so strongly implanted in our hearts by the great Director of all our passions? No—it is too precious! I would give up half the *reality* of joy for the sweet anticipation. Stop—I have gone too far—for indeed I could *not* resign my visit to you, though I might hope and anticipate for years!

"Just as I had written the above, father interrupted me with an invitation to ride. We have just returned from a long, delightful drive. Though Ballston cannot compare with Plattsburgh for its rich and varied scenery, still there are romantic woods and shady paths which cannot fail to delight the true lover of nature.

* * * * * * * *

"So you do have the *blues*, eh? I had almost said I was glad of it; but that would be too cruel—I will only say, one does not like to be alone, or in any thing singular, and I too, once in a while, receive a visit from these provoking imps—are they not? You should not have blamed Scott only, (excuse me,) but yourself, for selecting such a book to chase away melancholy.

"You ask me if I remember those *story-telling* days? Indeed I do, and nothing affords me more pleasure than the recollection of those happy hours! If my memory could only retain the particulars of my last story, gladly would I resume and continue it when I meet you again. I will ease *your* heart of its fear for *mine*—your scolding did not break it. My dear H., it is not made of such brittle materials as to crack for a trifle. No, no! It would be far more prudent to save it entire for some greater occasion, and then make the crash as loud as possible—don't you think so? Oh nonsensical nonsense! Well,

'The greatest and the wisest men
Will fool a little now and then.'

But I believe I will not add another word, lest my pen should slide off into some new absurdity."

On the 1st of May, 1837, the family left New York for Ballston. They had scarce reached there when Mrs. Davidson had an attack of inflammatory rheumatism, which confined her to her bed, and rendered her helpless as an infant. It was Margaret's turn now to play the nurse, which she did with the most tender assiduity. The paroxysms of her mother's complaint were at first really alarming, as may be seen by the following extract of a letter from Margaret to Miss Sedgwick, written a short time afterwards:

"We at first thought she would never revive. It was indeed a dreadful hour, my dear madam—a sad trial for poor father and myself, to watch, as we supposed, the last agonies of one so beloved as my dear mother! But the cloud has passed by, and my heart, relieved from its burden, is filled, almost to overflowing, with gratitude and joy. After a few hours of dreadful suspense, reaction took place, and since then she has been slowly and steadily improving. In a few days, I hope, she will be able to ride, and breathe some of this delightful air, which cannot fail to invigorate and restore her. My own health has improved astonishingly since my coming here. I walk, and ride, and exercise as much as possible in the open air, and find it of great service to me. Oh how much I hope to see you here! * * * * Do, if possible, try the Ballston air once more. It has been useful to you once, it might be still more so now. You will find warm hearts to welcome you, and we will do all in our power to make your visit pleasant to you. The country does indeed look beautiful! The woods are teeming with wild flowers, and the air is full of melody. The soft, wild warbling of the birds is far more sweet to me than the most laboured performances of art; *they* may weary by repetition, but what heart can resist the influence of a lovely day ushered in by the morning song of those sweet carollers! and even to sleep, as it were, by their melodious evening strain. How I wish you could be here to enjoy it with me."

The summer of 1837 was one of the happiest of her fleeting existence. For some time after the family removed to Ballston she was very much confined to the house by the illness of her mother, and the want of a proper female companion to accompany her abroad. At length, a Mr. and Mrs. H., estimable and intimate friends, of a highly intellectual character, came to the village. Their society was an invaluable acquisition to Margaret. In company with them she was enabled to enjoy the healthful recreations of the country; to ramble in the woods; to take exercise on horseback, of which she was extremely fond, and to make excursions about the neighbourhood; while they exerted a guardian care to prevent her, in her enthusiastic love for rural scenery, from exposing herself to any thing detrimental to her health and strength. She gave herself up, for a time, to these exhilarating exercises, abstaining from her usual propensity to overtask her intellect, for she had imbibed the idea that active habits, cheerful recreations, and a holiday frame of mind would effectually re-establish her health. As usual, in her excited moods, she occasionally carried these really healthful practices to excess, and would often, says her mother, engage, with a palpitating heart, and a pulse beating at the rate of one hundred and thirty in a minute, in all the exercises usually prescribed to *preserve* health in those who are in full possession of the blessing. She was admonished of her danger by several attacks upon her lungs during the summer, but as they were of short duration, she still flattered herself that she was getting well. There seemed to be almost an infatuation in her case. The exhilaration of her spirits was at times so great as almost to overpower her. Often would she stand by the window admiring a glorious sunset, until she would be raised into a kind of ecstasy; her eye would kindle; a crimson glow would mount into her cheek, and she would indulge in some of her reveries about the glories of heaven, and the spirits of her deceased sisters, partly uttering her fancies aloud, until turning and catching her mother's eye fixed painfully upon her, she would throw her arms round her neck, kiss away the tears, and sink exhausted on her bosom. The excitement over, she would resume her calmness, and converse on general topics. Among her writings are fragments hastily scrawled down at this time, showing the vague aspirations of her spirit, and her vain attempts to grasp those shadowy images that sometimes flit across the poetic mind.

Oh for a something more than this,
To fill the void within my breast;
A sweet reality of bliss,
A something bright, but unexpress'd!

My spirit longs for something higher
Than life's dull stream can e'er supply;
Something to feed this inward fire,
This spark, which never more can die.

I'd hold companionship with all
Of pure, of noble, or divine;
With glowing heart adoring fall,
And kneel at nature's sylvan shrine.

My soul is like a broken lyre,
  Whose loudest, sweetest chord is gone;
A note, half trembling on the wire—
  A heart that wants an echoing tone.

When shall I find this shadowy bliss,
  This shapeless phantom of the mind?
This something words can ne'er express,
  So vague, so faint, so undefined?

Language! thou never canst portray
  The fancies floating o'er my soul!
Thou ne'er canst chase the clouds away
  Which o'er my changing visions roll!

And again—

Oh I have gazed on forms of light,
  Till life seem'd ebbing in a tear—
Till in that fleeting space of sight
  Were merged the feelings of a year.

And I have heard the voice of song,
  Till my full heart gush'd wild and free,
And my rapt soul would float along
  As if on waves of melody.

But while I glow'd at beauty's glance,
  I long'd to feel a deeper thrill:
And while I heard that dying strain,
  I sigh'd for something sweeter still.

I have been happy, and my soul
  Free from each sorrow, care, regret;
Yet even in these hours of bliss
  I long'd to find them happier yet.

Oft o'er the darkness of my mind
  Some meteor thought has glanced at will;
'T was bright—but ever have I sigh'd
  To find a fancy brighter still.

Why are these restless, vain desires,
  Which always grasp at something more
To feed the spirit's hidden fires,
  Which burn unseen—unnoticed soar?

Well might the heathen sage have known
  That earth must fail the soul to bind;
That life, and life's tame joys, alone,
  Could never chain the ethereal mind.

The above, as we have before observed, are mere fragments, unfinished and uncorrected, and some of the verses have a vagueness incident to the mood of mind in which they were conceived, and the haste with which they were penned; but in these lofty, indefinite aspirations of a young, half-schooled, and inexperienced mind, we see the early and impatient flutterings of a poetical genius, which, if spared, might have soared to the highest regions.

In a letter written to Miss Sedgwick during the autumn, she speaks of her health as having rapidly improved. "I am no longer afflicted by the cough, and mother feels it unnecessary now to speak to me as being ill; though my health is, and probably always will be, very delicate."—"And she really did appear better," observes her mother, "and even I, who had ever been nervously alive to every symptom of her disease, was deluded by those favourable appearances, and began to entertain a hope that she might yet recover, when another sudden attack of bleeding at the lungs convinced us of the fallacy of our hopes, and warned us to take every measure to ward off the severity of the climate in the coming winter. A consultation was held between her father and our favourite physician, and the result was that she was to keep within doors. This was indeed sad, but, after an evident struggle with her own mind, she submitted, with her accustomed good sense, to the decree. All that affection could suggest, was done, to prevent the effects of this seclusion on her spirits." A cheerful room was allotted to her, commanding an agreeable prospect, and communicating, by folding doors, to a commodious parlour; the temperature of the whole apartment was regulated by a thermometer. Hither her books, writing-table, drawing implements, and fancy work were transported. When once established in these winter quarters, she became contented and cheerful. "She read and wrote," says her mother, "and amused herself with drawing and needle work. After spending as much time as I dare permit in the more serious studies in which she was engaged, she would unbend her mind with one of Scott's delightful novels, or play with her kitten; and at evening we were usually joined by our interesting friends, Mr. and Mrs. H. It is now a melancholy satisfaction to me to believe that she could not, in her state of health, be happier, or more pleasantly situated. She was always charmed with the conversation of Mr. H., and followed him through all the mazes of philosophy with the greatest delight. She read Cousin with a high zest, and produced an abstract from it which gave a convincing proof that she understood the principles there laid down; after which she gave a complete analysis of the Introduction to the History of Philosophy, by the same author. Her mind must have been deeply engrossed by these studies, yet it was not visible from her manner. During this short winter she accomplished what to many would have been the labour of years, yet there was no haste, no flurry; she pursued quietly her round of occupations, always cheerful. The hours flew swiftly by; not a moment lagged. I think she never spent a more happy winter than this, with all its varied employments."

The following extract from a letter to one of her young friends, gives an idea of her course of reading during this winter; and how, in her precocious mind, the playfulness of the child mingled with the thoughtfulness of the woman.

"You ask me what I am reading. Alas! book-worm as I am, it makes me draw a long breath to contemplate the books I have laid out for perusal. In the first place, I am reading Condillac's Ancient History, in French, twenty-four volumes; Gibbon's Decline and Fall of the Roman Empire, in four large volumes. I have not finished Josephus. In my moments of recreation I am poring over Scott's bewitching *novels*. I wish we could give them some other name instead of *novels*, for they certainly should not bear the same title with the thousand and one productions of that class daily swarming from the press. Do you think they ought? So pure, so pathetic, so historical, and, above all, so true to human nature. How beautifully he mingles the sad with the grotesque, in such a manner that the opposite feelings they excite harmonize perfectly with each other. His works can be read over and over again, and every time with a growing sense of their beauties. Do you read French? If so, I wish we could read the same works together. It would be a great pleasure to me at least, and our mutual remarks might benefit each other. Supposing you will be pleased to hear of my amusements, however trifling, I will venture to name one, at the risk of lowering any great opinion you may have formed of my wisdom! A pet kitten!!! Yes, my dear Henrietta, a sweet little creature, with a graceful shape, playful temper, white breast, and dear little innocent eyes, which completely belie the reputed disposition of a *cat*. He is neither deceitful, ferocious, nor ungrateful, but is certainly the most rational being for an irrational one, I ever saw. He is now snugly lying in my lap, watching every movement of my pen with a quiet purr of contentment. Have you such a pet? I wish you had, that we both might play with them at the same time, sunset, for instance, and while so far distant, feel that we were enjoying ourselves in the selfsame way. You ask what I think of animal magnetism? My dear Hetty, I have not troubled my head about it. I hear of it from every quarter, and mentioned so often with contempt, that I have thought of it only as an absurdity. If I understand it rightly, the leading principle is the influence of one mind upon another; there is undoubtedly such an influence, to a reasonable degree, but as to throwing one into a magnetic sleep—presenting visions before their eyes of scenes passing afar off, it seems almost too ridiculous! Still it may be all *true!* A hundred years since, what would have been our feelings to see what is now here so common, a *steam engine*, breathing fire and smoke, gliding along with the rapidity of thought, and carrying at its *black heels* a train which a hundred men would fail to move. We know not but this apparent absurdity, this magnetism may be a great and mysterious secret, which the course of time will reveal and adapt to important purposes. * * * * * What are you studying? Do you play? Do you draw? Please tell me every thing. I wish I could form some picture of you to my mind's eye. It is so tormenting to correspond with a dear friend, and have no likeness of them in our fancy. I remember every thing as it used to be, but time makes great changes! Now here comes my saucy kitten, and springs upon the table before me as if he had a perfect right there. 'What do you mean, little puss? Come, sit for your portrait!' I hope, dear H., you will fully appreciate this painting, which I consider as my chef-d'œuvre, and preserve it as a faithful likeness of my inimitable cat. But do forgive me so much nonsense! But I feel that to you I can rattle off any thing that comes uppermost. It is near night, and the sun is setting so beautifully after the long storm that I could not sit here much longer, even if I had a whole page to fill. How splendid the moon must look on the bright waters of the Champlain this night! Good bye, good bye—love to all from all, and believe me, now as ever,

Your sincere friend,

MARGARET."

The following passages from her mother's memorandums, touch upon matters of more solemn interest, which occasionally occupied her young mind:

"During the whole of the preceding summer her mind had dwelt much upon the subject of religion. Much of her time was devoted to serious reflection, self-examination, and prayer. But she evidently shunned all conversation upon the subject. It was a theme she had always conversed upon with pleasure until *now*. This not only surprised but pained me. I was a silent but close and anxious observer of the operations of her mind, and saw that, with all her apparent cheerfulness, she was ill at ease; perfect silence was however maintained on both sides until the winter commenced, and brought us more closely together. Then her young heart again reposed itself, in confiding love, upon the bosom that heretofore had shared its every thought, and the subject became one of daily discussion. I found her mind perplexed, and her ideas confused by points of doctrine which she could neither understand nor reconcile with her views of the justice and benevolence of God, as exhibited in the Scriptures. Her views of the divine character and attributes had ever been of that elevated cast, which, while they raised her mind above all grosser things, sublimated and purified her feelings and desires, and prepared her for that bright and holy communion without which she could enjoy nothing. Her faith was of that character 'which casteth out fear.' It was sweet and soothing to depend upon Jesus for salvation. It was delightful to behold, in the all-imposing majesty of God, a kind and tender father, who pitied her infirmities, and on whose justice and benevolence she could rest for time and eternity. She had, during the summer, heard much disputation on doctrinal points, which she had silently and carefully examined, and had been shocked at the position which many professing Christians had taken; she saw much inconsistency, much bitterness of spirit, on points which she had been taught to consider not essential to salvation; she saw that the spirit of persecution and uncharitableness which pervaded many classes of Christians, had almost totally destroyed that bond of brotherhood which ought firmly to unite the followers of the humble Saviour; and she could not reconcile these feelings with her ideas of the Christian character. Her meekness and humility led her sometimes to doubt her own state. She felt that her religious duties were but too feebly performed, and that without divine assistance all her resolutions to be more faithful were vain. She often said, 'Mamma, I am far from right. I resolve and re-resolve, and yet remain the same.' I had shunned every thing that savoured of controversy, knowing her enthusiasm and extreme sensibility on the subject of religion; I dreaded the excitement it might create. But I now more fully explained, as well as I was able, the simple and divine truths of the Gospel, and held up to her view the beauty and benevolence of the Father's character, and the unbounded love which could have devised the atoning sacrifice; and advised her at present to avoid controversial writings, and make a more thorough examination of the Scriptures, that she might found her principles upon the evidences to be deduced from that groundwork of our faith, unbiassed by the opinions and prejudices of *any man*. I represented to her, that, young as she was, while in feeble health, researches into those knotty and disputed subjects would only confuse her mind; that there was enough of plain practical religion to be gathered from the Bible; and urged the importance of frequent and earnest prayer, which, with God's blessing, would compose the agitation of her mind, which I considered as essential to her inward peace.

On one occasion, while perusing Lockhart's Life of Scott with great interest, her mother ventured to sound her feelings upon the subject of literary fame, and asked her whether she had no ambition to have her name go down to posterity. She took her mother's hand with enthusiasm, kissed her cheek, and, retiring to the other room, in less than an hour returned with the following lines:

TO DIE AND BE FORGOTTEN.

A few short years will roll along,
 With mingled joy and pain,
Then shall I pass—a broken tone!
 An echo of a strain!

Then shall I fade away from life,
 Like cloud-tints from the sky,
When the breeze sweeps their surface o'er,
 And they are lost for aye.

The world will laugh, and weep, and sing,
 As gaily as before,
But cold and silent I shall be—
 As I have been no more.

The haunts I loved, the flowers I nursed
 Will bloom as sweetly still,
But other hearts and other hands
 My vacant place shall fill.

And even mighty love must fail
 To bind my memory here—
Like fragrance round the faded rose,
 'T will perish with the year.

The soul may look with fervent hope
 To worlds of future bliss;
But oh how saddening to the heart
 To be forgot in this!

How many a noble mind hath shrunk
 From death without a name:
Hath look'd beyond his shadowy realm,
 And lived and died for fame.

Could we not view the darksome grave
 With calmer, steadier eye,
If conscious that a world's regret
 Would seek us where we lie?

Faith points, with mild confiding glance,
  To realms of bliss above,
Where peace, and joy, and justice reign,
  And never-dying love!

But still our earthly feelings cling
  Around this bounded spot;—
There is a something burns within
  Which will not be forgot.

It cares not for a gorgeous hearse,
  For waving torch and plume;
For pealing hymn, funereal verse,
  Or richly sculptured tomb;

But it would live, undimm'd and fresh,
  When flickering life departs;
Would find a pure and honour'd grave,
  Embalm'd in kindred hearts.

Who would not brave a life of tears
  To win an honour'd name?
One sweet and heart-awakening tone
  From the silver trump of fame?

To be, when countless years have past,
  The good man's glowing theme?
To be—but I—what right have I
  To this bewildering dream?

Oh, it is vain, and worse than vain,
  To dwell on thoughts like these;
I, a frail child, whose feeble frame
  Already knows disease!

Who, ere another spring may dawn,
  Another summer bloom,
May, like the flowers of autumn, lie
  A tenant of the tomb.

Away, away, presumptuous thought,
  I will not dwell on thee!
For what, alas! am I to fame,
  And what is fame to me?

Let all these wild and longing thoughts
  With the dying year expire,
And I will nurse within my breast
  A purer, holier fire!

Yes, I will seek my mind to win
  From all these dreams of strife,
And toil to write my name within
  The glorious book of life.

Then shall old Time, who, rolling on,
  Impels me towards the tomb,
Prepare for me a glorious crown,
  Through endless years to bloom.

December, 1837.

The confinement to the house, in a graduated temperature, the round of cheerful occupations, and the unremitting care taken of her, produced a visible melioration of her symptoms. Her cough gradually subsided, the morbid irritability of her system, producing often an unnatural flow of spirits, was quieted; as usual, she looked forward to spring as the genial and delightful season that was to restore her to perfect health and freedom.

Christmas was approaching, which had ever been a time of social enjoyment in the family; as it drew near, however, the remembrance of those lost from the fireside circle was painfully felt by Mrs. Davidson. Margaret saw the gloom on her mother's brow, and kissing her, exclaimed, "Dear mother, do not let us waste our present happiness in useless repining. You see I am well, and you are more comfortable, and dear father is in good health and spirits. Let us enjoy the present hour, and banish vain regrets!" Having given this wholesome advice, she tripped off with a light step to prepare Christmas presents for the servants, which were to be distributed by St. Nicholas or Santa Claus, in the old traditional way. Every animated being, rational or irrational, must share her liberality on that day of festivity and joy. Her Jenny, a little bay pony on which she had taken many healthful and delightful rides, must have a gayer blanket, and an extra allowance of oats. "On Christmas morning," says her mother, "she woke with the first sound of the old house-clock striking the hour of five, and twining her arms around my neck, (for during this winter she shared my bed,) and, kissing me again and again, exclaimed—

'Wake, mother, wake to youthful glee,
The golden sun is dawning!'

then slipping a piece of paper into my hand, she sprang out of bed, and danced about the carpet, her kitten in her arms, with all the sportive glee of childhood. When I gazed upon her young face, so bright, so animated, and beautiful, beaming with innocence and love, and thought that perhaps this was the last anniversary of her Saviour's birth she might spend on earth, I could not suppress my emotions: I caught her to my bosom in an agony of tenderness, while she, all unconscious of the nature of my feelings, returned my caresses with playful fondness." The following verses were contained in the above-mentioned paper:

TO MY MOTHER AT CHRISTMAS.

Wake, mother, wake to youthful glee,
The golden sun is dawning!
Wake, mother, wake, and hail with me
This happy Christmas morning!

Each eye is bright with pleasure's glow,
Each lip is laughing merrily;
A smile hath pass'd o'er winter's brow,
And the very snow looks cheerily.

Hark to the voice of the waken'd day,
To the sleigh-bells gaily ringing,
While a thousand, thousand happy hearts
Their Christmas lays are singing.

'T is a joyous hour of mirth and love,
And my heart is overflowing!
Come, let us raise our thoughts above,
While pure, and fresh, and glowing.

'T is the happiest day of the rolling year,
But it comes in a robe of mourning
Nor light, nor life, nor bloom is here
Its icy shroud adorning.

It comes when all around is dark,
'T is meet it so should be,
For its joy is the joy of the happy heart,
The spirit's jubilee.

It does not need the bloom of spring,
Or summer's light and gladness,
For love has spread her beaming wing
O'er winter's brow of sadness.

'Twas thus he came, beneath a cloud
His spirit's light concealing,
No crown of earth, no kingly robe
His heavenly power revealing.

His soul was pure, his mission love,
His aim a world's redeeming;
To raise the darken'd soul above
Its wild and sinful dreaming.

With all his Father's power and love
The cords of guilt to sever;
To ope a sacred fount of light,
Which flows, shall flow for ever.

Then we shall hail the glorious day,
The spirit's new creation,
And pour our grateful feelings forth,
A pure and warm libation.

Wake, mother, wake to chasten'd joy,
The golden sun is dawning!
Wake, mother, wake, and hail with me
This happy Christmas morning.

"The last day of the year 1837 arrived. 'Mamma,' said she, 'will you sit up with me to-night until after twelve?' I looked inquiringly. She replied, 'I wish to bid farewell to the present, and to welcome the coming year.' After the family retired, and we had seated ourselves by a cheerful fire to spend the hours which would intervene until the year 1838 should dawn upon us, she was serious, but not sad, and as if she had nothing more than usual upon her mind, took some light sewing in her hand, and so interested me by her conversation, that I scarcely noticed the flight of time. At half past eleven she handed me a book, pointing to some interesting article to amuse me, then took her seat at the writing-table, and composed the piece on the departure of the old year 1837, and the commencement of the new one 1838. When she had finished the Farewell, except the last verse, it wanted a few minutes of twelve. She rested her arms in silence upon the table, apparently absorbed in meditation. The clock struck—a sort of deep thought passed over her expressive face—she remained solemn and silent until the last tone had ceased to vibrate, when she again resumed her pen and wrote, 'The bell! it hath ceased.' When the clock struck, I arose from my seat and stood leaning over the back of her chair, with a mind deeply solemnized by a scene so new and interesting. The words flowed rapidly from her pen, without haste or confusion, and at one o'clock we were quietly in bed."

We again subjoin the poem alluded to, trusting that these effusions, which are so intimately connected with her personal history, will be read with greater interest, when given in conjunction with the scenes and circumstances which prompted them.

ON THE DEPARTURE OF THE YEAR 1837, AND THE COMMENCEMENT OF 1838.

Hark to the house-clock's measured chime,
As it cries to the startled ear,
"A dirge for the soul of departing time,
A requiem for the year."

Thou art passing away to the mighty past,
Where thy countless brethren sleep,
Till the great Archangel's trumpet-blast,
Shall waken land and deep.

Oh the lovely and beautiful things that lie
On thy cold and motionless breast!
Oh the tears, the rejoicings, the smiles, the sighs,
Departing with thee to their rest.

Thou wert usher'd to life amid darkness and gloom,
But the cold icy cloud pass'd away,
And spring, in her verdure, and freshness, and bloom,
Touch'd with glory thy mantle of gray.

The flow'rets burst forth in their beauty—the trees
In their exquisite robes were array'd,
But thou glidedst along, and the flower and the leaf,
At the sound of thy footsteps, decay'd.

And fairer young blossoms were blooming alone,
And they died at the glance of thine eye,
But a life was within which should rise o'er thine own,
And a spirit thou couldst not destroy.

Thou hast folded thy pinions, thy race is complete,
And fulfill'd the Creator's behest,
Then, adieu to thee, year of our sorrows and joys,
And peaceful and long be thy rest.

Farewell! for thy truth-written record is full,
And the page weeps, for sorrow and crime;
Farewell! for the leaf hath shut down on the past,
And conceal'd the dark annals of time.

The bell! it hath ceased with its iron tongue
To ring on the startled ear,
The dirge o'er the grave of the lost one is rung—
All hail to the new-born year!

All hail to the new-born year!
To the child of hope and fear!
He comes on his car of state,
And weaves our web of fate,
And he opens his robe to receive us all,
And we live or die, and we rise or fall,
In the arms of the new-born year!

Hope! spread thy soaring wings!
Look forth on the boundless sea,
And trace thy bright and beautiful things
On the veil of the great To Be.

Build palaces broad as the sky,
And store them with treasures of light,
Let exquisite visions bewilder the eye,
And illumine the darkness of night.

We are gliding fast from the buried year,
And the present is no more,
But hope, we will borrow thy sparkling gear,
And shroud the future o'er.

Our tears and sighs shall sleep
In the grave of the silent past;
We will raise up flowers—nor weep
That the air hues may not last.

We will dream our dreams of joy,
  Ah, fear! why darken the scene?
Why sprinkle that ominous tear,
  My beautiful visions between?

Hath not sorrow swift wings of her own,
  That thou must assist in her flight?
Is not daylight too rapidly gone,
  That thou must urge onward the night?

Ah! leave me to fancy, to hope,
  For grief will too quickly be here;
Ah! leave me to shadow forth figures of light,
  In the mystical robe of the year.

'T is true, they may never assume
  The substance of pleasure,—the real,—
But believe me, our purest of joy
  Consists in the vague—the ideal.

Then away to the darksome cave,
  With thy sisters, the sigh and the tear,
We will drink, in the crystal wave,
  To the health of the new-born year.

"She had been for some time thinking of a subject for a poem, and the next day, which was the first of January, came to me in great perplexity and asked my advice. I had long desired that she would direct her attention to the beautiful and sublime narratives of the Old Testament, and now proposed that she should take the Bible and examine it with that view. After an hour or two spent in research, she remarked that there were many, very many subjects of deep and thrilling interest; but if she now should make a failure, her discouragement would be such as to prevent her from ever making another attempt. 'I am now,' she said, 'trying my wings; I will take a lighter subject at first: if I succeed, I will then write a more perfect poem, founded upon Sacred History.'"

She accordingly took as a theme a prose tale, in a current work of the day, and wrote several pages with a flowing pen, but soon threw them by dissatisfied. It was irksome to employ the thoughts and fancies of another, and to have to adapt her own to the plan of the author. She wanted something original. "After some farther effort," says Mrs. Davidson, "she came to me out of spirits and in tears. 'Mother,' said she, 'I must give it up after all.' I asked the reason, and then remarked that as she had already so many labours upon her hands, and was still feeble, it might be the wisest course. 'Oh mother,' said she, 'that is not the reason; my head and my heart are full: poetic images are crowding upon my brain, but every subject has been monopolised: "there is nothing new under the sun."' I said, 'My daughter, that others have written upon a subject is not an objection. The most eminent writers do not always choose what is new.' 'Mother, dear mother, what can I say upon a theme which has been touched by the greatest men of this or some other age? I, a mere child; it is absurd in me to think of it.' She dropped beside me on the sofa, laid her head upon my bosom, and sobbed violently. I wiped the tears from her face, while my own were fast flowing, and strove to soothe the tumult of her mind. * * * When we were both more calm, I said, 'Margaret, I had hoped that during this winter you would not have commenced or applied yourself to any important work; but if you feel in that way, I will not urge you to resign an occupation which gives you such exquisite enjoyment.'"

Mrs. Davidson then went on to show to her that, notwithstanding the number of poets that had written, the themes and materials for poetry are inexhaustible. By degrees Margaret became composed, took up a book and read. The words of her mother dwelt in her mind. In a few days she brought her mother the introduction to a projected poem to be called Lenore. Mrs. Davidson was touched at finding the remarks she had made for the purpose of soothing the agitation of her daughter had served to kindle her imagination, and were poured forth with eloquence in those verses. The excitement continued, and the poem of Lenore was completed, corrected, and copied into her book by the first of March; having written her plan in prose at full length, containing about the same number of lines as the poem. "During its progress," says Mrs. Davidson, "when fatigued with writing, she would take her kitten, and recline upon her sofa, asking me to relate to her some of the scenes of the last war. Accordingly, I would while away our solitude by repeating anecdotes of that period; and before Lenore was completed she had advanced several pages in a prose tale, the scene of which was laid upon Lake Champlain during the last war. She at the same time executed faces and figures in crayon, which would not have disgraced the pencil of an artist. Her labours were truly immense. Yet a stranger coming occasionally to the house would hardly observe that she had any pressing avocations."

The following are extracts from a rough draught of a letter written to Miss Sedgwick about this time.

"My dear Madam,

"I wish I could express to you my pleasure on receiving your kind and affectionate letter. So far from considering myself neglected by your silence, I felt it a great privilege to be permitted to write to you, and knew that I ought not to expect a regular answer to every letter, even while I was longing, day after day, to receive this gratifying token of remembrance. Unless you had witnessed, I fear you would hardly believe my extravagant delight on reading the dear little folded paper, so expressive of your kind recollection. I positively danced for joy; bestowed a thousand caresses upon every body and every thing I loved, dreamed of you all night, and arose next morning (with a heart full,) to answer your letter, but was prevented by indisposition, and have not been able until now to perform a most pleasing duty by acknowledging its receipt. My health during the past winter has been much better than we had anticipated. It is true I have been with dear mother, entirely confined to the house, but being able to read, write, and perform all my usual employments, I feel that I have much more reason to be thankful for the blessings continued to me, than to repine because a few have been denied. But spring is now here in name, if not in reality, and I can assure you my heart bounds at the thought of once more escaping from my confinement, and breathing the pure air of Heaven, without fearing a blight or consumption in every breeze. Spring! What pleasure does that magic syllable convey to the heart of an invalid, laden with sweet promises, and bringing before his mind visions of liberty, which those who are always free cannot enjoy. Thus do I dream of summer, I may never see, and make myself happy for hours in anticipating pleasures I may never share. It is an idle employment, and little calculated to sweeten disappointment. But it has opened to me many sources of delight otherwise unknown; and when out of humour with the present, I have only to send fancy flower-gathering in the future, and I find myself fully repaid. Dear mother's health has also been much better than we had feared, and her ill turns less frequent and severe. She sits up most of the day, walks around the lower part of the house, and enjoys her book and her pen as much as ever. * * * * * * You speak of your intercourse with Mrs. Jameson. It must indeed be an exquisite pleasure to be intimately associated with a mind like hers. I have never seen any thing but extracts from her writings, but must obtain and read them. I suppose the world is anxiously looking for her next volume. * * * We have been reading Lockhart's Life of Scott. Is it not a deeply interesting work? In what a beautiful light it represents the character of that great and good man!

No one can read his life or his works without loving and venerating him. As to 'the waters of Helicon' we have but a few niggardly streams in this, our matter-of-fact village; and father in his medical capacity has forbidden my partaking of them as freely as I could wish. But no matter, they have been frozen up, and will flow in 'streams more salubrious' beneath the milder sky of spring."

In all her letters we find a solicitude about her mother's health, rather than about her own, and indeed it was difficult to say which was most precarious.

The following extract from a poem written about this time to "Her Mother on her fiftieth Birthday" presents a beautiful portrait, and does honour to the filial hand that drew it.

Yes, mother, fifty years have fled
With rapid footsteps o'er thy head;
Have past with all their motley train,
And left thee on thy couch of pain!
How many smiles and sighs and tears,
How many hopes and doubts and fears
Have vanish'd with that lapse of years.

Oh that we all could look like thee,
Back on that dark and tideless sea,
And 'mid its varied records find
A heart at ease with all mankind,
A firm and self-approving mind—
Grief that had broken hearts less fine
Hath only served to strengthen thine.

Time that doth chill the fancy's play
Hath kindled thine with purer ray:
And stern disease, whose icy dart
Hath power to chill the breaking heart,
Hath left thine warm with love and truth,
As in the halcyon days of youth.

The following letter was written on the 26th of March, to a female cousin resident in New York.

"DEAR KATE: This day I am fifteen, and you can, you will, readily pardon and account for the absurd flights of my pen, by supposing that my tutelary spirits, nonsense and folly, have assembled around the being of their creation, and claimed the day as exclusively their own; then I pray you to lay to their account all that I have already scribbled, and believe that, uninfluenced by these grinning deities, I can think and feel, and love, as I love you with all warmth and sincerity of heart. Do you remember how we used to look forward to sweet fifteen as the pinnacle of human happiness, the golden age of existence? You have but lately passed that milestone in the highway of life; I have just reached it, but I find myself no better satisfied to stand still than before, and look forward to the continuance of my journey with the same ardent longing I felt at fourteen.

"Ah, Kate, here we are, two young travellers starting forth upon our long pilgrimage, and knowing not whither it may conduct us! *You* some months my superior in age, and many years in acquaintance with society, in external attractions, and all those accomplishments necessary to form an elegant woman. *I*, knowing nothing of life but from books, and a small circle of friends, who love me as I love them; looking upon the *past* as a faded dream, which I shall have time enough to study and expound when old age and sorrow come on; upon the *present* as a nursling, a preparative for the *future;* and upon that future, as what? a mighty whirlpool, of hopes and fears, of bright anticipations and bitter disappointments, into which I shall soon plunge, and find there, in common with the rest of the world, my happiness or misery." * * *

The following to a young friend, was also written on the 26th of March.

"My Dear H.: You must know that winter has come, and gone, and neither mother nor myself have felt a single breeze which could not force its way through the thick walls of our little dwelling. Do you not think I am looking gladly forward to April and May, as the lovely sisters who are to unlock the doors of our prison house, and give us once more to the free enjoyment of nature, without fearing a blight or a consumption in every breath? And now for another, and even more delightful anticipation—your visit! Are you indeed coming? And when are you coming? Do answer the first, that I may for once have the pleasure of framing delightful visions without finding them dashed to the ground by the iron hand of reality; and the last, that I may not expect you too soon, and thus subject myself to all the bitterness of "hope deferred." Come, for I have so much to say to you, that I cannot possibly contain it until summer; and come quickly, unless you are willing to account for my wasted time as well as your own, for I shall do little else but dream of you and your visit until the time of your arrival. You cannot imagine how those few words in your little *good for nothing* letter have completely upset my wonted gravity. Do not disappoint me. It is true, mother and I are both feeble and unable to go out with you and show you the lions of our little village; but if warm welcomes can atone for the want of ceremony, you shall have them in abundance: but it seems to me that I shall want to pin you down in a chair, and do nothing but look at you from morning till night. As to coming to Plattsburgh, I think if we cannot do so in the spring, (which is doubtful,) we certainly shall in the course of the summer. Brother M. wrote to me yesterday, saying that he would spend the month of August in the country, and if nothing occurred to prevent, we would take our delightful trip by the way of Lake George. Oh it will be so pleasant! But my anticipations are now all bent upon a nearer object. Do not allow a slight impediment to destroy them. We expect in May to move to Saratoga. We shall then have a more convenient house, better society, and the benefit of a school in which I can practise music and drawing, without being obliged to attend regularly. We shall then be a few miles nearer to you, and at present that seems something desirable to me. I have read and own three volumes of Scott's life, and was much disappointed to find that it was not finished in these three, but concluded the remainder had not yet come out. Are the five volumes all? it is indeed a deeply interesting work. I am very fond of biography, for surely there can be nothing more delightful or instructive than to trace in the infancy and youth of every noble mind the germs of its future greatness. Have you read a work called Letters from Palmyra, by Mr. Ware of New York? I have not yet seen it, but intend to do so soon. It is written in the character of a citizen of Rome at that early period, and it is said to be a lively picture of the manners and customs of the imperial city, and still more of the magnificence of Palmyra, and its splendid queen Zenobia. It also contains a beautiful story. I have lately been reperusing many of Scott's novels, and intend to finish them. Was ever any thing half so fascinating! Oh how I long to have you here and tell you all these little things in person. Do write to me immediately, and tell me when we may expect you; I shall open your next with a beating heart. Do excuse all the blunders and scrawls of this hasty letter. You must receive it as a proof of friendship, for to a stranger, or one who I thought would look upon it with a cold and critical eye, I certainly should not send it. I believe you and I have entered into a tacit agreement to forgive any little mistakes, which the other may chance to commit. Croyez moi ma chère amie votre

MARGUERITE."

The spirits of this most sensitive little being became more and more excited with the opening of spring. "She watched," says her mother, "the putting forth of the tender grass and the young blossoms as the period which was to liberate her from captivity. She was pleased with every body and every thing. She loved every thing in nature, both animate and inanimate, with a warmth of affection which displayed the benevolence of her own heart. She felt that she was well, and oh! the bright dreams and imaginings the cloudless future presented to her ardent mind—all was sunny and gay."

The following letter is highly expressive of the state of her feelings at that period.

"A few days since, my dearest cousin, I received your affectionate letter, and if my heart smote me at the sight of the well-known superscription, you may imagine how unmercifully it thumped on reading a letter so full of affection, and so entirely devoid of reproach for my unkindly negligence. I can assure you, my dear coz, you could have no better way of striking home to my heart the conviction of my error; and I resolved that hour, that moment, to lay my confessions at your feet, and sue for forgiveness; I knew you were too gentle to refuse. But alas! for human resolves! We were that afternoon expecting brother M. Dear brother! And how could I collect my floating thoughts and curl myself up into a corner with pen, ink and paper before me, when my heart was flying away over the sand-hills of this unromantic region, to meet and embrace and welcome home the wanderer? If it can interest you, picture to yourself the little scene: Mother and I breathless with expectation, gazing from the window, in mute suspense, and listening to the '*phiz, phiz*,' of the great steam-engine. Then when we caught a rapid glance of his trim little figure, how we bounded away over chairs, sofas, and kittens, to bestow in reality the greeting fancy had so often given him. Oh! what is so delightful as to welcome a friend! Well, three days have passed like a dream, and he is gone again. I am seated at my little table by the fire. Mother is sewing beside me. Puss is slumbering on the hearth, and nothing external remains to convince us of the truth of that bright sunbeam which had suddenly broken upon our quiet retreat, and departed like a vision as suddenly. When shall we have the pleasure of welcoming *you* thus, my beloved cousin? Your flying call of last summer was but an aggravation. Oh! may all good angels watch over you and all you love, shake the dew of health from their balmy wings upon your smiling home, and waft you hither, cheerful and happy, to sojourn awhile with the friends who love you so dearly! All hail to spring, the bright, the blooming, the renovating spring! Oh! I am so happy—I feel a lightness at my heart, and a vigour in my frame that I have rarely felt. If I speak, my voice forms itself into a laugh. If I look forward, every thing seems bright before me. If I look back, memory calls up what is pleasant, and my greatest desire is that my pen could fling a ray of sunshine over this scribbled page, and infuse into your heart some of the cheerfulness of my own.

I have been confined to the house all winter, as it was thought the best and only way of restoring my health. Now my symptoms are all better, and I am looking forward to next month and its blue skies with the most childish impatience. By the way, I am not to be called a child any more; for yesterday I was *fifteen*, what say you to that? I feel quite like an old woman, and think of putting on caps and spectacles next month."

It was during the same exuberance of happy feeling, with the delusive idea of confirmed health, and the anticipation of bright enjoyments, that she broke forth like a bird into the following strain of melody.

Oh, my bosom is throbbing with joy,
  With a rapture too full to express;
From within and without I am blest,
  And the world, like myself, I would bless.

All nature looks fair to my eye,
  From beneath and around and above,
Hope smiles in the clear azure sky,
  And the broad earth is glowing with love.

I stand on the threshold of life,
  On the shore of its wide-rolling sea,
I have heard of its storms and its strife,
  But all things are tranquil to me.

There 's a veil o'er the future—'t is bright
  As the wing of a spirit of air,
And each form of enchantment and light
  Is trembling in Iris hues there.

I turn to the world of affection,
  And warm, glowing treasures are mine;
To the past, and my fond recollection
  Gathers roses from memory's shrine.

But oh, there 's a fountain of joy
  More rich than a kingdom beside;
It is holy—death cannot destroy
  The flow of its heavenly tide.

'T is the love that is gushing within—
  It would bathe the whole world in its light;
The cold stream of time shall not quench,
  The dark frown of woe shall not blight.

These visions of pleasure may vanish,
  These bright dreams of youth disappear,
Disappointment each air hue may banish,
  And drown each frail joy in a tear.

I may plunge in the billows of life,
  I may taste of its dark cup of woe,
I may weep, and the sad drops of grief
  May blend with the waves as they flow.

I may dream, till reality's shadow
O'er the light form of fancy is cast;
I may hope, until hope, too, despairing
Has crept—to the grave of the past.

But though the wild waters surround me,
Misfortune, temptation, and sin,
Though fear be about and beyond me,
And sorrow's dark shadow within;

Though age, with an icy-cold finger,
May stamp his pale seal on my brow
Still, still in my bosom shall linger
The glow that is warming it now.

Youth will vanish, and pleasure, gay charmer,
May depart on the wings of to-day,
But that spot in my heart shall grow warmer,
As year after year rolls away.

"While her spirits were thus light and gay," says Mrs. Davidson, "from the prospect of returning health, my more mature judgment told me that those appearances might be deceptive—that even now the destroyer might be making sure his work of destruction; but she really seemed better, the cough had subsided, her step was buoyant, her face glowed with animation, her eye was bright, and love, boundless, universal love, seemed to fill her young heart. Every symptom of her disease assumed a more favourable cast. Oh how my heart swelled with the mingled emotions of hope, doubt, and gratitude! Our hopes of her ultimate recovery seemed to be founded upon reason, yet her father still doubted the propriety of our return to Lake Champlain; and as Saratoga held out many more advantages than Ballston as a temporary residence, he decided to spend the ensuing year or two there; and then we might perhaps, without much risk, return to our much-loved and long-deserted home on the banks of the Saranac. Accordingly a house was taken, and every preparation made for our removal to Saratoga on the first of May. Margaret was pleased with the arrangement."

The following playful extract of a letter to her brother in New York, exhibits her feelings on the prospect of their change of residence:

"I now most humbly avail myself of your most gracious permission to scribble you a few lines in token of my everlasting love. 'This is to inform you I am very well, hoping these few lines will find you in possession of the same blessing'—notwithstanding the blue streaks that flitted over your pathway a few days after you left us. Perhaps it was occasioned by remorse, at the cruelty of your parting speech; perhaps it was the reflection of a bright blue eye, upon the deep waters of your soul; but let the cause be what it may, 'black spirits or white, blue spirits or grey,' I hope the effect has entirely disappeared, and you are no longer tinged with its most doleful shadow. A blue sky, a blue eye, or the blue dye of the violet, are all undeniably beautiful, but this tint when transferred from the works of nature to the brow of man, or the stockings of woman, becomes a thing to ridicule or weep at. May your spirits henceforth, my dear brother, be preserved from this ill-omened influence, and may your feet and ankles never be graced with garments of a hue so repulsive. Oh, brother, we are all in the heat of moving; we, I say—you will account for the use of that personal pronoun on the authority of the old proverb, 'What a dust we flies raise,' for, to be frank with you, I have little or nothing to do with it, but poor mother is over head and ears in boxes, bedclothes, carpets, straw and discussions. Our hall is already filled with the fruits of her labours and perseverance, in the shape of certain blue chests, carpet cases, trunks, boxes, &c., all ready for a move. Dear mother is head, hands, and feet for the whole machine; our *two helps* being nothing but cranks, which turn when you touch them, and cease their rotary movement when the force is withdrawn. Heigho! We miss our good C——, with her quick invention and hopeful hand. * * * * * Oh, my dear brother, I am anticipating so much pleasure next summer, I hope it will not all prove a dream. It will be so delightful when you come up in August and bring cousin K—— with you; tell her I am calculating upon this pleasure with all my powers of fore-enjoyment—tell her also, that I am waiting most impatiently for that annihilating letter of hers, and if it does not come soon, I shall send her another cannonade, ere she has recovered the stunning effects of the first. Oh dear! I have written a most disunderstandable letter, and now you must excuse me, as I have declared war against M——, and after mending my pen, must collect all my scattered ideas into a fleet, and launch them for a combat upon a whole sea of ink."

"The exuberance of her spirits," says her mother, "as the spring advanced, and she was enabled once more to take exercise in the open air, displayed itself in every thing. Her heart was overflowing with thankfulness and love. Every fine day in the latter part of April, she either rode on horseback or drove out in a carriage. All nature looked lovely to her, not a tree or shrub but conveyed some poetical image or moral lesson to her mind. The moment, however, that she began to take daily exercise in the open air, I again heard with agony the prophetic cough. I felt that all was over! She thought that she had taken cold, and our friends were of the same opinion. 'It was a slight cold which would vanish beneath the mild influence of spring.' I, however, feared that her father's hopes might have blinded his judgment, and upon my own responsibility consulted a skilful physician, who had on many former occasions attended her. She was not aware of my present alarm, or that the physician was now consulted. He managed in a playful manner to feel her pulse, without her suspicions. After he had left the room, 'Madam,' said he, 'it is useless to hold out any false hopes; your daughter has a seated consumption, which is, I fear, beyond the reach of medical skill. There is no hope in the case; make her as happy and as comfortable as you can; let her enjoy riding in pleasant weather, but her walks must be given up; walking is too great an exertion for her.' With an aching heart I returned to the lovely unconscious victim, and found her tying on her hat for a ramble. I gently tried to dissuade her from going. She caught my eye, and read there a tale of grief, which she could not understand, and I could not explain. As soon as I dared trust my voice, I said, 'My dear Margaret, nothing has happened, only I have just been speaking with Dr. ——, respecting you, and he advises that you give up walking altogether. Knowing how much you enjoy it, I am pained to mention this, for I know that it will be a great privation.' 'Why, mamma,' she exclaimed, 'this cold is wearing off, may I not walk then?' 'The Doctor thinks you should make no exertion of that kind, but riding in fine weather may have a happy effect.' She stood and gazed upon my face long and earnestly; then untied her hat and sat down, apparently ruminating upon what had past; she asked no questions, but an expression of thoughtfulness clouded her brow during the rest of the day. It was settled that she was to ride out in fine weather, but not to walk out at all, and in a day or two she seemed to have forgotten the circumstance altogether. The return of the cough, and profuse night perspirations, too plainly told me her doom, but I still clung to the hope, that, as she suffered no pain, she might, by tender judicious treatment, continue yet for years. I urged her to remit her labours; she saw how much my heart was in the request, and promised to comply with my wishes. On the first of May we removed to Saratoga. One short half hour in the railroad-car completed the journey, and she arrived fresh, cheerful, and blooming in her appearance, such an effect had the excitement of pleasure upon her lovely face."

On the day we left Ballston she wrote a "Parting Word" to Mrs. H., who had been one of our most intimate and affectionate visitors throughout the winter, and whose husband had assisted her much in her studies of moral philosophy, as well as delighted her by his varied and instructive conversation.

A PARTING WORD TO MY DEAR MRS. H.

Ballston Spa, April 30, 1838.

At length the awful morn hath come,
  The parting hour is nigh,
And I sit down 'mid dust and gloom,
  To bid you brief "good-bye."

Each voice to fancy's listening ear
  Repeats the doleful cry,
And the bare walls and sanded floor
  Re-echo back "good-bye."

So must it be; but many a thought
  Comes crowding on my mind,
Of the dear friends, the happy hours,
  The joys we leave behind.

How we shall miss your cheerful face,
  For ever bright and smiling,
And your sweet voice, so often heard,
  Our weary hours beguiling!

How shall we miss the kindly hearts,
  Which none can know unloving,
Whose thoughts and feelings none can read,
  Nor find his own improving!

And he, whose converse, hour by hour,
  Hath lent old Time new pinions,
Whose hand hath drawn the shadowy veil
  From wisdom's broad dominions;

Whose voice hath poured forth priceless gems,
  Scarce conscious that he taught,
Whose mind of broad, of loftiest reach,
  Hath shower'd down thought on thought.

True, we may meet with many a dear
  And cherish'd friend, but yet
Oft shall we cast a backward glance
  Of wistful, vain regret.

When evening spreads her sombre veil,
  To fold the slumbering earth,
When our small circle closes round
  The humble, social hearth—

Oft shall we dream of hours gone by,
And con these moments o'er,
Till we half bend our ears to catch
Your footsteps at the door,
And then turn back and sigh to think
We hear those steps no more!

But though these dismal thoughts arise
Hope makes me happy still;
There is a drop of comfort lurks
In every draught of ill!

By pain and care each joy of earth
More exquisite is made,
And when we meet, the parting grief
Shall doubly be o'erpaid.

In disappointments deep too quick
Our fairest prospects drown,
Let not this hope, which blooms so bright,
Be wither'd at his frown!

Come, and a mother's pallid cheek
Shall brighten at your smile,
And her poor frame, so faint and weak,
Forget its pains the while.

Come, and a glad and happy heart
Shall give the welcome kiss,
And puss shall purr, and frisk, and mew,
In token of her bliss.

Come! and behold how I improve
In dusting—cleaning—sweeping;
And I will hear, with patient ear,
Your lectures on housekeeping.

And now, may all good angels guard
Your path where'er it lie;
May peace reign monarch in your breast,
And gladness in your eye.

And may the dews of health descend
On him you cherish best,
To his worn frame their influence lend,
And calm each nerve to rest!

And may we meet again, nor feel
The parting hour so nigh—
Peace, love, and happiness to all,
Once more—once more, "good-bye!"

"She interested herself," continued Mrs. Davidson, "more than I had anticipated in the arrangement of our new habitation, and in forming plans of future enjoyment with our friends when they should visit us; I exerted myself to please her taste in every thing, although she was prohibited from making the slightest physical exertion herself. The house settled, then came the flower-garden, in which she spent more time than I thought prudent; but she was so happy while thus engaged, and the weather being fine, and the gardener disposed to gratify and carry all her little plans into effect, I, like a weak mother, wanted resolution to interfere, and have always reproached myself for it, although not conscious that it was an injury at the time. Her brother had invited her to return to New York with him when he came to visit us in June, and she was now impatiently counting the days until his arrival. Her feelings are portrayed in a letter to her young friend H."

"Saratoga, June 1, 1838.

"June is at last with us, my dear cousin, and the blue-eyed goddess could not have looked upon the green bosom of her mother earth attired in a lovelier or more enchanting robe. I am seated by an open window, and the breeze, laden with the perfumes of the blossoms and opening leaves, just lifts the edge of my sheet, and steals with the gentlest footsteps imaginable to fan my cheek and forehead. The grass, tinged with the deepest and freshest green, is waving beneath its influence; the birds are singing their sweetest songs; and as I look into the depths of the clear blue sky the rich tints appear to flit higher and higher as I gaze, till my eye seems searching into immeasurable distance. Oh! such a day as this, it is a luxury to breathe. I feel as if I could frisk and gambol like my kitten from the mere consciousness of life. Yet with all the loveliness around me I reperuse your letter, and long for wings to fly from it all to the dull atmosphere and crowded highways of the city. Yes! I could then look into your eyes, and I should forget the blue sky; and your smile, and your voice would doubly compensate me for the loss of green trees and singing birds. There are green trees in the heart which shed a softer perfume, and birds which sing more sweetly. 'Nonsense! Mag is growing sentimental!' I knew you would say so, but the streak came across me, and you have it at full length. In plainer terms, how delighted, how more than delighted I shall be when I do come! when I do come, Kate! oh! oh! oh!—what would our language be without interjections, those expressive parts of speech, which say so much in so small a compass! Now I am sure you can understand from these three syllables all the pleasure, the rapture I anticipate; the meeting, the parting, all the component parts of that great whole which I denominate a visit to New York! No, not to New York! but to the few dear friends whose society will afford me all the enjoyment I expect or desire, and who, in fact, constitute all my New York.

June 2d. I had written thus far, dear Kate, when I was most agreeably interrupted by a proposal for a ride on horseback; my sheet slid of itself into the open drawer, my hat and dress flew on as if by instinct, and in ten minutes I was galloping full speed through the streets of our little village with father by my side. I rode till nearly tea-time, and came home tired, tired, tired; oh, I ache to think of it. My poor letter slept all night as soundly as its writer, but now that another day has dawned, the very opposite of its predecessor, damp, dark, and rainy, I have drawn it forth from its receptacle, and seek to dissipate all outward gloom, by communing with one the thought of whom conveys to my mind any thing but melancholy. Oh, Kate, Kate, in spite of your disinterested and sober advice to the contrary, I shall come, I shall soon come, just as soon as M. can and will run up for me. Yet, perhaps, in the end I shall be disappointed. My happy anticipations resemble the cloudless sky of yesterday, and who knows but a stormy to-morrow may erase the brilliant tints of hope as well as those of nature. * * * * * * Do write quickly, and tell me if I am to prepare. If you continue to feel as when you last wrote, and still advise me not to come, I shall dispose of your advice in the most approved manner, throw it to the winds, and embark armed and equipped for your city, to make my destined visit, and fulfil its conditions by fair means or foul, and bring you home in triumph. Oh! we shall have fine times. Oh dear, I blush to look back upon my sheet and see so many I's in it."

The time of her brother's coming drew near. He would be with us at nine in the morning. At eleven they were to start. I prepared all for her departure with my own hand, lest, should I trust it to a domestic to make the arrangements, she would make some exertion herself. She sat by me while thus engaged, relating playful anecdotes, until I urged her to retire for the night. On going into her room an hour or two afterwards, I was alarmed to find her in a high fever. About midnight she was taken with bleeding at the lungs. I flew to her father, and in a few minutes a vein was opened in her arm. To describe our feelings at this juncture is impossible. We stood gazing at each other in mute despair. After that shock had subsided her father retired, and I seated myself by the bedside to watch her slumbers, and the rising sun found me still at my post. She awoke, pale, feeble and exhausted by the debilitating perspiration which attended her sleep. She was surprised to find that I had not been in bed; but when she attempted to speak I laid my finger upon her lips and desired her to be silent. She understood my motive, and when I bent my head to kiss her, I saw a tear upon her cheek. I told her the necessity of perfect quiet, and the danger which would result from agitation. Before her brother came, she desired to rise. I assisted her to do so, and he found her quietly seated in her easy chair, perfectly composed in manner, and determined not to increase her difficulties by giving way to feelings which must at that time have oppressed her heart. My son was greatly shocked to find her in this state. I met him and urged the importance of perfect self-possession on his part, as any sudden agitation might in her present alarming state be fatal. Poor fellow! he subdued his feelings and met her with a cheerful smile which concealed a heart almost bursting with sorrow. The propriety of her taking this jaunt had been discussed by her father and myself for a number of weeks. We both thought her too ill to leave home, but her strong desire to go, the impression she had imbibed that travelling would greatly benefit her health, and the pleading of friends in her behalf, on the ground that disappointment would have a more unfavourable effect than the journey possibly could have, all had their effect in leading us to consent. It was possible it might be of use to her, although it was at best an experiment of a doubtful nature. But this attack was decisive: yet caution must be used in breaking the matter to her in her present weak state. Her brother stayed a day or two with us, and then returned, telling her that when she was able to perform the journey, he would come again and take her with him. After he left us, she soon regained her usual strength, and in a fortnight her brother returned and took her to New York.

The anxiety of Mrs. Davidson was intense until she received her first letter. It was written from New York, and in a cheerful vein, speaking encouragingly of her health, but showing more solicitude about the health and well being of her mother than of her own. She continued to write frequently, giving animated accounts of scenes and persons.

The following extract relates to an excursion, in company with two of her brothers, into West Chester county, one of the pleasantest, and, until recently, the least fashionably known, regions on the banks of the Hudson.

"At three o'clock, we were in the Singsing steamer, with the water sparkling below, and the sun broiling over head. In the course of our sail a huge thundercloud arose, and I retreated, quite terrified, to the cabin. But it proved a refreshing shower. Oh! how sweet, how delightful the air was! When we landed at the dock, every thing looked so fresh and green! We mounted into a real country vehicle, and rattled up the hill to the village inn, a quiet, pleasant little house. I was immediately shown to my room, where I stayed until tea-time, enjoying the prospect of a splendid sunset upon the mountains, and resting after the fatigues of the day. At seven, we drank tea, a meal strongly contrasted with the fashionable meagre unsocial city tea. The table was crowded with every thing good, in the most bountiful style, and served with the greatest attention by the landlord's pretty daughter. I retired soon after tea, and slept soundly until daybreak. After breakfast, we sent for a carriage to take us along the course of the Croton, to see the famous water-works, but, to our disappointment, every carriage was engaged, and we could not go. In the afternoon, a party was made up to go in a boat across the river, and ascend a mountain to a singular lake upon its summit, where all the implements of fishing were provided, and a collation was prepared. In short it was a pic-nic. To this we were invited, but on learning they would not return until nine or ten in the evening, that scheme also was abandoned. Towards night we walked around the village, looked at the tunnel, and visited the ice-cream man, and in spite of my various disappointments, I retired quite happy and pleased with my visit. The next day was Sunday, and we proposed going to the little Dutch church, a few miles distant, and hearing the service performed in Dutch; but lo! on drawing aside my curtains in the morning, it rained, and we were obliged to content ourselves as well as we could until the rain was over. After dinner the sun again peeped out, as if for our special gratification, and in a few minutes a huge country wagon, with a leathern top and two sleek horses, drew up to the door. We mounted into it, and away we rattled over the most beautiful country I ever saw. Oh! it was magnificent! Every now and then the view of the broad Hudson, with its distant hills, and the clouds resting on their summits, burst upon our view. Now we would ascend a lofty hill, clothed with forests, and verdure of the most brilliant hues; now dash down into a deep ravine with a stream winding and gurgling along its bed, with its tiny waves rushing over the wheel of some rustic mill, embosomed in its shade and solitude. Every now and then the gable end of some low Dutch building would present itself before us, smiling in its peaceful stillness, and conveying to the mind a perfect picture of rural simplicity and comfort, although, perhaps, of ignorance. At length we paused upon the summit of a gentle hill, and judge of my delight when I beheld below me the old Dutch church, the quiet, secluded, beautiful little churchyard, the running stream, the path, and the rustic bridge, the ever memorable scene of Ichabod's adventure with the *headless horseman.* There, thought I, rushed the poor pedagogue, his knees cramped up to his saddle-bow with fear, his hands grasping his horse's mane, with convulsive energy, in the hope that the running stream might arrest the progress of his fearful pursuer, and allow him to pass in safety. Vain hope! scarce had he reached the bridge when he heard, rattling behind him, the hoofs of his fiendish companion. The church seemed in a blaze to his bewildered eyes, and urging on, on, he turned to look once more, when, horror of horrors! the head, the fearful head, was in the act of descending upon his devoted shoulders. Ha! ha! ha! I never laughed so in my life. Well, we rode on through the scene of poor Andre's capture, and dashed along the classic valley of Sleepy Hollow. After a long and delightful drive, we returned in time for tea. After tea we were invited into Mrs. F.'s parlour, where, after a short time, were collected quite a party of ladies and gentlemen. At nine we were served with ice-cream, wine, &c. I retired very much pleased and very much fatigued. Early in the morning we rose with the most brilliant sun, breakfasted, mounted once more into the wagon, and rattled off to the dock. Oh! that I could describe to you how fresh and sweet the air was. I felt as if I wanted to open my mouth wide and inhale it. We gave M. our parting kisses, and soon found ourselves once more, after this charming episode, approaching the mighty city. We had a delightful sail of two or three hours, and again rode up to dear aunt M.'s, where all seemed glad at my return. I spent the remainder of the day in resting and reading."

In these artless epistles, continues Mrs. Davidson, there is much of character, for who could imagine this constant cheerfulness, this almost forgetfulness of self, these affectionate endeavours, by her sweetly playful account of all her employments while absent, to dispel the grief which she knew was preying upon my mind on account of her illness? Who could conceive the pains she took to conceal from me the ravages which disease was daily making upon her form? She was never heard to complain, and in her letters to me, she hardly alludes to her illness. The friends to whom I had entrusted her, during her short period of absence, sometimes feared that she would never be able to reach home again. Her brother told me, but not until long after her return, that on her way home she really fainted several times from debility—and that he took her from the boat to the carriage as he would have done an infant.

On the sixth of July, I once more folded to my heart this cherished object of my solicitude; but oh, the change which three short weeks had wrought in her appearance struck me forcibly. I was so wholly unprepared for it, that I nearly fainted. After the excitement of the meeting (which she had evidently summoned all her fortitude to bear with composure) was over, she sat down by me, and passing her thin arm around my waist, said, "Oh, my dear mamma, I am home again at last; I now feel as if I never wanted to leave you again; I have had a delightful visit, my friends were all glad to see me, and have watched over me with all the kindness and care which affection could dictate, but oh, there is no place like home, and no care like a mother's care; there is something in the very air of home, and in the sound of your voice, mother, which makes me happier just now, than all the scenes which I have passed through in my little jaunt; oh, after all, home is the only place for a person as much out of health as I am." I strove to suppress my emotions, while I marked her pale cheek and altered countenance. She fixed her penetrating eyes upon my face, kissed me, and drawing back to take a more full survey of the effects which pain and anxiety had wrought in me, kissed me again and again, saying, "she knew I had deeply felt the want of her society, and now once more at home, she should so prize its comforts as to be in no haste to leave it again." She was much wasted, and could hardly walk from one room to another; her cough was very distressing; she had no pain, but a languor and depression of spirits, foreign to her nature. She struggled against this debility, and called up all the energies of her mind to overcome it; her constant reply to inquiries about her health, by the friends who called, was the same as formerly, "Well, quite well—mother calls me an invalid, but I feel well." Yet, to me, when alone, she talked more freely of her symptoms, and I thought I could discern from her manner, that she had apprehensions as to the result. I had often endeavoured to acquire firmness sufficient to tell her what was her situation, but she seemed so studiously to avoid the disclosure, that my resolution had hitherto been unequal to the task. But I was much surprised one day, not long after her return from New York, by her asking me to tell her, without reserve, my opinion of her state. The question wrung my very heart; I was wholly unprepared for it, and it was put in so solemn a manner, that I could not evade it, were I disposed to do so. I knew with what strong affection she clung to life, and the objects and friends which endeared it to her; I knew how bright the world upon which she was just entering appeared to her young fancy, what glowing pictures she had drawn of future usefulness and happiness. I was now called upon, at one blow, to crush these hopes, to destroy the delightful visions, which had hovered around her from her cradle until this very period; it would be cruel and wrong to deceive her, in vain I attempted a reply to her direct and solemn appeal, and my voice grew husky; several times I essayed to speak, but the words died away on my lips; I could only fold her to my heart in silence, imprint a kiss upon her forehead, and leave the room to avoid agitating her with feelings I had no power to repress.

The following extract from a letter to her brother in New York, dated a short time after this incident occurred, and which I never saw until after her departure, will best portray her own feelings at this period.

"As to my health at present, I feel as well as when you were here, and the cough is much abated, but it is evident to me, that mother thinks me not so well as before I left home; I do not myself believe that I have gained any thing from the visit, and in a case like mine, standing still is certainly loss, but I feel no worse. However, I have learned that feelings are no criterion of disease. Now, brother, I want to know what Dr. M—— discovered, or thought he discovered, in his examination of my lungs; father says nothing—mother, when I ask, cannot tell me, and looks so sad! Now, I ask you, hoping to be answered. If you have not heard the doctor say, I wish you would ask him, and write to me. If it is more unfavourable than I anticipate, it is best I should know now; if it is contrary, how much pain and restlessness and suspicion, will be spared me by the knowledge. As to myself, I feel and know that my health is in a most precarious state, that the disease we dread has perhaps fastened upon me, but I have an impression that if I make use of the proper remedies and exercise, I may yet recover a tolerable degree of health. I do not feel that my case is incurable; I wish to know if I am wrong. I have rode on horseback twice since you left me; dear, dear brother, whât a long egotistic letter I have written you! do forgive me, my heart was full, and I felt that I must unburden it. I wish you would write me a long letter. Do not let dear mother know at present the questions I have asked you." * * * * * * *

From this period she grew more thoughtful. There was even a solemnity in her manner which I never before observed. Her mind, as I mentioned before, had been much perplexed by some doctrinal points. To solve these doubts I asked if I should not send for some clergyman. She said no. She had heard many discussions on these subjects, and they had always served rather to confuse than to convince her. "I would rather converse with you alone, mother." She then asked me if I thought it essential to salvation that she should adopt any particular creed. I felt that I was an inefficient, perhaps a blind guide, yet it was my duty not only to impart consolation, but to explain to her my own views of the truth. I replied that I considered faith and repentance only, to be essential to salvation; that it was very desirable that her mind should be settled upon some particular mode of faith; but that I did not think it absolutely necessary that she should adopt the tenets of any established church, and again recommended an attentive perusal of the New Testament. She expressed her firm belief in the divinity of Christ. The perfections of his character, its beauty and holiness excited her admiration, while the benevolence which prompted the sacrifice of himself to save a lost world, filled her with the most enthusiastic gratitude. It was a source of regret that so much of her time had been spent in light reading, and that her writings had not been of a more decidedly religious character. She lamented that she had not chosen scriptural subjects for the exercise of her poetical talent, and said, "Mamma, should God spare my life, my time and talents shall for the future be devoted to a higher and holier end." She felt that she had trifled with the gifts of Providence, and her self-condemnation and grief were truly affecting. "And must I die so young? My career of usefulness hardly commenced? Oh! mother, how sadly have I trifled with the gifts of heaven! What have I done which can benefit one human being?" I folded her to my heart, and endeavoured to soothe the tumult of her feelings, bade her remember her dutiful conduct as a daughter, her affectionate bearing as a sister and a friend, and the consolation which she had afforded me through years of suffering! "Oh my mother," said she, "I have been reflecting much of late upon this sad waste of intellect, and had marked out for myself a course of usefulness which, should God spare my life—" Here her emotions became too powerful to proceed. At times she suffered much anxiety with regard to her eternal welfare, and deeply lamented her want of faithfulness in the performance of her religious duties; complained of coldness and formality in her devotional exercises, and entreated me to pray with and for her. At other times, her hopes of heaven would be bright, her faith unwavering and her devotion fervent. Yet it was evident to me, that she still cherished the hope that her life might be prolonged. Her mother had lingered for years in a state equally hopeless, and during that period had been enabled to attend to the moral and religious culture of her little family. Might not the same kind Providence prolong *her life?* It would be vain to attempt a description of those seasons of deep and thrilling interest. God alone knows in what way my own weak frame was sustained. I felt that she had been renovated and purified by Divine Grace, and to see her thus distressed when I thought that all the consolations of the Gospel ought to be hers, gave my heart a severe pang.

"Many of our friends now were of opinion that a change of climate might benefit, perhaps restore her. Heretofore, when the suggestion had been made, she shrunk from the idea of leaving her home for a distant clime. Now her anxiety to try the effect of a change was great. I felt that it would be vain, although I was desirous that nothing should be left untried. Feeble as she now was, the idea of her resigning the comforts of home, and being subject to the fatigues of travelling in public conveyances, was a dreadful one, and yet if there was a rational prospect of prolonging her life by these means, I was anxious to give them a trial. Dr. Davidson, after much deliberation on the subject, called counsel. Dr. ——— came, and when, after half an hour's pleasant and playful conversation with Margaret, he joined us in the parlour, oh! how my poor heart trembled. I hung upon the motions of his lips as if my own life depended on what they might utter. At length he spoke, and I felt as if an icebolt had passed through my heart. He had never thought, though he had known her many years, that a change of climate would benefit her. She had lived beyond his expectations many months, even years; and now he was convinced, were we to attempt to take her to a southern climate, that she would die on the passage. Make it as pleasant as possible for her at home, was his advice. He thought that a few months must terminate her life. She knew that we had confidence in the opinion of this, her favourite physician. When I had gained firmness enough to answer her questions, I again entered the room and found her composed, though she had evidently been strongly agitated, and had not brought her mind to hear her doom. Never, oh! never to the latest hour of my life, shall I forget the look she gave me when I met her. What a heart-rending task was mine! I performed it as gently as possible. I said the doctor thought her strength unequal to the fatigue of the journey; that he was not so great an advocate for change of climate as many persons; that he had known many cases in which he thought it injurious, and his best advice was, that we should again ward off the severity of the winter by creating an atmosphere within our house. She mildly acquiesced, and the subject was dropped altogether. She sometimes read, and frequently, from mere habit, held a book in her hand when unable to digest its contents, and within the book there usually rested a piece of paper, upon which she occasionally marked the reflections which arose in her mind, either in poetry or prose."

We here interrupt the narrative of Mrs. Davidson, to insert a copy of verses addressed by Margaret to her brother, a young officer in the army, and stationed at a frontier post in the far west. They were written in September, about two months before her death, and are characterized throughout by her usual beauty of thought and tenderness of feeling; but the last verse, which alludes to the fading verdure, and falling leaf, and gathering melancholy, and lifeless quiet of the season, as typical of her own blighted youth and approaching dissolution, has something in it peculiarly solemn and affecting.

TO MY SOLDIER BROTHER IN THE FAR WEST.*

'T is an autumn eve, and the tints of day
  From the west are slowly stealing,
And clouds round the couch of the setting sun
  Are gently and silently wheeling.
'T is the scene and the hour for the soul to bathe
  In its own deep springs of feeling,
And my thoughts, from their galling bonds set free,
Have fled to the "far, far west" to thee!

And perchance, 'mid the toils of thy varied life,
  Thou also art pausing awhile,
To behold how beautiful all things look
  In the sunlight's passing smile;

* This copy of verses has come to hand since the publication of the first edition of this memoir.

And perchance recollections of kindred and home
  Thy cares for a moment beguile;
Thy thoughts have been *mine* in their passage to thee,
And though distant, far distant, our spirits are free!

I know thou art dreaming of home,
  And the dear ones sheltered there;
Of thy mother, pale with the pain of years,
  And thy sire with his silvered hair;
And with *them* blend thoughts of thy boyish years,
  When the world looked all so fair,
When thy cheek flushed high at the voice of praise,
  And thy breast was unknown to care;
And while memory burns her torch for thee,
I know that these thoughts and these dreams will be!

But when, in the shade of the autumn wood,
  Thy wandering footsteps stray,
When yellow leaves and perishing buds
  Are scattered in thy way;
When all around thee breathes of rest,
  And sadness and decay—
With the drooping flower, and the falling tree,
Oh! brother, blend thy thoughts of me!

"The following fragments," continues Mrs. Davidson, "appear to be the very breathings of her soul during the last few weeks of her life, written in pencil, in a hand so weak and tremulous that I could with difficulty decipher them word by word with the aid of a strong magnifying glass.

"Consumption! child of woe, thy blighting breath
Marks all that 's fair and lovely for thine own,
And, sweeping o'er the silver chords of life,
Blends all their music in one deathlike tone."

1838.

"What strange, what mystic things we are,
With spirits longing to outlive the stars.
* * * * * * * * but even in decay
Hasting to meet our brethren in the dust.
As one small dewdrop runs, another drops
To sink unnoticed in the world of waves."

"O it is sad to feel that when a few short years
Of life are past, we shall lie down, unpitied
And unknown, amid a careless world;
That youth and age and revelry and grief
Above our heads shall pass, and we alone
Shall sleep! alone shall be as we have been,
No more.

These are unfinished fragments, a part of which I could not decipher at all. I insert them to give an idea of the daily operations of her mind during the whole of this long summer of suffering. Her gentle spirit never breathed a murmur or complaint. I think she was rarely heard to express even a feeling of weariness. But here are a few more of those outpourings of the heart. I copy these little effusions with all their errors; there is a sacredness about them which forbids the change even of a single letter. The first of the fragments which follow was written on a Sabbath evening in autumn, not many weeks before her death.

It is autumn, the season of rapid decay,
When the flow'rets of summer are hasting away
  From the breath of the wintry blast,
And the buds which oped to the gazer's eye,
And the glowing tints of the gorgeous sky,
And the forests robed in their emerald dye,
  With their loveliest blossoms have past.

'T is eve, and the brilliant sunset hue
Is replaced by a sky of the coldest blue,
  Untouched by a floating cloud.
And all nature is silent, calm and serene,
As though sorrow and suffering never had been
On this beautiful earth abroad.

'T is a Sabbath eve, and the longing soul
Is charm'd by its quiet and gentle control
  From each wayward and wandering thought,
And it longs from each meaner affection to move,
And it soareth the troubles of earth above
To bathe in that fountain of light and love,
  Whence our purest enjoyments are caught.

1838.

But winter, O what shall thy greeting be
  From our waters, our earth, and our sky?
What welcoming strains shall arise for thee
  As thy chariot-wheels draw nigh?
Alas! the fresh flowers of the spirit decay
  As thy cold, cold steps advance,
And even young Fancy is shrinking away
  From the chill of thy terrible glance;
And Hope with her mantle of rainbow hue
  Hath fled from thy freezing eye,
And her bright train of visions are melting in air
  As thy shivering blasts sweep by.
Thy * * * * * *

Oct. 1838.

THE NATURE OF THE SOUL.

The spirit, what is it? Mysterious, sublime,
  Undying, unchanging, for ever the same,
It bounds lightly athwart the dark billows of time,
  And moves on unscorched by its heavenly flame.

Man owns thee and feels thee, and knows thee divine;
  He feels thou art his, and thou never canst die;
He believes thee a gem from the Maker's pure shrine,
  A portion of purity holy and high.

'T is around him, within him, the source of his life,
Yet too weak to contemplate its glory and might;
He trembling shrinks back to dull earth's humble strife,
And leaves the pure atmosphere glowing with light.

Thou spark from the Deity's radiant throne,
I know thee, yet shrink from thy greatness and power;
Thou art mine in thy splendour, I feel thee my own,
Yet behold me as frail as the light summer flower.

I strive in my weakness to gaze on thy might,
To trace out thy wanderings through ages to come,
Till like birds on the sea, all exhausted, at length
I flutter back weary to earth as my home.

Like a diamond when laid in a rough case of clay,
Which may crumble and wear from the pure gem enclosed,
But which ne'er can be lit by one tremulous ray
From the glory-crown'd star in its dark case reposed.

As the cool weather advanced, her decline became more visible, and she devoted more and more of her time to searching the Scriptures, self-examination and subjects for reflection, and questions which were to be solved by evidences deduced from the Bible. I found them but a few days before her death, in the sacred volume which lay upon the table, at which she usually sat during her hours of retirement. She had been searching the holy book, and overcome by the exertion, rang the bell, which summoned me to her side, for no person but myself was admitted during the time set apart for her devotional exercises.

Subjects for reflection.

1st. The uniform usefulness of Christ's miracles.

2d. The manner in which he overthrows all the exalted hopes which the Jews entertain of a temporal kingdom, and strives to explain to them the entire spirituality of the one he has come to erect.

3d. The deep and unchangeable love for man, which must have impelled Christ to resist so many temptations and endure so many sufferings, even death, that truth might enlighten the world, and heaven and immortality become realities instead of dreams.

4th. The general thoughtlessness of man with regard to his greatest, his only interest.

5th. Christ's constant submission to the will of his Father, and the necessity of our imitating the meek and calm and gentle qualities of his character, together with that firmness of purpose and confidence in God which sustained him to the end.

6th. The necessity of so living, that we need not fear to think each day our last.

9

7th. The necessity of religion to soothe and support the mind on the bed of sickness.

8th. Self-examination.

9th. Is Christ mentioned expressly in Scripture as equal with God and a part?

10th. Is there sufficient ground for the doctrine of the Trinity?

11th. Did Christ come as a prophet and reformer of the world, or as a sacrifice for our sins, to appease the wrath of his Father?

12th. Is any thing said of infant baptism?

Written in November, 1838.

About three weeks before her departure, I one morning found her in the parlour, where, as I before observed, she spent a portion of her time in retirement. I saw that she had been much agitated, and seemed weary. I seated myself by her and rested her head on my bosom, while I gently pressed my hand upon her throbbing temples to soothe the agitation of her nerves. She kissed me again and again, and seemed as if she feared to trust her voice to speak lest her feelings should overcome her. As I returned her caresses, she silently put a folded paper in my hand. I began to open it, when she gently laid her hand on mine, and said in a low tremulous tone, "Not now, dear mother! I then led her back to her room, and placed her upon the sofa, and retired to examine the paper. It contained the following lines.

TO MY MOTHER.

Oh mother, would the power were mine
  To wake the strain thou lov'st to hear,
And breathe each trembling new-born thought,
  Within thy fondly listening ear,
As when in days of health and glee,
My hopes and fancies wander'd free.

But, mother, now a shade has past
  Athwart my brightest visions here,
A cloud of darkest gloom has wrapt
  The remnant of my brief career!
No song, no echo can I win,—
The sparkling fount has died within.

The torch of earthly hope burns dim,
  And Fancy spreads her wings no more;
And oh, how vain and trivial seem
  The pleasures that I prized before.
My soul, with trembling steps and slow,
  Is struggling on through doubt and strife:
Oh! may it prove, as time rolls on,
  The pathway to eternal life—
Then, when my cares and fears are o'er,
I'll sing thee as in days of yore.

I said that hope had pass'd from earth :
'T was but to fold her wings in Heaven,
To whisper of the soul's new birth,
Of sinners saved and sins forgiven.
When mine are wash'd in tears away,
Then shall my spirit swell my lay.

When God shall guide my soul above,
By the soft cords of heavenly love,
When the vain cares of earth depart,
And tuneful voices swell my heart,
Then shall each word, each note I raise,
Burst forth in pealing hymns of praise,
And all not offered at His shrine,
Dear mother, I will place on thine.

It was long before I could gain sufficient composure to return to her. When I did so, I found her sweetly calm, and she greeted me with a smile so full of affection, that I shall cherish the recollection of its brightness until my latest breath. It was the last piece she ever wrote, except a paraphrase of four lines of the hymn, "I would not live always," which was written within the last week of her life.

"I would not live always thus fettered by sin,
Temptation without, and corruption within,
With the soul ever dimmed by its hopes and its fears,
And the heart's holy flame ever struggling through tears."

Thus far in preparing this memoir, we have availed ourselves almost entirely of copious memoranda, furnished us at our own request by Mrs. Davidson; but when the narrator approached the closing scene of this most affecting story, the heart of the mother gave out, and she found herself totally inadequate to the task. Fortunately, Dr. Davidson had retained a copy of a letter, written by her in the midst of her affliction to Miss Sedgwick, in reply to an epistle from that lady, expressive of the kindest sympathy, and making some inquiries relative to the melancholy event. We subjoin that letter entire, for never have we read any thing of the kind more truly eloquent or deeply affecting.

"Saratoga Springs.

"Yes, my dear Miss Sedgwick, she is an angel now; calmly and sweetly she sunk to her everlasting rest, as a babe gently slumbers on its mother's bosom. I thank my Father in heaven that I was permitted to watch over her, and I trust administer to her comfort during her illness. I know, my friend, you will not expect either a very minute or connected detail of the circumstances preceding her change from me at this time, for I am indeed bowed down with sorrow. I feel that I am truly desolate, how desolate I will not attempt to describe. Yet in the depth of grief I have consolations of the purest, most soothing and exalted nature. I would not, indeed I could not murmur, but rather bless my God that he has in the plenitude of his goodness made me, even for a brief space on earth, the honoured mother of such an angel. Oh my dear Miss Sedgwick, I wish you could have seen her during the last two months of her brief sojourn with us. Her meekness and patience, and her even cheerful bearing were unexampled. But when she was assured that all the tender and endearing ties which bound her to earth were about to be severed, when she saw that life and all its bright visions were fading from her eyes—that she was standing at the entrance of the dark valley which must be traversed in her way to the eternal world, the struggle was great, but brief—she caught the hem of her Saviour's robe and meekly bowed to the mandate of her God. Since the beginning of August, I have watched this tender blossom with intense anxiety, and marked her decline with a breaking heart; and although from that time until the period of her departure, I never spent a whole night in my bed, my excitement was so strong that I was unconscious of the want of sleep. Oh, my dear madam, the whole course of her decline was so unlike any other death-bed scene I ever witnessed; there was nothing of the gloom of a sick chamber; a charm was in and around her; a holy light seemed to pervade every thing belonging to her. There was a sacredness, if I may so express it, which seemed to tell the presence of the Divinity. Strangers felt it, all acknowledged it. Very few were admitted to her sick room, but those few left it with an elevation of heart new, solemn, and delightful. She continued to ride out as long as the weather was mild, and even after she became too weak to walk she frequently desired to be taken into the parlour, and when there, with all her little implements of drawing and writing, her books, and even her little work-box and basket beside her, she seemed to think that by these little attempts at her usual employments she could conceal from me, for she saw my heart was breaking, the ravages of disease and her consequent debility. The New Testament was her daily study, and a portion of every day was spent in private in self-examination and prayer. My dear Miss Sedgwick, how I have felt my own littleness, my total unworthiness, when compared with this pure, this high-souled, intellectual, yet timid, humble child; bending at the altar of her God, and pleading for pardon and acceptance in his sight, and grace to assist her in preparing for eternity. As her strength wasted, she often desired me to share her hours of retirement and converse with her, and read to her, when unable to read herself.

"Oh! how sad, how delightful, how agonizing is the memory of the sweet and holy communion we then enjoyed. Forgive me, my friend, for thus mingling my own feelings with the circumstances you wished to know; and, oh! continue to pray that God will give me submission under this desolating stroke. She was my darling, my almost idolized child—truly, truly, you have said, the charm of my existence. Her symptoms were extremely distressing, although she suffered no pain. A week before her departure, she desired that the sacrament of the Lord's Supper might be administered to her. 'Mother,' said she, 'I do not desire it because I feel worthy to receive it; I feel myself a sinner, but I desire to manifest my faith in Christ by receiving an ordinance instituted by himself but a short time before his crucifixion.' The Holy Sacrament was administered by Mr. Babcock. The solemnity of the scene can be better felt than described. I cannot attempt it. After it was over, a holy calm seemed to pervade her mind, and she looked almost like a beatified spirit. The evening following, she said to me, 'Mother, I have made a solemn surrender of myself to God: if it is his will, I would desire to live long enough to prove the sincerity of my profession, but his will be done; living or dying I am henceforth devoted to God.' After this some doubt seemed to intrude; her spirit was troubled. I asked her if there was any thing she desired to have done, any little arrangements to be made, any thing to say which she had left unsaid, and assured her that her wishes should be sacred to me. She turned her eyes upon me with an expression so sad, so mournfully sweet—'Mother, "When I can read my title clear to mansions in the skies," then I will think of other matters.' Her hair, which when a little child had been often cut to improve its growth, was now very beautiful; and she usually took much pains with it. During the whole course of her sickness I had taken care of it. One day, not long before her death, she said, evidently making a great effort to speak with composure, 'Mother, if you are willing I will have my hair cut off; it is troublesome; I should like it better short.' I understood her at once: she did not like to have the idea of death associated with those beautiful tresses which I had loved to braid. She would have them taken off while living. I mournfully gave my consent, and she said, 'I will not ask you, my dear mother, to do it; my friend, Mrs. F—— will be with me to-night, and she will do it for me.' The dark rich locks were severed at midnight. Never shall I forget the expression of her young faded face as I entered the room. 'Do not be agitated, dear mamma, I am more comfortable now. Lay it away, if you please, and to-morrow I will arrange and dispose of it. Do you know that I view my hair as something sacred? It is a part of myself, which will be re-united to my body at the resurrection.'

"She had sat in an easy chair or reclined upon a sofa for several weeks. On Friday the 22d of November, at my urgent entreaty, she consented to be laid upon the bed. She found it a relief, and sunk into a deep sleep, from which she was only awoke when I aroused her to take some refreshment. When she awoke, she looked and spoke like an angel, but soon dropped asleep as before. Oh! how my poor heart trembled, for I felt that it was but the precursor to her long last rest, although many of our friends thought she might yet linger some weeks. A total loss of appetite, and a difficulty in swallowing, prevented her from taking any nourishment throughout the day, and when we placed her in the easy chair, at night, in order to arrange her bed, I offered her some nice food, which I had prepared, and found she could not take it. My feelings amounted almost to agony. She said 'Do not be distressed. I will take it by and by.' I seated myself beside her, and she said, 'Surely, my dear mother, you have many consolations. You are gathering a little family in heaven to welcome you.' My heart was full; when I could speak, I said, 'Yes, my love, I feel that I am indeed gathering a little family in heaven to bid you welcome, but when they are all assembled there, how dreadful to doubt whether I may ever be permitted to join the circle!' 'Oh hush, dear, dear mother, do not indulge such sad thoughts; the fact of your having trained this little band to inhabit that holy place, is sufficient evidence to me that you will not fail to join us there.' I was with her myself that night, and a friend in the neighbourhood sat up also. On Saturday morning, after I had taken half an hour's sleep, I found her as quiet as a sleeping infant. I prepared her some food, and when I awoke her to take it, she said, 'Dear mother, I will try if it is only to please you.' I fed her as I would have fed a babe. She smiled sweetly and said, 'Mother, I am again an infant.' I asked if I should read to her; she said yes, she would like to have me read a part of the gospel of John. I did so, and then said, 'My dear Margaret, you look sweetly composed this morning. I trust all is peace within your heart.' 'Yes, mother, all is peace, sweet peace. I feel that I can do nothing for myself. I have cast my burden upon Christ.' I asked if she could rest her hopes there in perfect confidence. 'Yes,' she replied, 'Jesus will not fail me—I can trust him.' She then sank into a deep sleep, as on the preceding day.

"In the afternoon, Mr. and Mrs. H. came from Ballston. They were much affected by the change a few days had made in her appearance. I awoke her, fearing she might sleep too long, and said her friends had come. She extended her arms to them both, and kissed them, saying to Mr. H. that he found her a late riser, and then sank to sleep again. Mrs. H. remained with us that night. About sunset I spoke to her. She awoke and answered me cheerfully, but observing that I was unusually depressed, she said, 'Dear mother, I am wearing you out.' I replied, 'My child, my beloved child, it is not that; the thought of our separation fills me with anguish.' I never shall forget the expression of her sweet face, as she replied, 'Mother, my own dear mother, do not grieve. Our parting will not be long. In life we were inseparable, and I feel that you cannot live without me. You will soon join me, and we shall part no more.' I kissed her pale cheek, as I bent over her, and finding my agitation too strong to repress, I left the room. She soon after desired to get up; she said she must have a coughing fit, and she could bear it better in the chair. When there she began to cough, and her distress was beyond description; her strength was soon exhausted, and we again carried her to the bed. She coughed from six until half past ten. I then prevailed on her to take some nutritious drink, and she fell asleep.

"My husband and Mrs. H. were both of them anxious that I should retire and get some rest, but I did not feel the want of it, and impressed as I was with the idea that this was the last night she would pass on earth, I could not go to bed. But others saw not the change, and to satisfy them, I went at twelve to my room, which opened into hers, There I sat listening to every sound. All seemed quiet. I twice opened the door, and Mrs. H. said she slept, and had taken her drink as often as directed, and again urged me to go to bed. A little after two I put on my night dress, and laid down. Between three and four Mrs. H. came in haste for ether. I pointed to the bottle, and sprang up. She said, 'I entreat, my dear Mrs. Davidson, that you do not rise; there is no sensible change, only a turn of oppression.' She closed the door, and I hastened to rise, when Mrs. H. came again, and said Margaret has asked for her mother. I flew—she held the bottle of ether in her own hand, and pointed to her breast. I poured it on her head and chest. She revived. 'I am better now,' said she. 'Mother, you tremble, you are cold; put on your clothes.' I stepped to the fire, and threw on a wrapper, when she stretched out both her arms, and exclaimed, 'Mother, take me in your arms.' I raised her, and seating myself on the bed, passed my arms around her waist; her head dropped upon my bosom, and her expressive eyes were raised to mine. That look I never shall forget; it said, 'Tell me, mother, is this death?' I answered the appeal as if she had spoken. I laid my hand on her white brow—a cold dew had gathered there. I spoke, 'Yes, my beloved, it is almost finished; you will soon be with Jesus.' She gave one more look, two or three short fluttering breaths, and all was over—her spirit was with its God—not a struggle or groan preceded her departure. Her father just came in time to witness her last breath. For a long half hour I remained in the same position with the precious form of my lifeless child upon my bosom. I closed those beautiful eyes with my own hand. I was calm. I felt that I had laid my angel from my own breast, upon the bosom of her God. Her father and myself were alone. Her Sabbath commenced in heaven. Ours was opened in deep, deep anguish. Our sons, who had been sent for, had not arrived, and four days and nights did Ellen, (our young nurse, whom Margaret dearly loved,) and I, watch over the sacred clay. I could not resign this mournful duty to strangers. Although no son or relative was with us in this sad and solemn hour, never did sorrowing strangers meet with more sympathy, than we received in this hour of affliction, from the respected inhabitants of Saratoga. We shall carry with us through life, the grateful remembrance of their kindness. And now, my dear madam, let me thank you for your kind consoling letter, it has given me consolation. My Margaret, my now angel child, loved you tenderly. She recognised in yours a kindred mind, and I feel that her pure spirit will behold with delight your efforts to console her bereaved mother."

She departed this life on the 25th of November, 1838, aged fifteen years and eight months; her earthly remains repose in the grave-yard of the village of Saratoga.

"A few days after her departure," observes Mrs. Davidson in a memorandum, "I was searching the library in the hope of finding some further memento of my lost darling, when a packet folded in the form of a letter met my eye. It was confined with a needle and thread, instead of a seal, and secured more firmly by white sewing silk, which was passed several times around it; the superscription was, 'For my mother, private.' Upon opening these papers, I found they contained the results of self-examination, from a very early period of her life, until within a few days of its close. These results were noted and composed at different periods. They are some of the most interesting relics she has left, but they are of too sacred a nature to meet the public eye. They display a degree of self-knowledge and humility, and a depth of contrition, which could only emanate from a heart chastened and subdued by the power of the divine grace."

We here conclude this memoir, which, for the most part, as the reader will perceive, is a mere transcript of the records furnished by a mother's heart. We shall not pretend to comment on these records; they need no comment, and they admit no heightening. Indeed, the farther we have proceeded with our subject, the more has the intellectual beauty and the seraphic purity of the little being we have endeavoured to commemorate broken upon us; and the more have we shrunk at our own unworthiness for such a task. To use one of her own exquisite expressions, she was "A spirit of heaven fettered by the strong affections of earth;" and the whole of her brief sojourn here, seems to have been a struggle to regain her native skies. We may apply to her a passage from one of her own tender apostrophes to the memory of her sister Lucretia.

——One who came from heaven awhile
  To bless the mourners here,
Their joys to hallow with her smile,
  Their sorrow with her tear.

Who joined to all the charms of earth
  The noblest gifts of heaven;
To whom the Muses at her birth
  Their sweetest smiles had given.

Whose eye beamed forth with fancy's ray,
  And genius pure and high;
Whose very soul had seemed to bathe
  In streams of melody.

The cheek which once so sweetly beamed,
  Grew pallid with decay,
The burning fire within consumed
  Its tenement of clay.

Death, as if fearing to destroy,
  Paused o'er her couch awhile;
She gave a tear for those she loved,
  Then met him with a smile.

END OF THE MEMOIR.

REMAINS.

A TALE.

WRITTEN AT THE AGE OF FIFTEEN.

About the close of the year 1813 there stood on the banks of the Saranac a small neat cottage, which peeped forth from the surrounding foliage, the image of rural quiet and contentment; the scenery around it was wildly yet beautifully romantic; the clear blue river, glancing and sparkling at its feet, served only as a preparative for another and more magnificent view, where the stream, gliding on to the west, was buried in the broad white bosom of Champlain, which stretched back, wave after wave, in the distance, until lost in faint blue mists that veiled the sides of its guardian mountains, seeming more lovely in their indistinctness.

On the borders of the Saranac the little village of Plattsburgh had sprung up, in picturesque wildness, amid the loveliest haunts of nature, imparting to the mind, by its indications of man's presence with the joys and sufferings ever attendant in his train, a deeper interest than a scene of solitary nature would ever have inspired. Of all the low-roofed and shaded dwellings which rose around, the one named above, although less indicative of wealth, was by far the most striking, from its peculiarly beautiful situation. The old-fashioned piazza, which extended in front of the building, was shaded with vines and honeysuckle just budding into life; the turf on the bank of the river was of the richest and brightest emerald, and the wild rose and sweetbriar, which twined over the neat enclosure, seemed to bloom with more delicate freshness and perfume within the bounds of this earthly paradise. It was May—the blue waves of the Saranac, so lately released from their icy bondage, bounded along with music and gladness, to meet and mingle with its parent lake; the fairy isles, so beautifully throned on its sparkling bosom, robed in all the rich luxuriance of spring, and the song of the birds floated forth on the balmy air like a strain of seraph melody.

The proprietor of this lowly mansion was a grey-haired and respectable physician, whose life had been spent in toiling to mitigate the terrors of disease, and to obtain a support for his lovely and delicate family. A few words may serve to describe a character so open and ingenuous, and a fate so common to dispositions like his. Early in life he evinced a studious and scientific turn of mind, and had seized upon the profession of medicine with all the earnestness of youth. Thirsting for knowledge, he plunged into its deepest waters, and, after a few years of unremitting study, entered upon life with a character of firm and unbending integrity, and an almost childlike simplicity of manners and ignorance of the ways of the world. This was a disposition illy calculated to gain wealth or even competence; he knew not how to snatch the golden sands that lay within his grasp; he could not be servile to the rich or tyrannical to the poor, and passed through life unblest with other riches than those of an approving conscience, and the tributes of respect and love from those whose welfare he had promoted at the expense of his own. At the age of twenty-five he saw and loved a beautiful and high-spirited girl, and obeying the impulse of affection rather than the calm reasonings of prudence, he united her fortunes with his own, and settled down for life in this lowly and humble retreat we have vainly attempted to describe. At the time of our simple tale, he was far in the decline of life, but still performing his professional duties. He found his happiness in promoting the comfort of his family and enjoying the quiet pleasures of his cheerful fireside. The circle which had once closed around it was now sadly diminished by the inroads of death, but three lovely plants still clung by the side of their parent tree, and although one of these remaining blossoms seemed already fading from the eyes of her idolizing parents, there was much of pure and refined enjoyment in this lowly cottage, unknown in the haunts of wealth and worldly pleasure. The two eldest children were sisters; the one was seventeen, and the other had nearly attained her sixteenth year. Emily, the eldest, notwithstanding her youth, was the belle of the little village, and the life of her family circle. Her form and face might have been taken for the model of a Hebe—all health and gaiety—her complexion of pure red and white, had never been blanched by the cold touch of disease, and her smiling lip, with its childlike dimples, seemed bidding defiance to care and sorrow, with all their retinue of sighs, tears, and wrinkles; her dark auburn hair curled in natural and tiny ringlets on her soft white neck and shoulders; her full hazel eye wore an expression of habitual smiling archness, and her birdlike voice was for ever bursting forth in snatches of wild and untaught melody. Oh! dearly did her father love, at the close of the long, weary day, to draw forth his beloved flute and practise some soul-stirring air, while the voice of the light-hearted maiden blent with its notes, and her feet danced lightly to its measure. Such was Emily, whose sprightliness and native good sense had rendered her the favourite of her father.

But how shall I describe, in words, the high-souled, the almost ethereal Melanie? Oh! that memory could paint on other tablets than on those of the heart! Oh! that we could transfer to lifeless paper the warm and glowing images which she has there implanted! *then* might I picture that fragile form, which seemed every day fading into more spiritual fragility; that broad, high brow, through which the blue veins coursed like silken threads, so feeble and transparent; that veil of dark and luxuriant hair parted so meekly above it, and flowing, in long, waving tresses, on her neck; that cheek, now pale as the snow of December, now flushed with a hue too intense for health; and *that eye*, one moment melting with the warmest tears of earthly emotion, and the next, sparkling with the radiant light of angelic inspiration! She seemed not a being of the *present*, all her confidence in the happiness of earth was buried with the *past*, and all her hopes of pure, exalted blessedness were merged in the vast *future* of eternity. Ardent and enthusiastic in her temperament, she had loved. Highly and poetically imaginative, she had invested the object of her affection with the highest and most exalted qualities of our nature, and when stern, unbending truth dissolved those bright dreams of fancy in which she had lived and revelled—when she beheld in sober reality that *he* upon whom she had bestowed her affections was unworthy of the sacred trust, her mind received a shock only to be felt or imagined by a spirit like her own—gentle, confiding, and, at the same time, bearing within itself a standard of lofty honour, of pure sentiment, and high and heavenly virtue, by which she judged of the world around her, it was indeed an overwhelming blow; but *hers* was not the mind to waste itself in fruitless repinings, and bury all its wealth of intellect and affection in the grave of one disappointed hope: far from it! Upon its first short voyage on the cold waters of life, her little bark had been wrecked, and it now turned back to the quiet haven of home with a meek and gentle confidence, to bestow upon her family that love which was still treasured in her heart, and direct her powers of mind to higher and holier purposes than before. But if her spirit was strong in misfortune, her delicate frame partook not of that strength: although the stream of affliction had passed over the fragile flower, it had planted in the pale blossom the germs of decay—she seemed a spirit in the home and with the friends of her childhood—she was *with* them, but not *of* them. The light faded from her eye, the buoyancy from her step, and her voice no longer mingled with the gay-hearted carols of her sister. Her hopes were now rested upon a firmer foundation than that of earth, and while she walked day by day more deeply into "the valley of the shadow of death," her soul and its pure and heavenly faith waxed brighter and brighter to the close. The dark mists of receding time seemed to blend with the brilliant foreshadowings of a blessed eternity, and impart to her manners an habitual and subdued mournfulness, changed at times to the loftiest elevation, as she caught some unwonted flash from that far land of light towards which she was slowly and hopefully journeying.

Her heart, with its warm and glowing tenderness, still clung to the beings of her early love, and when she saw how deeply they mourned her visible decline, with a sad sweetness she resumed her wonted avocations, though each word and act was tinged with the lofty and spiritual enthusiasm of her nature. If she read, her mind sought fitting aliment in the holy sublimity of Milton, or the melancholy force and grandeur of Young; if she drew, faces and forms of aerial and unearthly beauty sprung from her pencil; and if she sung, the wild and tremulous melody of her voice thrilled while it charmed the listener. She was dying! For the brief space of sixteen years she had been a habitant of earth—she had tasted of its purest joy and its keenest sorrow, and now, with a calm and trustful earnestness, she was hastening to the home of the weary. Still there were deep and tender ties which bound her below. Her mother she adored; her spirited and highly-gifted little brother she watched with a mother's fondness; the sister, the beautiful and light-hearted Emily, she loved with more than sisterly affection; and her country, again threatened by the power of a foreign throne, while scarcely shadowed by the banner of its new-born freedom—her country, its struggles and its welfare, was still a theme of deep and engrossing interest. Such was Melanie Mentreville—such, as far as language can imperfectly pourtray, the lovely yet too unearthly form unfolded to my "mind's eye," like an aerial vision—such the gentle yet elevated spirit which is mingling with every dream of fancy, and would fain embody itself in words.

Those who seek in these few pages for a regular and eventful *tale*, will rise disappointed from the perusal; it is nothing more than a faint and imperfect sketch of sentiments and scenes which have long since passed away, with their actors, "to dim burial isles of the past," and which, still living as vividly as ever in the ideal world of memory, I would once more introduce upon the stage of life as beings of real and actual existence.

It was a glorious evening in May; the sun was just retiring to his couch in the west, arrayed in all the splendid livery of a northern sunset; the groves of pine and elm upon the lake shore were bathed in his golden hue, and their tall shadows were reflected in the clear depths beneath; the distant mountains of Vermont, which bounded the horizon, were shrouded with a veil of dream-like glory, blending shade by shade with the blue tints above, till heaven and earth seemed one; and that heaven! oh that pen could describe its calm and solemn magnificence; the clouds of amber and gold, tinted and fringed with crimson, floating over the pure depths, moving as in sleep to their bright western home, while a rich blending of purple and green rose up from the horizon as if darting to meet them on their mid-career. It was at this glorious sunset hour that the two sisters had repaired to the piazza of their little cottage to breathe the invigorating air of spring; and each to enjoy with their peculiar feelings the lovely and solemnizing influence of the scene. With the last ray of the golden sunlight playing over her pale upraised features, Melanie stood beside one of the vine-wreathed columns, her head resting on her hand, and her full dark eyes bent earnestly upon the wild and purified drapery of the heavens, now fading into dimness, now combining and bursting forth hues more gorgeous than before. Emily was bending over a rose-tree in the little enclosure, twining a fairy wreath of the wild sweetbriar, while the lively air which she almost unconsciously warbled, as if in unison with the character of the scene, died away in tones of plaintive and tremulous sweetness. For a few moments the silence was unbroken, until Emily, springing lightly to her sister's side, exclaimed, while her fine features beamed with an expression of affectionate gaiety, "How can you look so sad, Melanie, when all around us is breathing the very spirit of happiness? Do not the clouds you gaze upon make your heart feel light and airy as themselves! Will not these sweet flowers I have twined for you, impart something of their own hue to your cheek and your thoughts?"

Melanie gently took the wreath from her hand and replied, "You mistake me, sister, I am not sad—never perhaps did I experience a moment of more exquisite joy, for I thought, that ere those clouds had many times fleeted away to their bright homes in the west, my freed spirit might soar above them and the great orb which imparts their brilliance; to the source of all light, all love; that ere those flowers had faded with the blasts of autumn, I might rest in that fair land, where flowers of undying bloom bathe for ever in the river of the waters of life; where there is no more winter to chill the bright buds of nature, or the far more fragile blossoms of the heart."

"Oh, Melanie! Melanie!" said Emily passing her arm around her sister's neck, and bursting into tears; "you will break my heart. Would you so gladly leave us all—father and mother, and me—and—"

"No, no," replied Melanie, earnestly; "but even though you should see me no more, I feel, I know, that I shall *not* leave you, my own, my only sister. The thought may be a presumptuous one, but something within tells me that I shall see you, shall love you as dearly as now—

perhaps, even be permitted to watch over and protect you, and oh, Emily, were not *this* happiness!"

She replied only by a warmer pressure of the pale hand within her own, and borne away by the suggestions of her wild fancy, Melanie continued—

"Yes, Emily, though this weak and wasted frame may be gone from among you, my spirit shall be with you; yours will be the blessed task of soothing the pillow of disease, when our beloved parents shall tread the pathway I have trodden; but think not that Melanie, the child of their love, will be far from them in that parting hour—when you are in sorrow, my soul shall plead for you at the throne of eternal mercy—and when you are happy, my voice shall whisper in your soul of that Heavenly Father, from whose treasures of love cometh all happiness on earth, and all your hopes of blessedness in Heaven! Do not weep, Emily, I shall love you all with a purer and holier love. My kind-hearted and ingenuous father, my high-souled, my beloved mother: you, my sweet blossom; and you also, my noble little brother," she added, as the lovely boy bounded over the threshold, and she placed her hand carelessly on his long dark curls.

"Oh! sister, sister!" cried Alfred with all the eagerness of boyhood, "oh! the sights I have seen to-day! I have crossed the river in a canoe, and I have been up to the old fort, and I have seen the militia-men training, and the flags, and the drums, and the big cannon, and all!—didn't you hear it fire? Sister Emma and Mr. Selden said I should be a soldier. Shall I not, dear sister?" and with a martial air the miniature hero strode up and down the piazza as if courting admiration.

"Fie, Alfred!" replied Emily, to whose lips the smile had returned as before, "has the red coat and the gay epaulettes charmed you so soon? Remember, my little brother, that the life of a soldier is a life of hardships, and his employment a fierce and deadly one; those glittering bayonets have made many a mother childless, and those gay cockades cover many a worthless or deceitful brain. No! never be a soldier, Alfred."

"Say not so, Emily," exclaimed Milanie; "though we now smile at the proud step and flashing eye of the mimic warrior, I can read his fate in them. If his life is spared, that sprightly and slender form will expand into the tall and athletic man, and the spark that is now warming into life his unfledged fancy, will strengthen into a glowing and unquenchable flame; and as it now prompts to those tones and gestures of mock defiance and command, it will lead him on to deeds of high and lofty daring. Yes! thou wilt be a soldier, my little Alfred—noble, generous, high-souled, and brave; all, all—" her voice trembled as she added, "all I once thought another."

"Yes, I *will* be a soldier," echoed the youthful candidate for fame—"a brave and an honourable soldier;" and he bounded away through the open door, while the hall rang with his shouts.

For a few moments Melanie stood with her hands clasped upon her bosom as if in mental prayer for the interesting boy whose fate she had prophesied; and Emily seemed buried in deep revery, her head bowed, and her hand unconsciously pulling the leaves from a splendid moss rose, which was half concealed in her bosom. The silence was at length broken by the soft voice of Milanie. "Whence came that sweet rose, sister Emily?" The maiden started from her revery, blushed deeply, and drew the bud from the folds of her handkerchief.

"Forgive me, Melanie—I—Walter—Mr. Selden left it for you, and I—I forgot to give it you."

A faint sweet smile passed over Melanie's delicate features as she replied—"Keep it, Emily; save as a proof of *brotherly* kindness, his gifts are valueless to me."

Emily gazed upon the calm and gentle face before her with a mingled expression of doubt and joyful inquiry. "Do you not—tell me, dear sister,—I fear it cannot be—your heart belies your words?"

Melanie took her trembling hand in both her own, and replied, while a shade of deep sadness mingled with the affectionate simplicity of her manner.

"No, my beloved sister, you wrong me; what I say is the true, the only language of my heart. I will own to you that *once* had I known Walter Selden, I might have returned with ardour what I now view with pain as an unfortunate and misplaced attachment. You believe it not, Emily, but I am dying. Is it for me, whose every thought and hope should rest upon that world of spirits to which I am hastening, to twine my affections around an earthly idol? Is it for me, whose wayward love hath once been crushed and blighted, to bid it arise Phœnix-like from the ashes of its destruction, with new hope and new confidence? And more than all, is it for me to encourage a visionary attachment, which would blast the hopes, the young affections of a sister dearer than life? Blush not, Emily; I have read the pure volume of your heart perhaps more clearly than yourself; I have long studied its pages with pain, yet not without a deep, strong hope for the future. When I am gone, Emily, his now ardent passion will be buried in my grave; he will only remember me as a sad and pleasing vision; and as day by day that impression waxes fainter, he will behold the loveliness, the worth of your mind and person; and although it is denied to me below, my rejoicing spirit shall behold the union of those two my heart loves best, my sister and my friend."

Emily threw herself in tears upon the neck of her sister. "Oh! Melanie, Melanie, my kind, my generous Melanie! how can I believe that any one who has looked upon that bright, heavenly face, could ever cast one glance upon a simple, unideal child of earth like me?"

"And the loveliest of earth's creation," was Melanie's fond reply as she passed her hand over the silken ringlets and blushing cheek of the tearful maiden.

* * * * * * * *

A year had past by; the flowers had again bloomed, and were again fading, and time (as ever) had brought many a change upon his restless pinions. The little village of Plattsburg still looked forth as sweetly from amid its groves and streams; the Saranac flowed on with as glad a music; the billows rolled as proudly on the broad bosom of Champlain, but armed fleets in all their dreadful array now rode upon its waters; the voice of the distant cannon echoed back from its shores, and martial music pealed long and loud through those once quiet abodes of peace. It was September, 1814, that year which commenced with bloodshed and dismay, and closed with a triumph that shall never fade from the annals of our history, while America hath a heart to warm with the glow of patriotism, or a voice to perpetuate the memory of the brave. Upon the tenth morning of this memorable month we would re-open the scene of our simple drama; a morning which rose upon our feeble band of intrepid patriots in doubt and anxiety, and inspired in the breasts of their numerous and well-regulated foes, new hopes, new confidence of victory. Well might they look around upon that mighty and veteran host of fourteen thousand warriors, who had conquered in Spain, France, and the Indies, and forward upon that weak but well-disciplined band of fifteen hundred, commanded by the brave Macomb, and predict the triumph which, in all human probability, must necessarily ensue. After a long period of alternate success and defeat, the British forces poured in their utmost strength upon the northern frontier, and determined, by a decisive attack upon the comparatively unprotected village, to open a free passage into the heart of that country which they had laboured so long and so fruitlessly to subdue. Their officers were men who sought in foreign victories a glory which should enrol their names for ever upon the pages of England's history; they fought for distinctions, for titles, for wealth, and they knew not the force of a feeble arm, when directed and nerved by that holy patriotism which could toil and bleed, ere it would yield one single minutia of that independence bequeathed to them by the valour of their immortal sires.

On the morning of the fifth, the land force, commanded by Sir George Prevost, had approached the village of Plattsburgh, and their fleet was prepared to make the attack by water at the same time that the army entered the town, and overcame the feeble resistance which it expected to meet.

Meanwhile the village presented a scene of deep and thrilling interest. The small force which remained after the departure of the American army for Lake Erie was collected by their gallant leader, General Macomb, in fort Moreau, situated on the borders of the lake, a short distance from the banks of the Saranac. Here they had planted their cannon, and collected their means of defence; here they were to conquer, or if courage and skill proved vain, here they were to die. Guards and sentinels were posted at intervals along the streets, parties of volunteers were continually sallying forth to harass the enemy, and prepare themselves for the decisive struggle, and expresses were riding back and forth on their foaming steeds, shouting to the eager listener the position of the army, as it approached nearer and nearer, or hastening in silence to the fort to discharge some embassy of mighty and mysterious import. The greater part of the peaceful inhabitants had fled from the scene of bloodshed and commotion, and many a gun and bayonet were glittering in the windows of their peaceful dwellings, thus converted into barracks for the use of the soldiery, or hospitals for the wounded.

The mists of the morning had just rolled from the bosom of the waters, and the sun, struggling through the dense clouds, had just kissed the light foam upon its surface, when a tall, manly youth was seen approaching the guards on the northern bank of the Saranac with a hurried, anxious, yet half-hesitating air. His form was slight and graceful in the extreme, and the partly military dress which he wore displayed to advantage its symmetry of proportion. He carried his long rifle in one hand, and a massive old-fashioned sword was fastened by an embroidered belt to his side; his lips were firmly compressed, but his dark blue eyes were fixed upon the ground, as if some sad, subduing thought had mingled with the sterner occupants of his mind. As he approached the sentinels, each touched his cap in respect, and he passed on unquestioned, until pausing at the gate of Dr. Mentreville's

10 *

cottage, he slowly and softly raised the latch; a curtain was drawn aside, a pale face peeped from the window, a light step was heard in the hall, and Emily stood upon the threshold. A year had wrought many changes in the person of this lovely girl; her form was taller and more womanly, but had lost much of its roundness; sorrow and midnight watching had faded the roses on her cheek, and tears had been its frequent visitants; but her features, in their morning freshness and gorgeous bloom, had never seemed half so lovely. A flush sprang to her face, and a light to her eye, as she stepped forward to meet the stranger, and extended her hand with a frank and affecting simplicity. "Walter!" "Emily!" His heart seemed too full for another word, and he raised his eyes to hers with a look of sad and apprehensive inquiry.

"Oh! do not ask me," she replied, bursting into tears. "Oh! that I could give you some gleam of comfort; that I could lay down my worthless life for my sweet sister! But it may not be, her frame grows hourly weaker, and her mind more strong; she seems all *soul*—a spirit of Heaven fettered by the strong affections of earth; but yet, Walter," she added, wiping the blinding tears from her eyes, "when I look upon her I can scarcely find it in my heart to grieve; she seems so placid and so happy, like an infant returning to the arms of its parent: it is only when I look upon myself, and dear mother, and father, and *you*, and think how lonely, how desolate we shall be, that I feel the full weight of sorrow."

"Desolate! desolate indeed!" replied the young man, and unable longer to control his emotion he turned from her, and leaning his head upon the little column where Melanie had so often rested, gave vent to his excited feelings in a flood of tears. But a moment, and it was over—he had paid his tribute upon the altar of sorrowing affection, and he awoke to the remembrance of sterner and more pressing duties.

"Forgive me, Emily!" his cheek burning with shame at this transitory weakness—"surely the being for whose early fate I have shed these unmanly tears must form my best apology; yet I would not give way to sorrow upon a day like this, when every man should bring a cool head and a strong arm to the succour of his country."

Emily's pale cheek turned yet more pallid, as she exclaimed, "Walter, do you—have you indeed joined yourself with those doomed men?" and her eye rested on the sword and rifle, which she had not before perceived.

"And have I not, Emily? Would you, would Melanie own me as her—her friend? Would she not blush to hear my shame? Would not the blood of my grandsire, who fought so bravely in the Revolution, burn and scorch in the veins of his dastardly son, if I refused to join the brave band in defence of my native village, of my family, and of you, sweet Emily—and—and Melanie?"

"And if you are defeated"—

He smiled encouragingly.

"Why, *then*, Emily, we must yield like men, only with our lives. But we shall not be defeated—we shall conquer! Brave hearts and determined hands will do more in the hour of conflict than closed ranks and mere animal force."

"And when is this dreadful hour to come? When do you expect the final attack?"

"I should be tempted to conceal it, little trembler," replied the youth, "did I not feel that I have already too long neglected the chief object of my visit. From the reports of the expresses and scouts who have returned, we expect the enemy to-morrow morning, when we shall probably be assailed by land and water. This place will be the scene of bloodshed and confusion: you cannot remain here—you must fly."

"I know it, I know it!" exclaimed Emily; "father is already gone in search of wagons to convey our effects; but my sister, my poor sister, it seems almost sacrilege to disturb and perhaps hasten her parting moments by this precipitation; and the idea is so distressing, she longs so to die in her own old home. I can read it in every look, though she will not name it, lest we subject ourselves to danger for her sake. You know, Walter, we should have fled long since, as at the time of the former invasion, but ever since that short sojourn with strangers, she has seemed to fade more rapidly. It was breaking up all the sweet associations and habits which alone seem binding her to earth, and now, when she has so short a time to live, oh! it is a cruel, cruel task!" and the affectionate girl wept faster than before.

"I feel it all, dear Emily," said Walter, "but were it not more cruel that her gentle spirit should part amid the roar of cannon and the shouts of the combatants? Then, if the British conquer, the last sounds which would meet her ear, would be those of insult and lawless triumph. No, no, it is impossible—you must fly. Would to God my duties did not call me for the space of two hours, that I might see you all in safety, and then return, with a light heart, to my post. But that cannot be; by especial favour I have obtained leave to make you this hasty visit, and, upon my return, the band of volunteers which I have joined proceed to the bank above the old bridge, the station deemed most advantageous for this section of our small force. So you see, dear Emily, I cannot aid you; but you say your father is gone—where, and with what hopes of success?"

"He started before daylight this morning, to obtain more easy conveyance for our dear invalid than our old-fashioned family vehicle affords, and wagons to convey the family and our most valuable effects; but you know calamity and terror make us selfish, and the inhabitants having fled, he found not the proper means of conveyance for dear Melanie in the village, and he hastened on some ten or twelve miles in the country to obtain them, and we do not expect him to return until sunset."

"Good heavens!" exclaimed Walter, "the British forces will have advanced between him and our village, and he cannot return to you. Why did I not know this before?"

Scarcely had he spoken, when Mrs. Mentreville appeared on the threshold of the open door, at the porch of which they had been conversing. Her figure was about the middle height and delicately formed, and her features retained the traces of much former beauty, but deep and unremitting anxiety had wasted a form naturally feeble, and an expression of calm but unutterable grief was seated in her full dark eye. As she advanced, she caught the expression of alarm in the face of young Selden and her daughter, and after the first silent greeting was over she inquired, "What were you saying, Walter? Do not fear to tell me; nothing can alarm me now."

In brief words Walter repeated his apprehensions that her husband might be prevented from returning, and their flight would shortly become impossible.

"Then we will remain," replied Mrs. Mentreville firmly. "If we are successful, all is well; if we fail, the British officers are gentlemen as well as soldiers—they have mothers, wives, and daughters—they will protect us. I only fear the effect of the excitement and turmoil upon our beloved sufferer."

Walter sighed deeply.

"God will protect you, my dear madam. I wish *I* could trust more implicitly to the faith and honour of our enemies. But Dr. Mentreville may still return—all may yet be well. My term of absence is almost expired—can I not see Melanie?" and he lowered his voice almost to a whisper, as if he feared to breathe aloud a name so sacred.

The mother replied not, but silently taking the hand of the young man, she led him into the chamber of the dying girl. It seemed not like the abode of death and disease. The spirit, trembling, hovering within its boundaries, appeared to sanctify its resting place. There was no gloom, or darkness, or dreariness, for they found no place in the mind of Melanie, and why should they surround her frame without? She was all purity, gentleness, elevation—and an air of soft soothing melancholy pervaded the scene of her last sufferings. The windows opening upon the river were closed, for there were sights and sounds of too animating and warlike a nature to meet the acute eye or sensible ear of the dying maiden; but a casement beside her couch was thrown back, and the little flower-garden beneath it, which she had so often tended, sent up the perfume of its last fading blossoms into her chamber, while the quivering poplar-trees waved and sighed her requiem before it, and the luxuriant vines twined their small tendrils round the lattice. The sunlight, broken and softened by the green branches, fell in chastened splendour upon the floor, and tinged with a yet more heavenly radiance the pale, bright features of Melanie. The couch had been placed beside the open casement, that, as she reclined upon its pillows, she might yet look around upon the scenes so dear to her; and well do those who witnessed remember the unearthly loveliness of her form and face, and the alternate sadness—a glorious hope in its expression, as she bade a mental farewell to the cherished scenes of earth, or looked forward to the blessed home which she was seeking. There was one by her side who watched with unwearied care and childish simplicity every look and motion. It was the little Alfred. She dearly loved the ardent and enthusiastic boy, and his young heart clung with all its ardour and enthusiasm to the one who most deeply awakened and cherished the incipient romance of his nature. Now that he beheld her thus fading from before him, he hovered for ever by her bed-side, and hung, like one entranced, upon each trembling accent of her voice. This deep and subdued affection had unlocked a new fountain in his little breast, and it flowed on, overwhelming all the petty selfishness of childhood, and quenching all save the flame of military ardour, which still burnt silently and slowly, though subdued by this new and overpowering sentiment of love for his gentle and intellectual sister. It was affecting to mark the struggle of these two passions in his young mind. At the sound of the distant cannon, the roll of the drum, or the shouting of the express as he rode furiously by, he would start from his seat, while his eye kindled, and his step involuntarily kept pace with the music; then, as the thought of Melanie rushed over his mind, he would turn to the bed, take her hand gently in his own little palm, and whisper softly, "Sister, did it disturb you? He was seated on his little stool by her side, cutting miniature soldiers from the little branches of a wild rose-tree, and watching every change in his sister's face, when Mrs. Mentreville, Emily, and Walter entered. Melanie raised her head from the pillow on which she reclined, and extended her hand feebly as Selden approached.

"Walter, this is kind," said she; "I feared I should not see you before the engagement, and then we may never meet again." The youth spoke not, but kissed the pale hand which rested in his own. She continued: "I see that you have joined them, that you are going forth to add one more brave heart and arm to our adventurous band. I knew it. Go, Walter, go! and my blessing and the blessing of God go with you. If you conquer, you will find your reward in that peace which you have fought to bestow; if you fall, it will be in the performance of your duty, and you will share the grave of our bravest and best. Oh!" she added, clasping her hands, and her eyes kindling with enthusiasm, "Oh! that the shout of victory might be the last earthly sound wafted to my spirit as it seeks the portal of a brighter world! With the voice of triumph floating around its pathway, how blessed might be its departure!" There was a moment's deep silence; every heart seemed too full for speech, till the soft sweet voice of Melanie again fell, like a bird whisper, upon the ears of the motionless group: "Walter, do not deceive me; is it safe for my dear mother and sister to remain in this village, abandoned as it will be to the soldiery in case of defeat? God only knows how deeply I have longed to breathe my last in this dear home of my infancy, but, for the love of mercy, let not this idle fancy endanger the safety or comfort of those I love dearer than myself." Walter replied that it was deemed necessary to fly, and that her father had gone in search of the easiest means of conveyance for her. She sighed deeply. "My own dear father!—But I shall not need him." Immediately rallying her spirits, while the faint sunlight smile, so peculiar to herself, played over her features, she again extended her hand. "Let me not detain you, Walter, from the performance of those duties which now devolve upon you. Go! When I hear the shouts and tumult of the battle, I will pray for you, if on earth—I will watch over you, if released from its fetters. Oh! do not look so sad! If I saw not the mournful faces of those I love, my soul feels so happy I could almost think it Paradise. When I am gone, remember me as a dream, a moonlight vision which never formed itself into reality till it had fled; as a being whose shadow has flitted over the past, whose life is only in the future. I have only two hopes, two wishes upon earth; one for my country, the other—" She paused, and gazed fondly upon Walter and Emily as they stood beside her. The quick glance of Emily caught her meaning, and, throwing herself upon Melanie's bosom, she looked imploringly in her face. "Fear not, my sweet blossom," whispered Melanie, "I cannot, will not say aught which you could wish unsaid." Then turning to Selden, she said, "Farewell; may God protect and prosper you, my *brother!*"

The tears rushed to the young man's eyes as he cast one long, mournful look upon the delicate and spiritual features, and kissed the small wan fingers which he again pressed, but mastering his emotion with a strong effort, he turned from the room, and paused a moment in the hall, ere he could collect sufficient courage to leave the spot which contained a being so lovely (as he feared) *for ever.* As he stood thus, with his hand upon his brow and his eyes bent upon the floor, a slight noise behind him attracted his attention. He turned; it was little Alfred. He had stolen unperceived from the room, and was examining Walter's rifle with looks of earnest and admiring attention, and too much absorbed to be conscious of the owner's presence; he was, in fancy, loading, presenting, firing, and performing all the military evolutions of which he was master; when he at length perceived Walter, he sprang to his side, and raising his bright face, exclaimed in an eager whisper—

"Oh! Mr. Selden! Mr. Selden! take me with you to the battle; I will not trouble you; I will load your gun, and I will take my little bow and arrow, and fight as the Indians do; and I will make the British run—do, do—take me!"

"Will you not be afraid, my dear boy?" said Walter, scarcely conscious that he spoke.

A smile of contempt curled the boy's red lip.

"Afraid! what honourable soldier was ever afraid?" and forgetting his caution one moment, he laughed aloud. The spark had been awakened in his little bosom, and it required all the soft dews of feeling and reflection to quench its flame.

"Hush, hush, Alfred!" said Selden; "would you leave your sister, your dear sister, and perhaps never see her more?" The boy looked down; his heart swelled, and his lip trembled; but his desire was still strong. "Your father is gone, and would you leave your mother and sisters defenceless? What will become of them if the British conquer?"

Here was a double motive; here were united the two ruling passions, and he clapped his hands in the eagerness of his joy.

"Yes, yes, I will stay and protect them; and mother shall call me her little soldier, and sister Emmy will not be afraid, and no one shall touch dear Melanie." And he stole back contented to the stool by his bedside, to indulge his young fancy, in dreams of war, and victory, and defence.

Walter departed; and in a short time after the sound of martial music, of the drum and fife, and the trampling of many feet, disturbed the silence of Melanie's chamber. Mrs. Mentreville and Emily cast an anxious glance upon the apparently sleeping sufferer, and softly raised the curtain of the window. It was the band of volunteers marching out to their post. It was mostly composed of the young men of the village, led by an older and more experienced commander. Their hearts were beating high with hope and expectation, and they kept pace with a proud and even step to the lively national air which swelled in loud strains upon the breeze. As they passed the house of Dr. Mentreville, many an eye was turned, and many a glance fixed eagerly upon the beautiful face of Emily, as she leaned from the window; but she knew it not, she saw, she thought of but *one*. The rest passed before her like a colourless picture, and she beheld the form of Walter Selden, vivid and distinct from the pageantry around him. His eye caught hers, fixed with such an earnest and speaking gaze upon his features! Then first flashed the truth like an electric spark through his mind—the idea that that young and guileless maiden might feel in him an interest deeper than that of a sister or a friend. A burning flush rose to his cheeks and brow: he bowed low; a white handkerchief fluttered from the window, and it was again closed. All had passed in an instant, but it was one of those which contained more of existence than many a long, long year: in that one look, unseen save by its object, the unconscious girl had betrayed the secret most dear, most sacred to her heart; the one which she had fancied, had believed, no grief, no mental torture could force her to reveal. She turned from the window, hid her blushing face in her hands, and burst into tears.

"Come hither, Emily," said Melanie, and opened her arms, while the weeping girl threw herself into them and sobbed upon her sister's bosom. Melanie clasped her hands over the silken tresses of the young mourner, and raised her head as in prayer. Oh! that I had a purer pencil than those of earth to paint the forms, the expression, of those two lovely beings! Some hovering angel might have transferred that scene to his immortal tablets, and laid it up among the records of heaven, as one bright spot shining forth from the dark annals of misery and crime. Emily, the type of all earth's loveliest, warm with its noblest passions, all the generous impulses of youth, weeping upon the bosom of a dying sister; and that sister, forgetful of herself, of all beside, praying for the dear one, while her face beamed with all the hallowed love, of the gentle compassion of a purified being, and her dark eyes kindled with a glow reflected only from the heaven they sought. The day rolled on, that long, long dreary day; the village was still in the tumult of preparation; the expresses rode by more furious than ever; the British forces were rapidly approaching the village, but still the father, the husband came not, and fears for his safety mingled with the agony of his helpless family. Mrs. Mentreville was a woman of acutely delicate and sensitive feelings, but they were mastered and controlled by a firm judgment, a strong and independent mind. She had long seen, with that anguish which a mother only can know, the certain but gradual decline of her beloved Melanie.

This child had been her favourite. There was something in the pure and lofty enthusiasm of her character which touched a responsive chord in her own bosom. What others had never seen, or only marked as the idle fancies of a romantic girl, revealed to her the inmost recesses of a nature composed of deep sensibilities, quiet, unobtrusive affections, and lofty aspirations after something higher and holier than earth. She had studied her carefully; she loved her to idolatry, and she only who has nurtured, who has wept over the death-bed of such a child, can understand the bitterness of grief which converted her whole soul into a fountain of agony. She saw how deeply it distressed Melanie to behold her sorrow, and many an hour banished herself from her bedside, that spot most sacred upon earth, that she might drink unperceived from the darkness of her affliction, and in solitude, and silence, struggle to subdue her heart into accordance with the will of her Heavenly Father.

Night drew on; the sky, which had been clear, became suddenly overcast; the sunbeams no longer played upon the quivering poplars, or sparkled gladly in the blue depths of the Saranac, and a dark thunder-gust rolled in black volumes from the west. The wing of the storm, as it slowly unfolded in the heavens, cast a deep leaden shadow on the waves of the Champlain; and the white foam gathered upon the crest of each receding billow, as it rolled with an angry murmur to the shore. The thunder growled faintly in the distance; pale flashes of light burst at intervals from the rent clouds, and large threatening drops fell with their sullen patter on the roof. Every thing betokened the approach of a fearful, though transient storm; and a fervent prayer for the safety of her husband burst from the lips of Mrs. Mentreville, as she closed the door of the cottage and returned to the chamber of Melanie. As the tempest strengthened, the lightning streamed in with broad and livid flashes, and the thunder rolled on its tremendous pathway; each crash more loud and terrific than the last. Mrs. Mentreville, seated on Melanie's couch, supported her head upon her bosom, and an expression of deep awe rested upon her pale features. Emily knelt by the bedside and concealed her face in its drapery, and even the stout heart of little Alfred quailed, as peal after peal burst and gleamed above them and around them. He lisped no word of fear, but grasped the hand of Melanie in his own, gazed wistfully upon her placid and spiritual features, as if something whispered within him that no danger could assail, no bolts from the artillery of heaven descend upon a form and soul so heavenly. No terror, no dread was on the face of Melanie; resting upon her mother's bosom, she gazed on the dark rolling masses of the tempest-cloud, and trembled not at the livid flames, or the pealings of the loud-voiced thunder; her soul seemed bursting from her eyes in one long gaze of solemn adoration; her spirit was lifted above the warring elements; it was casting its burden of deep and silent worship at the footstool of the *Almighty.* The storm for an instant paused: the thunder-peals died away in a low muttering growl, and an awful silence reigned in the heavens and on the earth; the angel of the tempest had retired 'neath the veil of blackness, to gather the scattered thunderbolts in his hand, and to wreathe the winged lightnings on his brow. Again he came upon his wild career—on, on, in more terrific majesty; the dark cloud parted with a fearful chasm, while from its bosom poured a sheet of flame, broad, livid, terrible, and a fierce crash, as of a shattered world, pealed along the heavens. A low shriek burst from the lips of Emily, and Alfred pressed his sister's hand with a convulsive energy. The grasp recalled Melanie's wandering senses; she drew him closer to her bosom, and whispered in accents low but distinct, heard like an angel's murmur amid the roaring of the storm, "Fear not, my little brother; it is the same voice which breathes in melody among the flowers of spring; the same hand which paints the rainbow and the rose. Fear not, it is your Father and your God! He sendeth forth the spirit of his love, and heaven and earth are bathed in the fountain of its glory, he stretcheth out the arm of his power and the hills tremble and are shaken. Yea," she added, clasping her hands and looking upwards with an expression of fervent solemnity, "yea; thou only art great who coverest thyself with light as with a garment; who stretchest out the heavens like a curtain; who makes the clouds thy chariot; who walkest upon the wings of the wind."

It was midnight. The storm had departed as it came; the wind sighed mournfully, yet sweet amid the dripping branches; the black masses rolled from the firmament, and the moon, struggling through their gloom, cast her feeble and trembling beams on the still agitated waters; the waves rose and fell with a faint wailing murmur, like the sobs of a weeping child; and the hearts of the anxious mourners seemed to beat in unison with their sad cadence. A taper was burning on the hearth in Melanie's chamber, but the curtain was withdrawn, and the pure cold rays of the moon trembled faintly upon a being, pure and heavenly as themselves. She slept—in the hush of that midnight hour, surrounded by those best loved on earth, she slept. Oh! the peace, the unearthly beauty of that sleep. Her head lay back upon the pillow, her bright dark hair shaded with its rich tresses the exquisite features of her face; the serenity of heaven seemed resting on her broad, pale brow; her dark eyelids lay motionless on their snowy pillow, and nought could reveal to the beholder that he gazed on an inhabitant of earth, save the brilliant flush which mantled upon her cheek, as if death, fearing utterly to destroy a work so beautiful, had breathed a deeper crimson on the fresh rose of health, and placed it 'mid the lilies of disease. Emily was kneeling, beside her, her face bathed in tears, and her eyes now bent with a wistful sadness upon her sleeping sister, now raised as in prayer to Heaven; a petition seemed trembling upon her lips, but it would wing its way no farther; she dared not pray for fetters to enchain the struggling spirit; she could not even wish to recall the fluttering prisoner to its cage of clay, and the prayer died unuttered on her tongue. Then her mind wandered far away from that shaded room and its midnight stillness. She saw the morning dawn above the opposing ranks; she heard the shouts of the commanders, the sharp report of the rifles, and the deafening roar of the cannon, and she saw *one* form amid the thousands, and, as when she last beheld it, she saw that form *alone;* she marked his every movement, and when her quick fancy beheld the "leaden death," flying around him, her breath was checked convulsively, and the colour went and came upon her cheek, and then with the swiftness and waywardness of thought, her mind returned to their last meeting, their last look; and her face became one burning flush when she thought how much, how all *too* much that look betrayed. As she raised her head from the counterpane in which it had been buried, her eyes again rested upon the features of Melanie, and still more deeply did she blush at her own selfishness in thinking of aught beside the cherished sufferer and the duty she owed to her beloved mother. Where was that mother now? Why was not *she* too bending over the slumbers of the dying one? Oh! had you asked her bleeding heart, an answer had been poured forth in tones of the bitterest agony which the hand of sorrow could draw forth from its broken strings. Grief—grief, too deep for utterance, too violent for restraint, had driven her from the bedside of Melanie. With a burning brain and throbbing nerves, she had stolen unnoticed from the side of Emily, and stepped forth upon the broad piazza, to breathe for one moment the coolness of the midnight air; it soothed, it refreshed her, and throwing herself upon the seat beneath Melanie's window, a burst of tears relieved her agitated feelings. The scene was solemn, and to the reflecting mind it was one of deep interest, for the shade of an eventful morrow seemed hanging darkly over it; torches were glancing to and fro in the distant fort; boats were crossing and recrossing the river; the bridges were destroyed, and the voice of the sentinel was heard at intervals, as he loudly demanded the countersign from some belated traveller. In addition to her other cares, Mrs. Mentreville was now seriously alarmed for the safety of her husband: at every casual footstep, at every shadow which obscured the moonlight, she started from her seat, and an anxious "is it he?" trembled unconsciously upon her lips. In the silent solemnity of that midnight hour her mind reverted to her own early days, when loving and beloved, she had first entered that humble cottage, a youthful and happy *wife*, and when after the lapse of years she had still found herself an adored and cherished *mother*, the centre of all the social affections, the *parent tree* which shadowed, nourished, and supported the fresh young tendrils that twined around it; *now* there was a deep, deep void within her heart. Death had breathed upon her paradise; he had laid his cold hand upon those delicate vines; he had torn them asunder; had gathered all but three young blossoms to twine around and wither on his clay-cold brow. Her affection for the dead was now transferred with tenfold ardour to the living; the buoyancy and hope of youth was gone; but love, a mother's love, can never perish, and her spirit, chastened and subdued by the hand of affliction, clung to Melanie as to some guardian angel, some being of superior mould, who seemed unfitted for the cares and buffetings of life, and yet foreboding fancy had never dared to whisper she could die; and now the dreadful summons had arrived; she saw it in the flushed and fevered cheek, the throbbing pulse, the eye of piercing brilliancy; she heard it in the tremulous accents of her beloved one,—they mingled all the sweetness of heaven, and all the sadness of earth; and the memory of those tones stole over her mind like a soothing murmur, as she buried her face in her hands, and the tears stole silently between them. She was startled from her revery by a sound like the distant trampling of horses' feet; she turned—the sound came nearer—"It is he!" and she rushed down the steps of the piazza, and with her hand upon the gate leaned anxiously over the little enclosure. She scarcely breathed. It was a horseman riding furiously down the little hill to the right, and as he passed in the moonlight, hope could deceive her no longer; it was *not* he, it was the express; he dashed along through the row of sentinels, and waving his cap in the air, his hoarse voice broke painfully upon the silence of the night.

"The enemy! the enemy!" he shouted, "they have come on by forced marches; they are now encamped within two miles; they will be here by daybreak," and he dashed on, arousing the sleeping echoes, till the trampling of his horse's feet, and the tones of his stentorian voice were alike lost in the distance. Mrs. Mentreville slowly and mechanically returned to the piazza, and a thousand agonizing thoughts swept like a burning torrent through her brain. The British army was rapidly approaching; the conflict would probably take place at daybreak; her husband had gone to secure them a place of refuge, but he returned not; perhaps he was a prisoner in the British camp, and she, a helpless woman, with one young and timid daughter, and one, so dear a one, just dying, was left alone in the deserted village, exposed to the cruel insults of the British soldiery, should they conquer, and to all the terror and tumult of a desperate conflict even should they fail. Oh! that was a night of agony, and never, through all the vicissitudes of after life, did one thought, one feeling then endured fade from the volume of her memory. As the thoughts of danger and the necessity of exertion passed through her mind, she wiped the tears from her eyes, and whispered within herself, "This weakness will not do; I have a part to perform. I am the only guardian of my three dear ones; we cannot fly, and if the British conquer, as I fear they must, I will appeal for protection to their officers! they have wives and children." * *

* * * * * * * *

POETICAL REMAINS.

TO MY MOTHER.

Mother! thou bid'st me touch the lyre,
And wake its sweetest tones for thee;
To kindle fancy's dying fire,
And light the torch of poetry.

Mother! how sweet the word, how pure,
As if from heaven the accents came;
If aught can rouse the dormant soul,
It is that cherish'd, honour'd name.

Deep in the heart's recess it dwells;
It lives with being's earliest dawn;
With reason's light expands and swells,
And dies with parting life alone.

Mother! 't is childhood's first essay,
Breathed in its trembling tones of love;
It lights the heart, through life's long way,
And points to holier worlds above!

It is a name, whose mighty spell
Can draw the chain'd affections forth,
Can rouse the feelings from their cell,
And give each purer impulse birth.

Then will I wake my sleeping muse,
And strive to breathe my thoughts in song,
Though sweetest strains must fail to speak
The heart's affections, deep and strong.

PRIDE AND MODESTY.

Just where a wild and rapid stream
Roll'd back its waves in seeming pride,
Flowers of each softly varying hue
Were sweetly blooming, side by side.

Shaded by many a bending tree,
Their glowing cups with dew-drops fill'd,
Nature's fair daughters blushing stood,
And all their fragrant sweets distill'd.

Oh, 't was a wild and lovely spot,
  Which well might seem a spirit's home!
A lone retreat, a noiseless grot,
  Where earth's rude blasts could never come.

Within a broad and open glade,
  A tulip spread its gaudy hue,
While, 'neath the myrtle's clustering shade,
  A sweetly-drooping lily grew.

As the light zephyrs o'er them swept,
  And heighten'd many a rosy glow,
A strange, deep murmur round them crept,
  Like distant music, wild and low.

'T was the gay tulip's fragrant breath,
  Which many an answering echo woke,
As to her lowly neighbour, thus,
  With proud and haughty mien, she spoke:

"Away! frail trembling flower! nor dare
  To droop beside my glittering form!
Behold how bright my garments are,
  And mark each sweetly varying charm!

"Then hie thee to some lonely nook,
  Nor show thy pallid features here;
Go, murmur to some babbling brook,
  Where like thyself each scene is drear!

"Hast thou assurance thus to gaze
  On one who nature's self beguiles?
Hence! haste thee hence! and hide that face,
  Where parent nature never smiles."

She ceased—a sad, sweet whispering rose,
  Which thrill'd the zephyrs list'ning ear;
Soft as an angel's gentlest tone,
  Too heavenly for this mortal sphere.

'T was the pale lily's silvery voice,
  Which rose in low and thrilling tone,
Like breath of wild Eolian lyre,
  Moved by the wind-god's tenderest moan:

"Great queen!" the lovely gem replied,
  "I view thy charms, I own their power,
And void of envy, shame, or pride,
  Admire thy beauties of an hour.

"Full well I know my pallid brow
  Can never match the hues of thine;
Nor my white robes the colours wear,
  Which on thy dazzling garments shine.

"But the same hand hath form'd us both;
  And heaven-born nature smiled as sweet
As on thy form, when the low flower
  Was peeping from its green retreat.

"Here was I planted! let me here
Still live in purity and peace;
The lily's eye shall never weep
To gain the tulip's gaudy grace.

"But oh, forget not, 'mid the pomp
Of earthly kingdom, pride, and joy,
That boasted beauty must decay,
And withering age thy pleasures cloy.

"Receive the lily's kind advice,—
Retire from scenes of public life,
And pass thy days in solitude,
Apart from vanity and strife."

While the sweet murmur past away,
The stately rose as umpire came;
The lily shunn'd her proud survey,
The lordly tulip bent for shame.

In accents bland, but nobly firm,
The queen-like flow'ret soon replied,
In tones which charm'd the tender flower,
And humbled more the tulip's pride.

"Come hither, pure and lovely one,
With thee no garden plant can vie;
Not e'en the tulip's gaudy hues
Match with thy stainless, spotless dye.

"Come to my bosom, emblem fair
Of heavenly virtue's fairer form!
Here let me learn each modest grace,
While here I hush each wild alarm.

"Come to my bosom! what so pure,
So lovely as a modest one,
Who flies from folly's glittering lure,
And shuns the bright meridian sun!

"Let the proud tulip glitter still,
Robed in her scarf of varying hue;
Alone 'neath nature's eye we'll rest,
Cheer'd by her smile, and nurtured by her dew."

VERSIFICATION OF THE TWENTY-THIRD PSALM.

My shepherd is the faithful Lord,
I shall not want, I trust his word;
He lays me down in pastures green,
He leads me by the lake serene;
Comforts my soul, and points me on
To pure religion's holy shrine.

I wander through the vale of death,
Yet he supports me still;
He will receive my dying breath
If I perform his will.

Even in the presence of my foes
He doth a meal of plenty spread;
My cup with blessings overflows,
With oil he does anoint my head.

1831.

TO BROTHER L——.

The vessel lightly skims the wave,
And bounds across the waters blue,
Near shores where trees luxuriant spread,
And roses wildly blooming grew.

Yon islands see! so fair and bright,
Like gems upon the azure sea;
The waters dance like forms of light,
And waft my brother dear from me.

1831.

FOR MAMMA.

The rippling stream serenely glides,
And rising meets the swelling tides;
The fleeting lights of heaven around
Shine brightly o'er the vast profound.

The moon hath hid her silvery face,
So mark'd with beauty and with grace,
Majestic when she rides on high,
A gem upon the azure sky!

My thoughts, oh Lord, then turn to thee,
Of what *thou* art and I shall be;
Thy outstretch'd wings around me spread,
And guard with love my hapless head.

1831.

TO MAMMA.

Farewell, dear mother, for awhile
I must resign thy plaintive smile;
May angels watch thy couch of wo,
And joys unceasing round thee flow.

May the almighty Father spread
His sheltering wings above thy head.
It is not long that we must part,
Then cheer thy downcast, drooping heart.

Remember, oh remember me,
Unceasing is my love for thee!
When death shall sever earthly ties,
When thy loved form all senseless lies.

Oh that my soul with thine could flee,
And roam through wide eternity;
Could tread with thee the courts of heaven,
And count the brilliant stars of even.

Farewell, dear mother, for awhile
I must resign thy plaintive smile;
May angels watch thy couch of woe,
And joys unceasing round thee flow.

1831

TO A FLOWER.

The blighting hand of winter
Has laid thy glories low;
Oh, where is all thy beauty?
Where is thy freshness now?

Summer has pass'd away,
With every smiling scene,
And nature in decay
Assumes a mournful mien.

How like adversity's rude blast
Upon the helpless one,
When hope's gay visions all have passed,
And to oblivion gone.

Yet winter has some beauties left,
Which cheer my heart forlorn;
Nature is not of charms bereft,
Though shrouded by the storm.

I see the sparkling snow;
I view the mountain tops;
I mark the frozen lake below,
Or the dark rugged rocks.

How truly grand the scene!
The giant trees are bare,
No fertile meadows intervene,
No hillocks fresh and fair;

But the cloud-capp'd mountains rise,
Crown'd with purest whiteness,
And mingle with the skies,
That shine with azure brightness.

And solitude, that friend so dear
To each reflecting mind,
Her residence has chosen here
To soothe the heart refined.

1831.

STANZAS.

Roll on, roll on, bright orb of day;
 Roll on, thou beauteous queen of even;
Ye stars, that ever twinkling play,
 And sweetly grace the azure heaven.

Roll on, until thy God's command
 Shall rend the sky and tear the earth;
Till he stretch forth his mighty hand
 To check the voice of joyous mirth.

He spread the heavens as a scroll,
 He made the sea, he form'd the world;
The heavens again shall backward roll,
 And mountains from their base be hurl'd.

He form'd the lovely verdant green,
And aught of fair that e'er has been;
These beauties all shall pass away,
And in one shapeless ruin lay.

But God in his glory, the God of the sky,
Will continue through endless eternity;
For ever untainted, all holy and pure,
His love and his mercy shall ever endure.

ESSAY ON NATURE.

How just, how pure, how holy is the great Creator of the universe! When I gaze upon all the wonders of nature, the rippling stream, the distant mountain, the rugged rock, or the gently sloping hill, my mind turns to the first Great Cause of all; the Author of this mingled beauty, grandeur, and simplicity. God made this beautiful world for us, that we might be happy, and why are we not so? Because we do not seek *real* happiness. We are striving to obtain *worldly* pleasure; but what is *that*, compared with the happiness of a child of God? *He* feels and knows that his Saviour is ever dear; he weeps over his past follies with a sweet consciousness that they are all forgiven; that the kind Shepherd has brought back his lost sheep to the fold. He trusts in the goodness of his Creator. His faith is firm in the blessed Saviour who died for him; he has charity for *all*, love for *all*. Such is the Christian! His earthly sorrows seem light, for his thoughts are continually upon his just Preserver. What is man, frail, feeble man, but a flower of the field, that fades away with the rude blast of the autumnal storm! How infinite the love which sustains him!

Plattsburgh, 1832.

VERSES WRITTEN WHEN NINE YEARS OF AGE.

HOME.

Yonder orb of dazzling light
Sinks beneath the robe of night,
And the moon so sweetly pale,
Waits to lift her silver veil.
One by one the stars appear,
Glittering in the heavenly sphere,
And sparkling in their bright array,
Welcome in the close of day.
But home, that sacred, pure retreat,
Where dwells my heart in all that 's sweet,
And my own stream, where oft I 've stray'd,
And mark'd the beams that o'er it play'd,
Is far away, o'er the waters blue,
Far from my fondly straining view.

1832.

THE MAJESTY OF GOD.

With the lightning his throne, and the thunder his voice,
He rides through the troubled sky;
He bids all his angels in heaven rejoice,
And thunders his wrath from on high!
"On the wing of the whirlwind he fearlessly rides,"
O'er the heavens, the earth, and the ocean he strides;
The breath of his nostrils the lightning's flame,
All nature re-echoes his powerful name!

FROM THE FORTY-SECOND PSALM.

Why is my bosom fill'd with fear,
And why cast down my troubled soul?
Is not thy God, thy Saviour near,
And will he not thy fate control?

How mighty is my Saviour's hand,
How powerful his word,
And how can I, a sinful worm,
Address him as my Lord?

Jehovah sends his mighty breath
Across the placid sea;
The foaming waters proudly whirl,
As longing to be free.

Deep calleth unto deep aloud,
The raging billows follow thee;
Thou send'st the roaring waves abroad,
Which rush o'erwhelming over me.

Yet at the great I Am's command,
For me, the object of his care,
The shouting waters silent stand;
He still shall listen to my prayer.

1833.

HYMN OF THE FIRE-WORSHIPPERS.

Welcome, oh welcome, god of day!
Thy presence gives us peace!
All hail, eternal, glorious king,
Thy light shall never cease!

Transcendent Sun! oh list to one
Whose heart is fill'd with love;
Let the sweet airs lift high our prayers
To thee our God above.

Pure orb of light! resplendent, bright;
Oh, who may cope with thee?
And who may dare to view thee there,
And never bend the knee?

Before thy ray the guilty flee,
And dread thy cheerful beam,
Lest thy fierce eye their crimes descry,
And chill hope's trembling gleam.

To thee we bow, for on thy brow
Is majesty impress'd,
Glory thy shroud, thy throne the cloud,
Which circles o'er thy breast.

The blushing flower will own thy power;
It blooms alone for thee;
And though so frail, oh hear my wail,
My blessed guardian be!

When the first ray of brilliant day
Illumes the hill, the plain,
The songsters raise a hymn of praise,
Oh, listen to my strain.

When thy loved form, which braves the storm,
In ocean disappears,
One mournful cry ascends on high,
The night is spent in tears.

But lest we mourn for thy return,
And pine away in grief,
The orb of night supplies thy light,
And gives us sweet relief.

Then on my head, Eternal! shed
Thy warmest, purest beam,
And to my heart content impart,
With gratitude serene.

Then, when, at last, my sorrows past,
With thee in light I'll roam,
And by thy side securely ride,
Thy bosom for my home.
1833.

ENIGMA.

Sometimes I grace the maiden's brow,
And lend her cheek a brighter glow;
Or grim and strong, secure the wall
Of many a castle gate from all.
The palace boasts me always there,
To guard the walls and bless the fair;
The meanest cot I ne'er disdain,
Yet guard the portals of the brain.—Lock.

TO A LITTLE COUSIN AT CHRISTMAS.

My dear little George, oh did you but know
How delighted I'd be could I meet with you now;
Oh could I but print on your forehead a kiss,
To thy Margaret the moment were unalloy'd bliss.
Thy flowers and acorns I've cherished with care,
And to me they have seem'd more than lovely and fair,
For thoughts of the friends I have left far behind,
And sweet recollections will crowd on my mind,
As I gaze on the tokens presented by you,
And the sweet little letter you've written me too;
I fancy I see thee on bright Christmas day,
With Kitty and mother all sportive at play,
Admiring the bounty St. Nicholas gave
To the boy who was worthy his counsel so grave.
Oh could I but join thee, my beautiful boy,
In thy holiday pastimes and innocent joy!
Is "Aunty" still working on bonnets and capes?
Or examining flowers of all sizes and shapes?
Does Aiken's Collection still lie on her lap,
While her fingers are plaiting some ruffle or cap?
Is thy "dear little mother" still lively and gay,
Pleasing and pleased, as when I came away?
And Annie and Kitty, and grandfather too?
But 'tis time, my dear George, I bade you adieu.
Tell uncle, and brother, and all whom I love,
My letters alone my affection must prove.
1833.

ON READING CHILDE HAROLD.

The rainbow's bright and varying hue,
Mix'd with the soft celestial blue,
The brightest, fairest stars of night,
Which shed their radiance pure and bright,
If mingled in a wreath, would be
Too poor an offering for thee.

The morning sun should deck thy brow,
Now dazzling bright, and softening now;
But night's dark veil too oft doth cloud
The brow which genius should enshroud,
For vice has set her impress there,
Mingled with virtues pure and fair.

1833.

INVOCATION.

Oh, thou almighty Lord of heaven and earth!
From whom the world and man derive their birth,
My youthful heart with sacred love inspire,
And fill my soul with wild poetic fire.

And oh, thou pure, transcendent muse of heaven,
Descend upon an airy cloud of even,
With thy bright fingers touch the trembling chord,
And let it echo to my Saviour, Lord.

1833.

CHRISTMAS HYMN.

Hail to salvation's brilliant morn,
  Hail to the dawn of joy and peace,
When God's supreme, almighty power,
  Bade all our pains and sorrows cease.

Ye angels, sing your sweetest songs,
  And strike anew each golden lyre;
Let him to whom the praise belongs
  The sacred strain inspire.

The day the star of promise shone
  Bright in yon eastern sky,
It bore redemption in its light,
  A herald from on high.

It led a wise and chosen band,
  Who writhed beneath the rod
Of Herod's proud and kingly hand,
  To seek their infant God.

From his high throne in realms of bliss,
  Where love was in every breast,
From his glorious home he came to this,
  And in his descent we are blest.

For man's unconquerable pride,
  That we salvation might obtain,
This blessed Saviour bled and died,—
  And has the sacrifice been vain?

Oh Jesus, fill'd with sacred fire,
  May I devote this life to thee;
May love my youthful heart inspire,
  And glow to all eternity!

1833.

EVENING.

'Twas evening, and the sun's last ray
  Was beaming o'er the azure sky;
Earth bade farewell to cheerful day,
  Which sinks beneath the mountains high.

Those cloud-tipp'd mountains soared afar
  In that bright heaven of blue,
And seem'd to reach yon eastern star,
  Which glittering you might view.

Between its banks yon rippling stream
  Unruffled glides along,
In curling eddies onward flew
  Rocks, branches, trees among.

Beyond it raged the troubled sea,
  Which drew aloft its wave,
And ever furious, ever dark,
  The Sky it seem'd to brave.

How strangely, sweetly blended there
  The beautiful and grand,
The awful with the prospect fair,
  The terrible and bland!

Behold that tall majestic rock,
  O'erhanging yonder stream;
See, at its frowning foot is seen
  The pale moon's silvery beam.

1833.

ENIGMA.

In nature it holds a conspicuous part,
It lives in the ocean, and softens the heart;
The supporter of angels, in heaven it dwells,
And the number of demons reluctantly swells,
'T is a part of our faith, and it lives with the dead,
'T is devoid of religion, yet always in dread;
In the wavering candle all brightly it glows,
And with the meandering streamlet it flows.

Without it the name of the warrior were lost,
And the seaman would sink, on the wide ocean tost.
And now, my dear friend, if you guess what it means,
You may have the enigma for nought but your pains.

1833.

TO THE DEITY.

Almighty God! Father of heaven and earth,
Who form'd, from 'midst the vast expanse of chaos,
This spacious world—omnipotent and holy!
Before thee angels bow!—the countless host
Of those that praise thee, and that hover round
Thy sacred throne, shrink from the blaze of light,
And shadow with their wings their beaming brows,
Lest, on their senses thy transcendent glories
Burst with a stunning power, and absorb them
In one full flood of brilliance.
Oh thou! whose ever-seeing eye can pierce
The misty shades of night, and penetrate
The deep recesses of the human heart;
Parent of earth! how glorious are thy works!
Look on yon orb, whose ever-open eye
Sheds at his glance a pure, resplendent light,
Dispensing good. Night throws her sable veil
O'er hill and rock, o'er rivulet and ocean:
Then chaste Diana sheds her silver ray
O'er all: her throne, the fleecy cloud that floats
Over the vast expanse of heaven above us;
Her bright attendants are the brilliant stars,
That seem like guardian angels, who attend,
In virgin purity, to keep from ill
Our ever-rolling orb: beauty reigns over all,
And tinges nature with her softest touch.
If scenery so bright as this be *here*,
Oh, how can fancy paint the joys of heaven,
That pure and holy place, region of bliss!
There glides an amber stream, diffusing sweets,
And every tiny wave, which o'er the sands
Of purest gold rolls backward, washes up
Some pearl or diamond, gem of dazzling beauty,
While ambrosial zephyrs fan the air.
See, yonder angel, resting on the cloud,
His beaming eye upturn'd with holy awe.
Oh list! he chaunts his great Creator's praise;
His golden harp is never hush'd by wo;
There music holds her sweet, harmonious reign.
How pure the being who calls forth that lay:
Such clear, melodious symphony
Might well awake the dead from their last sleep.

1833.

TO MY SISTER LUCRETIA.

Though thy freshness and beauty are laid in the tomb,
Like the flow'ret, which droops in its verdure and bloom;
Though the halls of thy childhood now mourn thee in vain,
And thy strains will ne'er waken their echoes again;
Still o'er the fond memory they silently glide;
Still, still, thou art ours and America's pride.
Sing on, thou pure seraph, with harmony crown'd,
O'er the broad arch of heaven thy notes shall resound,
And pour the full tide of thy music along,
While a bright choir of angels re-echoes the song.
The pure elevation which beam'd from thine eye,
As it turn'd to its home, in yon fair azure sky,
Told of something unearthly,—it shone with the light
Of pure inspiration and holy delight.
"Round the rose that is wither'd a fragrance remains,
O'er beauty in ruins the mind proudly reigns."
Thy lyre has resounded o'er ocean's broad wave,
And the tear of deep anguish been shed o'er thy grave,
But thy spirit has mounted to regions on high,
To the throne of its God, where it never can die.
1833.

WRITTEN WHEN BETWEEN ELEVEN AND TWELVE.

PROPHECY.

Fair mortal, I linger to tell thee thy fate,
Like an angel above thy bright fortunes I wait:
Thy heart is a mixture of tender and sweet,
And thy bosom is virtue's own sacred retreat.
Simplicity soft and affection combine
To render thee lovely and almost divine.
Devoid of ambition, rest, dear one, secure,
For with thoughts so refined, and with feelings so pure,
What mortal would injure, what care would pursue
A being protected by heaven like you?
Bright beauty thou hast not, but something so fair
It may serve to protect thee from sorrow and care.
I pierce the light veil which would darken thy fate,
And angels of happiness round thee await;
I see a bright cherub supporting thy head,
While around thee the smiles of affection are shed;
I see thy aged arms around him prest,
Thy grey locks waving o'er his youthful breast—
I see thee on his tender bosom lay,
In silent pleasure breathe thy life away.
My tale is told—dear one, I linger now
To kiss with fervent love thy own fair brow.
1833.

ENIGMA.

On the brow of the monarch in triumph I stand,
I govern each measure, I rule each command;
Without me, his kingdom to atoms would fall,
But I share not his crown, and I rule not his hall.
I dance in the meadow, and play on the stream,
And I glimmer obscurely in Luna's pale beam.

I dwell in thy bosom, I 'm part of thy form,
But I ride on the tempest, and guide the fierce storm;
With the sea-nymph I rest on the moss-cover'd cliff,
And I weep with the mourner that life is so brief.
O'er the grave of the mighty in sorrow I bow,
And I rest in thy mind as thou 'rt watching me now.

Go look on the pillow of sorrow and care,
On the brow that is wither'd by darkest despair,
Stern affliction will meet you, but I am not there.
In the heart of the rich man, the court of the prince,
In the mariner's vessel, the warrior's lance,
In the tumult of war, on the brow of the fair,
Though millions surround them still I am not there.

In the home of the noble, the virtuous, the great,
In thy own lovely bosom, rejoicing I wait.
I wish I might dwell in that beautiful eye;
I wish I might float on yon pure azure sky;
I would lead you in triumph wherever I stray'd,
Where the sunbeam had lit, or the pale moon had play'd.

1834.

ESSAY ON THE SACRED WRITINGS.

The Bible!—what is it?—every heart which has read and justly appreciated that inestimable volume cannot fail to exclaim, "This is the work of a God!" Who is there that will not admire, (although he read with a doubting mind,) its force, dignity, beauty, and simplicity? Principles so pure, precepts so sublime, and thoughts so refined, who could have formed them but one inspired by a God, or God himself? 'T is our guide, our star to lead, the herald to usher us into a glorious eternity. When the mind is overwhelmed with care, what power can soothe like this sacred volume? Its pages beaming with truth and mercy, will shed a holy light over the troubled landscape, and impart a softer swell to the billows of adversity. It is the lighthouse by whose beams we should direct our path over the gloomy waves of life. Then why neglect it? Some may think it derogatory to their earthly dignity —"What will the world say?" Read it, and learn from its sublime precepts to stem the tide of worldly opinion. When all else fails you, this will remain the supporter of your rights; here is *real* dignity and grandeur, but it is the dignity of the *soul*, the grandeur of virtue, the dignity arising from a close alliance with the *Deity*. If He who thundered on Mount Sinai, and caused the silver founts to flow from rocks of adamant, will deign to approach so near us, is it for us to stand aloof, wrapped in the mantle of our own insignificance, and brave the tempest of life alone? Oh! how depraved that heart must be, which such condescension will fail to affect! and how happy the bosom for ever confiding in its God! calm in the midst of afflictions, resigned while the torments of grief pour on the soul; which, though borne down by sorrow, is fortified by virtue, and looks calmly and steadily forward to the calamities which it is certain will terminate in an endless communion with its Maker.

February 2d, 1834.

THE DESTRUCTION OF SODOM AND GOMORRAH.

Oh tremble, ye proud ones! oh tremble with fear!
For Jehovah has come in his wrath;
Stern vengeance is throned on his terrible brow,
And lightning attends on his path.
Oh shrink from the glance of his soul-quenching eye,
As he treads on the whirlwind, and comes from on high!

Oh, burst the dark shackles of sorrow and sin!
Before his dread presence in penitence bow;
Oh, dash the bright wine-cup in terror away,
And dare not to gaze on his broad flaming brow,
For the angel of mercy no longer is there,
To quiet your conscience, or soothe your despair.

The spirit of death o'er your city has pass'd,
His broad flaming weapon is waving on high;
Your sentence is heard in the whirlwind's rude blast,
'T is written in fear on yon lightning-crown'd sky;
Oh, powerless your arm, and unwielded your lance,
As he cometh with vengeance and fire on his glance.

The bride at the altar, the prince on his throne,
The warrior secure in his strongly-built tower,
For the soft voice of music hear sorrow's deep moan,
And shrink 'neath the hand of their God in his power;
The smile on the cheek is transform'd to a tear,
But repentance is lost in bewailing and fear.

Oh, turn to your God, in this moment of dread,
For mercy may rest 'neath the frown on his brow.
Oh, haste ere each fast-failing hope shall have fled,
Oh, haste in repentance and terror to bow.

The moment of grace and repentance has pass'd;
Your entreaties for pardon are useless and vain;
The sword of destruction is levell'd at last,
And Gomorrah and Sodom are ashes again.

1834.

VERSIFICATION FROM OSSIAN.

Oh thou, who rollest far above,
  Round as my father's shield in war!
From whence proceed thy beams, oh sun,
  Which shine for ever and afar?

All cold and pale, the feeble moon
  Shrinks back, eclipsed beneath thy power;
The western wave conceals its light
  At morning's bright resplendent hour.

But thou, unchanging, mov'st alone!
  Oh who may thy companion be?
The rugged rocks, the mountain's fall,
  But who may stand in might like thee?

The ocean shrinks and grows again,
  All earthly things will fade away,
But thou for ever art the same,
  Rejoicing in thy brilliant ray;
Rolling and rolling on thy way,
Enlightening worlds from day to day.

When o'er yon vault the thunders peal,
  And lightning in its pathway flies;
When tempests darken o'er the world,
  And cloud the once resplendent skies,
Thou rear'st on high thy noble form,
And laughest at the raging storm.

But now thou look'st to me in vain,
  For I behold thy beams no more;
I languish here in darkness now,
  On Erin's green and fertile shore.

I know not if thy yellow hair
  Is floating on the western clouds,
Or if the fleecy veil of morn
  Thy brilliant beauty lightly shrouds;
But thou, great sun, perhaps, like me,
  Shall days of rest and silence see.

Amid the clouds thy form may sleep,
  Regardless of the morning's voice;
Exult then, mighty orb of day,
  And in thy vigorous youth rejoice.

1834.

TO MY DEAR MAMMA.

ON RETURNING FROM A LONG VISIT TO NEW YORK.

Though my lyre has been silent, dear mother, so long
  That its chords are now broken, and loose, and unstrung,
If 't will call but one smile of delight to thy cheek,
  I will waken the notes which so long were unsung.

My lyre has been thrown all neglected aside,
  And other enjoyments I' ve sought for a while;
But though lured by their brilliance, still none can compare
  With my dear little harp and my mother's sweet smile.

With joy I return to my books and my pen,
  To my snug little home and its inmates so dear,
For while scribbling each thought of my half-crazy brain
  I can chase every sorrow and lull every fear.

Oh excuse my poor harp, if the lines do not rhyme,
  'T is so long since it warbled aught breathing of sense,
That the chords, though I' m striving to tune them aright,
  Still warble of folly and pleasure intense.

1834.

ON THE DEATH OF MRS. F. H. WEBB.

In vain I strike my youthful lyre,
  Some gayer music to impart,
And dissipate the gloom which hangs
  Too sadly round my mourning heart.

Oh, I would wish its low deep tones,
  Some gentler, sprightlier strains to borrow;
But still they only can respond
  The plaintive voice of heartfelt sorrow.

For she, the young, the bright, the gay,
  Has left us here to weep,
While cover'd with her parent clay,
  And wrapt in death's long sleep.

But memory still can paint the scenes
  Of past, but ne'er forgotten joy,
When we have sported wild and free,
  No sorrow pleasure's tide to cloy.

Thy form, as it was wont to be,
  Still mingles with each thought of home;
My earliest sports were join'd by thee,
  When graced by beauty's brightest bloom.

Again I view that hazel eye,
  With life and pleasure beaming;
Again I view that fair, white brow,
  Those dark locks o'er it streaming.

Again I view thy blushing cheek,
  The glow of love and pride,
When, 'mid the throng of smiling friends,
  A blooming, happy bride.

But more than these, the angel mind
  Should all our thoughts engage;
Oh, 't was unsullied and refined
  As is this spotless page.

How changed the scene! the star of hope
Has set in clouds of darkest night,
And she, the lovely and the gay,
Is laid in the grave with her beauty and light.

Oh, where shall the mother, all mourning and sad,
Oh, where shall she look for the child she adored!
And where shall the husband, half frantic with grief,
Find the wife in whose bosom his sorrows he pour'd!

How lonely and silent each well-beloved scene,
Each garden, each grove, which she loved to frequent;
The sweet flowers she nurtured so fondly and long,
In sorrow their heads to the damp ground have bent.

But a flow'ret more lovely, more tender and pure,
Is languidly drooping, no mother to guide;
The fond kiss of a mother it never can feel,
And to her the warm prayer of a mother's denied.

But the spirit we mourn has ascended on high,
And there it will watch o'er its little one's fate;
In whispers her voice will be heard from the sky,
With a mother's affection which ne'er can abate.

1834.

TO THE EVENING STAR.

Though yon broad vault of heavenly blue
Is spangled o'er with gems of light;
Though veil'd beneath its azure hue
Is glittering many a star so bright;

Though thousands wait around the throne
Of yon cold monarch, proudly fair;
Though all unite their dazzling powers
To vie with Luna's brilliance there;

Each star which decks her cloud-veil'd brow,
Or glitters in her snowy car,
Would shrink beneath thy dazzling ray,
Sweet little sparkling evening star!

No twinkling groups around thee throng,
Thy path majestic, lonely, bright!
A radiant softness shades thy form,
First wanderer in the train of night!

While gazing on thy glorious path,
It seems as though some seraph's eye
Look'd with angelic sweetness down,
And watch'd me from the glorious sky.

As the dim twilight steals around,
And thou art trembling far above,
I think of those no longer here,
Dear objects of my earliest love.

And the soft ray which beams from thee,
A soothing calmness doth impart;
And from each poignant sorrow free,
A sweet composure fills my heart.

Oh! then shine on thus pure and bright,
Pour on each mourning soul thy balm!
Soothe the sad bosom's rankling grief,
And fill it with thy heavenly calm!

Till meek, submissive, and resign'd,
It seeks above a purer joy;
And stays the fickle, wayward mind
On pleasures which can never cloy.

1834.

TO MY FATHER.

Oh, how I love my father's eye,
So tender and so kind!
Oh, how I love its azure dye,
The index of his mind!

Oh, how I love the silver hair
Which floats around his brow!
I love to press my father's form,
And feel his cheek's warm glow.

Oh what is like a parent's love?
What heart like his will feel,
When sorrow's waves are raging round,
And cares the thoughts congeal?

Would he not die his child to save?
Would not his blood be shed
That yet one darling might remain
To soothe his dying bed?

Oh, what is like a parent's care
To guard the youthful mind?
Oh, what is like a parent's prayer,
Unbounded grace to find?

Ah, yes! my father is a friend
I ever must revere,
And, if I could but cease to love,
His virtues I would fear.

1834.

ON NATURE.

"How beautiful is Nature!" Every soul,
Beating with warm and gentle feeling,
Must repeat with me these heartfelt words,
"How beautiful is Nature!" In the dark

Awful waving of the sky-crown'd forest,
Her gentle whisper, like an angel's voice,
Still breaks upon the stillness;—in the stream
Which ripples past, is heard her low, sweet murmur;
While on the varied sky, the frowning mount,
Her chainless hand majestical is laid!
What voice so sweet as hers? what touch so soft,
So delicate? what pencilling so divine?
Oh, can the warmest fancy ever picture
To the rapt soul, a scene more beautiful!
Say, can imagination, light as air,
Capricious as each varying wind which blows,
Create a model of more perfect loveliness,
More grace and symmetry? Can thought present
A tint more light, and yet more gorgeous,
Hues more sweetly mingled, one dim shadow,
Blending in grace more lovely with another?
Ah no! but 'tis the sin which dwells within
That casts a dark'ning shade o'er Nature's face—
Nought can there be more beauteous and divine;
But to the eye of discontent and wo,
Her gentle graces seem to mix with sorrow;
And to the chilling glance of stern despair,
Her sweetest smile is but a threatening cloud;
Just as the mind is turn'd she smiles or frowns,
And to each eye a different view appears.
The cheerful, happy heart, devoid of guilt,
Like a white tablet, opens to receive
Each passing hue, and as the colours flit
Over its surface, it becomes more tranquil,
And fit to take once more the forms of joy,
Which ever, as they glide so sweetly by,
Tinge the fond soul with happiness serene.
If dark, degrading sin had never cast
Its shade of gloom o'er Nature's lovely brow,
This world had been an earthly paradise.
An all-presiding God has deck'd our globe
With grace, and life, and light; each object glows
With heavenly tints, and every form
Contains some hidden beauty, which, to minds
Unburden'd with a consciousness of guilt,
Proclaims the power of Him who rules o'er all.
The falling snow-flake, or the humming bee,
Small though they seem, may still contain a world
Of knowledge and of skill, which human wisdom,
Mix'd with human guilt, can never fathom.
The smallest item in this wondrous plan,
Replete with grace, and harmony, and light,
Would form employment for a fleeting life?
Oh, 't were a home for angels! and a home
No angel might despise, if human guilt
Had never stain'd it with its crimson glow.
Our earth was once an Eden, and if sin

Had never tinged with blood its rippling streams,
And ne'er profaned its broad luxuriant fields
With scenes of wickedness and thoughts of woe,
Had thus remain'd; each heart o'erflowing
With delight and love; each bosom fill'd
With heavenly joy. How awful is the change!
And how tremendous the effect of sin
On nature and on man! The wayward soul,
Once open'd to degrading guilt, is deaden'd
To her beauty; and all the glowing charms
Which waken'd it to love and happiness,
Ere thus ensnared, are pass'd unnoticed now!
Oh, could we purify our souls from sin,
Would we desire a brighter heaven than this?
More glorious, more sublime, more varied,
Or more beauteous? The softly rippling stream,
The rising mountain, and the leafy wood,
Combine their charms to grace the splendid scene!
The light-crown'd firmament, the tinted sky,
And all the sweetly varying graces
Which bedeck the queenlike brow of nature,
Serve but to show the power of nature's God,
The mighty Lord of this immense creation!
The heavenly Maker of our lovely world.

1834.

TO THE INFIDEL.

Behold, thou daring sinner! canst thou say,
As rolls the sun along its trackless course,
A God has never form'd that orb of day,
Of life, and light, and happiness the source?

Who made yon dark blue ocean? Who
The roaring billow and the curling wave,
Dashing and foaming o'er its coral bed,
Of many a hardy mariner the grave?

Who made yon dazzling firmament of blue,
So calm, so beautiful, so brightly clear,
Deck'd with its stars and clouds of fleecy white,
Like the bright entrance to another sphere?

Who made the drooping flow'ret? Who
The snowy lily and the blushing rose —
Emblem of love, which sheds its fragrance round,
As with the tints of heaven it brightly glows?

Who raised the frowning rock? Who made
The moss and turf around its base to grow?
Who made the lofty mountains, and the streams
Which at their feet in rippling currents flow?

Say, was it not a God? and does not all
Bear the strong "impress of his mighty hand?"
Oh yes — his stamp is fix'd on all around —
All sprang to being at our Lord's command.

Oh, ask the mind! — oh, ask the immortal mind,
  And this will be stern reason's firm reply —
'T will echo over ocean's swelling tide:
  The hand that form'd us was a *Deity!*

1834.

ON THE MIND.

How great, how wonderful the human mind,
Which, in each secret fold, conceals some dread,
Mysterious truth; which spurns the fetters
Binding it to earth, yet draws them closer
Round it; which, yearning for a world more pure,
And more congenial with its heavenly thoughts,
Confines its soaring spirit to the region
Of death and sin! But oh, how glorious
The sublime idea, that though this frame,
Corrupt and mortal, mingle with the dust,
There is a spark within, which, while on earth,
Gives to the clay its energy and life,
And when that clay returneth to the dust
From whence it came, may rise triumphant
From the senseless clod, and soaring, mount on high,
To dwell with beings holy and divine;
And there, with its ever-growing ken,
Clasp the great universe; with angels there
To expand those heaven-born powers, which here
Were fetter'd with the earthly chains that bind
Misguided man—pride, sorrow, discontent,
And cold ambition, foolish and perverted—
But destined there to burn in all its light,
And urge the enfranchised on to seek
Glories still undiscover'd, wonders
As yet unknown. And can it be? Does this
Weak, trembling frame conceal within itself
A soul ethereal and immortal?
A glorious spark, sublime and boundless,
"Struck from the burning essence of its God,"
The great I AM, the dread Eternal?
Oh, how tremendous is the awful thought!
The soul shrinks back alarm'd, too weak to gaze
On its own greatness, or rather on the greatness
Of that God who made it! Yes! 'tis his work!
The moulding of his mighty hand! How dread,
How peerless, how incomparably great
The Governor and Former of this vast machine!
Who watches from on high its slightest thought,
And omnipresent and unbounded, sways
Each feeling and each impulse! and whose touch,
However slight, may turn its passions from
Their common channel, and whose breath can tune
Aright those delicate and hidden fibres,
Which, rudely touch'd, would yield their finest chords,
And thus destroy the harmony of all,

Leaving a blank and darken'd chaos
Where once was harmony and joy!
Oh ye that seek to guide perverse mankind,
Tamper not lightly with the human mind;
But when an erring friend from virtue strays,
Gently reprove, and do not seek to guide
Those hidden springs which God alone can fathom.
Oh 'tis a fearful thing to see the mind,
Derived from such a pure and holy source,
Debased by sin, by dark, offensive crime,
And render'd equal with the beasts that roam?
To see the wreck of all that once was good,
The shrinking remnant of a noble soul,
Like the proud ship, which for a while may stem
The roaring ocean, but o'ercome by storms,
With half its voyage done, is torn apart—
The sails, the stately masts, and, last of all,
The guiding helm—until the shatter'd hulk
Lies undefended from the sweeping blasts,
Threaten'd by frowning rocks;—but as some
Friendly hand may snatch from death's embrace
The shuddering crew, so may a Saviour's love
Redeem from endless wo the trembling sinner,
And lead his shrinking spirit up to heaven!
The mighty God who saw him err, can change,
Within the twinkling of an eye, his wayward heart,
And give to his apostate soul those pure
And blessed dreams of heaven,
Those hopes of immortality, which soothe
The dying Christian; and when his spirit
Ascends to dwell with Him it once despised,
Through the bright merits of our heavenly Lord,
It there may join in love and hope with all
The angel band, in singing praises
To their glorious King, the great Jehovah!
Oh that we too might cherish every virtue,
Prepare our minds for immortality,
Where undisturb'd they may expand,
And reach perfection in a future world.

1834.

ON THE HOPE OF MY BROTHER'S RETURN.

Why rejoices my heart at the passage of time,
As it sweeps on the wind o'er the fast-rolling year,
And bounds as the sun to his broad couch declines,
His bed in the ocean, majestic and clear?

I pause not to question if wise it may be,
But faster I'll hurry old Time on his way;
And while hours unnumber'd shall rapidly flee,
I'll laugh as they fade from the fast-closing day

When the icy-cold spell of stern winter shall break,
  And the snow shall dissolve like the dewdrops of morn;
When spring from his death-like embraces shall wake,
  And verdure and brilliance her brow shall adorn;

To my fancy the woodlands more sweetly will smile,
  The streamlets unshackled more tranquilly glide;
More softly shall nature each sorrow beguile,
  And disperse every thought which with grief may be dyed.

I will watch the bright flowers with their delicate bloom,
Aroused, as by magic, from winter's cold tomb,
For my heart will be gladden'd as near and more near
The period approaches when he will be here.
Oh June! how resplendent thy flowers shall appear,
The loveliest, the sweetest which bloom in the year!
For with me a fond brother your grace shall admire,
And each word from his lips shall new rapture inspire.
But these dreams, though enchanting, may prove to be vain,
He never may visit the loved scene again;
On his home the dread weight of affliction may rest,
And the cold hand of sorrow may chill the warm breast;
Or death from its bosom some dear one may sever
And stop the warm current of life-blood for ever.
But love will illumine the future with light,
And tinge every cloud with a colour as bright
As hope in her own sanguine bosom has planted,
Or fancy with all her illusions has granted.

1834.

TO MY MOTHER.

THE spring of life is opening
  Upon my youthful mind,
And every day the more I see,
  The more there is to find.

The path of life is beautiful
  When sprinkled o'er with flowers,
And I ne'er felt affliction's touch,
  Or watch'd the weary hours.

To guard my youthful couch from wo,
  An angel hovers near,
Watches my bosom's every throe,
  And wipes each childish tear.

It is my mother—and with her
  Through life I 'd sweetly glide,
And when my pilgrimage is o'er
  I 'd moulder at her side.

To her I dedicate my lay,
  'T is she inspires my song;
Oh that it might those charms possess,
  Which to the muse belong.

1834.

BOABDIL EL CHICO'S FAREWELL TO GRANADA.

THE youthful lyre would shrink from tales of woe,
Would tune with hope and love each quivering string;
But when truth bids the sorrowing numbers flow,
Its mournful chords responsive notes must ring.
'T is sweet to tell of laughing mirth and glee;
Its chords would vibrate but to purest joy;
And when deep anguish pours unmix'd and free,
Would haste with hope the sinking heart to buoy.

But faithful history still the page unfolds
Of war and blood; of carnage fierce and dark;
Of savage bosoms, cast in giant mould,
And hearts unwarm'd by pity's gentle spark.
Then cast your garb of merry music by,
Assume the mantle of unbrighten'd woe; —
A cloud is gathering o'er the peaceful sky,
And the warm sunbeams hide their golden glow.

Robed in a mantle of unrivall'd light,
The glorious sun was sinking o'er the plain,
And tinging, with a glow of radiance bright,
The towering domes and palaces of Spain.
Between the lofty mounts which rise around,
And form the deep ravine or shady dell,
Granada's towers in mighty grandeur stood,
And on the plain their darkening shadows fell.

The beams were gilding all her lofty towers,
As on Nevada's side Alhambra stood,
And o'er her spacious halls, her laurel bowers,
Her marble courts, they pour'd a dazzling flood.
Her gothic arches glitter'd in the ray,
While many a gushing fountain cool'd the air,
And o'er the blushing flowers diffused their spray,
Which bloom perennial in a world of care.

The golden lute upon the grape-vine hung,
O'er sparkling waves the fragrant orange rose,
And o'er the gilded roofs the sunbeams flung
A dazzling light, as when the diamond glows.
And can it be!—can scenes so fair as this
Know aught but joy unclouded, purest bliss?
Will heaven's bright orb its dazzling brilliance shed,
As if in mockery, upon sorrow's head?

Will skies of azure pour their softest light
On hearts which grief has sear'd, and woe doth blight?
Will earth rejoice, while earthly hearts are riven,—
While man, oppress'd, to dark despair is driven?
Retire, oh sun! reserve thy cheering rays
For calmer hours, for brighter, happier days!

Go shine on England's spires, or India's bowers,
But gaze not on Alhambra's humbled towers!

Cease, cease thy soft meanderings, sparkling river!
Wind sadly silent, gentle Guadalquivir!
No more thy waves through Moorish woodlands glance,
No more reflect the Moorish warrior's lance,
Nor view the tournament and sprightly dance.
Cease, for thy foam is red with Moslem blood!
Cease, for thy lords lie cold beneath thy flood!
Captive Boabdil leaves his rightful throne,
To others yields a kingdom once his own.

Behold yon gate![1] the ancient sages say
No stone shall loosen, till that awful day,
When yonder guardian hand, now firmly clasp'd,
The mystic key beneath its arch has grasp'd;
At that dread hour each crumbling stone shall fall,
And in one common ruin bury all;
But not till then, though first Alhambra lie
A shapeless ruin, 'neath a frowning sky.

Why should she last? the monument of shame,
Her legends disbelieved, degraded every name!
Her noblest chiefs reduced to toil,
Her maidens left, the conqueror's spoil!
Murder'd her children, scorn'd each lovely dame.
Oh, that the mystic hand had power
To veil Granada's shame;
That in one dark and awful hour,
Might perish each dishonour'd name.

Lo! on yon mount appears a mournful train!
Behold the newly-conquer'd slave of Spain!
El Chico, humbled, winds his sorrowing way,
For, with his home, he leaves the light of day.
Ill-fated prince! thine errors still I mourn;
A father's hatred caused each bursting sigh;
Thy youthful days were lonely and forlorn,
Condemn'd a father's cruelty to fly.

Thy heart was never form'd for kingly state;
It teem'd with softest feeling, gentlest thought!
Devoid of strength to battle with thy fate,
For peace in vain thy troubled bosom sought!

Though the brave may not tremble when war shall surround them,
Or shrink when the mantle of death shall have bound them,
Yet the eye which can gaze unconcern'd on the tomb,
Which can look without shrinking on death in its gloom,
Will dissolve like the dew, or some wizard's dark spell,
When it bids the sweet home of its childhood farewell.

The exiled monarch slowly turn'd away;
He could not bear to view those towers again,
Which proudly glitter'd in the sun's last ray,
As if to mock their wretched master's pain.

His weeping bride press'd trembling near his form,
  While sobs convulsive heaved her snowy breast;
But proud Ayxa bade their sorrows cease,
  With scornful glances which she scarce represt.

"Chide me not, mother," cried the mourning son,
  "Nor charge me with unmanly weakness now;
I grieve that Spain the royal prize has won,
  That proud Granada to her kings should bow."
He paused, and turn'd aside his glowing cheek;
  His wandering eyes Alhambra's palace met:
Those splendid domes, those towers for ever lost,
  Lost, when the sun of Moorish glory set.

"Yes! yonder towering spires are seized by Spain,
  Their king an exile from his native land;
Shall I ne'er view thy princely courts again,
  But yield resistless to the victor's brand?
Yes, thou art gone! thine ancient splendours fled!
  O'er thy gay towers the shroud of slavery thrown;
Thy proudest chiefs, thy noblest warriors dead,
  And all thy pride and all thy glory gone.

"Farewell to Alhambra, dear home of my childhood!
  Farewell to the land I so proudly have cherish'd;
Farewell to the streamlet, the glen, and the wild-wood,
  The throne of my fathers whose glory has perish'd!
'Neath the crest of Nevada the bright sun is setting,
  And tinging with gold yonder beautiful river,
And his rays seem to linger, as if half-regretting
  They must leave the clear waves where so sweetly they quiver.

"Farewell, thou bright valley! I leave thee with sorrow;
Thou wilt smile as serene 'neath the sun of the morrow;
But thine ill-fated monarch shall view thee no more,
He ne'er shall revisit thy beautiful shore."
He paused; and the accents of heart-rending grief
Were borne by the wind past each murmuring leaf.
Cease, cease these vain wailings!" Ayxa replied,
"Nor languish and weep like thy timid young bride;

Why mourn like a maid, who in sorrow will bend,[2]
For what as a man thou couldst never defend!
Then cease these vain wailings, which womanlike pour,
Or Ayxa la Horra will own thee no more;
Granada has fallen, her glory has fled,
Her warriors and chieftains now sleep with the dead;
But who has surrender'd her walls to our foe,
And branded her honour with shame's crimson glow?"

The tear to his eyelid unconsciously sprung,
But back the intruder he eagerly flung,
And cried, in a tone which with frenzy might blend,
"Defamed by my country, and scorn'd by my friend!"
They slowly ascended a rock towering high,
Which long shall re-echo Boabdil's last sigh;[3]

No prospect of beauty his mourning heart cheers,
And he murmurs farewell on the dark hill of tears.[4]

Though grief and remorse with terrors oppress'd him;
Though peace and affection ne'er tranquilly blest him;
Though his kingdom was captured, his warriors were dying,
Himself from the fury of Ferdinand flying;
Through the tumult of feeling his pride had sustain'd him,
Had his griefs but a mother's fond sympathy gain'd him;
But the pride of a princess affection o'ercame
And with basest dishonour she branded his name.

Reproachful invectives unthinking she shower'd,
"His country was fallen, its monarch a coward?"
The proud Ayxa loved her yielding son,
And would have died had death his glory won;
But she had hoped his rising fame to see,
Had long'd to view his vanquish'd foemen flee.

This cherish'd object of each glowing thought
   Stern disappointment now had torn away,
And left a gaping wound, with frenzy fraught;
   For hope and fancy pour'd no cheering ray.
The mother was forgot in stately pride,
   While bitter anguish drew the trembling tear;
He claim'd her pity—she could only chide,
   And laugh to scorn his cowardice and fear.

But the fair Zorahayda his beautiful bride,
To soothe his affliction, remain'd at his side;
Each thought found an answering chord in her bosom,
Which glow'd with affection's first beautiful blossom:
'Twas warm as the sunbeam, and bright as its glance;
'Twas clear as the ripples which fairy-like dance;
Each thought and each feeling which dwelt in her soul
Her eye and her countenance told him the whole.

Yes, she, the young, the beautiful, the gay,
To sorrow's dread abode love call'd away!
From her dark eye she wiped the starting tear,
And by his side repress'd each rising fear;
Though dark despair should dim each future day,
And even hope refuse her cheering ray,
Her fairy form would bless his wandering eyes,
Like some pure spirit from the glowing skies.

Reposing 'mid Alhambra's shady bowers,
She cheer'd his lonely and his weary hours;
But when, alas! his brow no longer wore
The crown, which proudly grac'd his front before,
When fickle Moors forsook his tottering throne,
When, glory, power, and kingly state were gone,
And threatening clouds were seen around to lower,
Then, then he felt the more her witching power.

Vanquish'd at last upon the battle field,
And forced Granada's lofty towers to yield,

Still the fair bud of promise brightly glow'd,
From her heart's depths the warm affections flow'd;
She sweetly soothed his cares, she blest his name,
And sorrow fann'd to light the kindling flame
Which burn'd within that tender, faithful mind,
To all his faults, and all his errors blind.

How sweet the communion of kindred minds,
When sorrow each hope hath blighted;
When the heart which is bursting with agony finds
One face with pure sympathy lighted.
And must he from the fair Zorahayda be banish'd,
Must the charm of existence for ever be broken?
Has every fond dream of prosperity vanish'd,
Must he sigh over love's wither'd token?

In the tower of Gomares he gather'd a few,
And his warriors, still faithful, he rallied,
The broad Moorish banner far over them flew,
And forth to the battle he sallied.
He return'd—and his eye was cast down in despair,
The glow on his cheek was still deeper;
"Farewell to Granada! our foemen are there!"[4]
Loudly echoes the voice of the weeper.

"Come, wife of my bosom! together we'll wander,
The storm of affliction together we'll brave;
And perchance in some distant and desolate region,
We may find a lone shelter, a home, and a grave,
I would not my spirit should quit its sad mansion
'Mid the taunts and revilings of conquering Spain,
Where the foot of the victor would tread o'er my ashes,
And reproach and dishonour would tarnish my name.

"Oh, gaze on yon parapets towering on high,
Those pillars of pride were but yesterday mine;
But to-day we are doom'd from their splendours to fly—
Weep not for my sorrows, I mourn but for thine;
Those halls shall re-echo the loud voice of grief,
Those fountains in murmurs respond to our sorrow,
But ne'er can they waken the bright smile again,
Which woe from gay pleasure a moment would borrow.

"Around those gay mansions and beautiful bowers
The foot of the stranger contemptuous shall press;
Unmark'd the bright fountains, uncultured the flowers,
No fair hand to cherish, no soft voice to bless,
Ill-fated Boabdil! thy name shall be hated!
The babe shall repeat it with moaning and tears,
And the eye which was sparkling, with pleasure elated,
Indignant shall glance on thy cowardly fears."

He paused, and led away his mourning bride,
In grief his solace, and in joy his pride.
But whither do his weary footsteps bend?[5]
What clime his broken heart one joy can lend?
Where can he now from shame despairing fly,—
Beneath what golden sun, what beaming sky?

On Afric's arid plains and yellow sands,
Leagued with the Moslem's wild and ruthless bands,
With desperate force he grasp'd the fatal lance,
And shrank not at the scimitar's broad glance;
Fighting for strangers' rights he bravely fell,
While his own land was sunk in slavery's spell;
Far from affection's soft and soothing hand,
Interr'd by strangers in a foreign land.

How strange the structure of the human heart,
Which springs anew 'neath sorrow's quivering dart;
Bursting from wild despair, from sullen gloom,
And fired by frenzy, hastening to the tomb.
Reckless of danger,—rushing to the strife,—
For strangers bleeding,—yielding even life,—
Thus did Boabdil sink on Afric's plain,
His name dishonour'd in his own bright Spain!

NOTES TO BOABDIL EL CHICO.

NOTE I.

"Behold yon gate! the ancient sages say."

On the keystone of the arch is engraven a gigantic hand; within the vestibule on the keystone of the portal is engraven in like manner a gigantic key. Those who pretend to some knowledge of Mahometan symbols affirm, that the hand is an emblem of doctrine, and the key of faith. The latter, they add, was emblazoned on the standard of the Moslems, when they subdued Andalusia, in opposition to the Christian emblem of the cross. According to Mateo, it is a tradition handed down from the oldest inhabitants, that the hand and key were magical devices, upon which the fate of the Alhambra depended.—The Moorish king who built it was a great magician, and, as some believe, had sold himself to the devil, and had lain the whole fortress under a magical spell. This spell, the tradition went on to say, would last till the hand on the outer arch should reach down and grasp the key, when the whole pile would tumble to pieces, and all the treasures buried beneath it by the Moors would be revealed.—*Irving.*

NOTE II.

"Why mourn as a maid, who in sorrow will bend."

It was here, too, his affliction was embittered by the reproaches of his mother Ayxa who had often assisted him in times of peril, and had vainly sought to instil into him a portion of her own resolute spirit—"Why mourn as a woman, for that which as a man you could not defend?"—*Irving.*

NOTE III.

"Which long shall re-echo Boabdil's last sigh."

Beyond the embowered regions of the Vega, you behold a line of arid hills. It was from the summit of one of these that the unfortunate Boabdil cast back his last look on Granada, and gave vent to the agony of his soul. It is the spot famous in song and history as "The Last Sigh of the Moor."—*Irving.*

NOTE IV.

"And he murmur'd farewell on the dark hill of tears."

Another name given to the hill on the summit of which he bade farewell to Granada.

NOTE V.

"But whither do his weary footsteps bend?"

After leaving the Alpuxarra mountains he proceeded to Africa, and died in defence of the territories of Muley Aben, King of Fez. On leaving Spain, a band of faithful followers and the members of his household collected on the beach, to bid him farewell. As the vessel in which he had embarked was slowly floating onward, they shouted, "Farewell, Boabdil! Allah preserve thee, El Zogoybi!" (or *the unlucky.*) The name thus given him sank so deeply into his heart, that he burst into a flood of tears, and was unable to speak from emotion.

1834.

THE SHUNAMITE.

THE sun had gently shed his twilight beams
O'er Shunam's graceful waving harvest fields,
And with his golden rays each object tinged,
Imparting to all nature hues of joy:
The western sky had caught his parting ray,
And with reflected glory shone above,
In all the lovely varied hues which deck
A summer sky; masses of floating cloud
Hung gorgeous in the clear, blue firmament,
Brilliant as are the fairest rainbow's hues;
While round them spread the light and silver haze,
Beyond whose fold the eye could just discern
The pure transparence of the azure heaven.
The scene was beautiful! A tranquil sleep
Seem'd on the brow of nature lightly resting!
It was an hour when the pure soul might rise
And dwell in sweet communion with its God,
And contemplation and unmingled love
Find for a while repose and silence there.
But where is she, the gentle, lovely mother,
Whose soul delighted in an hour like this?
Oh, why does not her footstep softly shake
From the moist grass the drops of pearly dew?
Say, have the glittering charms of wealth and pride
Allured her from the sweetest charms of nature?
Have the gay baubles she was wont to scorn
Enticed her from this lovely scene away?
It cannot be; perchance amid the sick
Or suffering poor, her pitying spirit
Finds sweet employment, while her liberal hand
Offers relief to the sad prisoners
Who on her bounty live. No! while her heart
Was free from care and racking anguish,
She could soothe another's grief; but *now*—
Alas! how alter'd now—her darling child,
The laughing, sprightly boy, who at her side
Was wont in childish frolic to remain—
Where is he now? The tones of his soft voice
Would soothe a mourner's heart, however sad,
Much more the mother's, who so dearly loved him—
Ay, *loved* him! for she now hath nought to love
Save the cold remnant of what once was life!
Yes! in the splendid mansion which but seems
To mock her heartfelt agony, she weeps,
And weeping, watches o'er the lifeless corpse
Of her adored, her beautiful, her boy.
Perhaps just heaven removed this cherish'd flower,
That her own heart, bereft of earthly joy,
Might cling more closely to her God and Maker.
I know not—but the blow was keenly felt,
And deeply, truly mourn'd.

The spacious room
With rich embroider'd tapestry was hung.
And, mingled with the massy, crimson folds,
Shone many a gem of burning lustre.
The floor was paved with polish'd marble,
And the lifeless form which lay before her
Was array'd in costly garments; but she,
Vainly communing there with icy death,
If at her feet lay all the wealth of nations,
One speaking glance of life from those sweet eyes
Now closed for ever, had been worth it all.
The boy lay gently cradled on the knee
Of the fond mother, and her crimson robe
Around his form was wrapt; while on one arm
His fair young head was pillow'd, and her brow,
Her aching brow, reclined upon the other.
The auburn curls around his temples clung,
Clustering in beauty there, and the blue veins,
So clearly seen 'neath the transparent skin,
Seem'd flowing still with life-blood; the long lash
Of his blue, half-closed eye appear'd to tremble
On his fair cheek, while the fast-rolling tears
Which from his mother's darker orbits fell,
Droop'd from his snowy brow, as they had rested
Upon a marble statue.
Her grief
Burst forth awhile in sobs and bitter groans;
But when the view of death had for a time
Met her dull vision, and the sight of sorrow
Grew more familiar, then her full heart
Burst forth in words, simple but plaintive.
Sweetly pathetic were the gentle tones
Of her melodious voice; no ear
Could listen but to pity, and no eye
That saw her but must gaze and weep.

LAMENT.

And art thou gone, my beautiful, my boy,
Thy sorrowing father's pride, thy mother's joy!
I had not thought, my child, to view thee so,
In death's cold clasp laid motionless and low!
I had not thought to close thy beaming eyes,
To hear thy dying groans, thy feeble cries.
Alas! that thus for thee my tears should flow!
I thought not that this form, so fair and bright,
Death with his chilling arrows e'er could blight;
And oh, my child, my child, it cannot be
That his cold hand hath rested upon thee!
That this fair form, so active but to-day,
Is now a senseless, lifeless mass of clay—
Dust of the earth, fit subject for decay!

How white thy brow! how beautiful thy skin!
The spirit must be resting still within!

The pure, warm blood thy lip is tinging still,—
The purple current seems each vein to fill!
Oh no, it cannot be! My boy, awake!
Rouse from this slumber, for thy mother's sake!
Rouse, ere that mother's mourning heart shall break!

It is not so! my boy is gone for ever,
And I shall view his face again, oh never!
Ah, my sweet boy, I' ve watch'd thine infant years
With joy and grief, alternate hopes and fears.
  For many a night I' ve borne thee on my knee,
  Full many an hour of care I've spent for thee;
Thy joy would glad me, and thy grief bring tears.

Fond fancy pictured thee a noble man,
The fairest work in nature's wondrous plan;
The foremost leader in each patriot band,
Redeeming Syria from her foeman's hand;
Fearless in battle, swiftest in the race,
Replete with courage, virtue, strength, and grace;
I saw thee generous, noble, active, mild,
And blest the hero as my darling child!

But oh, my God! these hopes were crush'd by thee;
How shall I murmur at thy dread decree!
Hush, rebel spirit! whispering conscience tells
I should not vent each troubled thought which swells
  In my torn heart—my woes I'll speak no more,
Nor each vain thought which there impatient dwells,
  Waiting for utterance at my bosom's door.
Rouse, dormant soul! nor sleep when needed most,
While thy frail bark on adverse seas is tost,
And all thy comfort, all thy hope is lost!
I'll hie me to the prophet's mountain home,
He shall redeem my darling from the tomb,
Or teach me how, resign'd, to bear my doom.

She ceased;
A glance of hope o'er her pale features flash'd,
And with unwonted energy she raised
Her feeble hands in prayer to heaven.
Once more she press'd her pallid lips upon
The marble forehead of her lovely boy,
Then rising, laid the cold and lifeless load
From off her bosom, strong in her despair;
Then wildly throwing back the silken folds
Which droop'd upon the wall, she rush'd along,
Through many a corridor and hall, illumed
With glittering lamps and gems of burning lustre.
Her sandall'd feet glanced lightly on the floor,
And her soft tread no answering echo gave;
But heavier far her footstep would have been,
Beneath the galling burden on her heart,
If all had been despair; but the small grain of hope
Which linger'd still within, her onward course

Served but to quicken; something in her soul
Seem'd battling with its sorrow, and a spark,
Lighted by hope, within, a tiny star,
Shone o'er the almost desert gloom of woe.
She hasted on; and soon her form was lost,
In its dim outline, amid the windings
Of her noble mansion. Where hath she gone?
Why at this moment leave her lifeless son?
What human voice can yield her heart relief?
What hand redeem her loved one from the dust?
Return, frail mourner! and indulge thy grief,
Where none are nigh to view its heartfelt pangs;
Return, nor seek one sympathetic heart
In the cold world around thee: thou wilt see,
Since rankling sorrow hath oppress'd thy soul,
All who with smiles attended thee before
Will gaze on thee in scorn, and mock thy tears,
Nor heed thy bitter groans. Oh better far
In thine own heart to hide each torturing grief,
And meet thy sorrow here. But she hath gone!
Twilight is stealing on, and she hath gone!
And where! — Gaze on yon rugged path, which leads
Far onward to the mountain's brow, and there
Behold her toiling on her weary way!
The thorny brambles meet along her path,
And close around o'ershadowing thickets grow —
But still she rushes on — the piercing thorn
Or fallen bough, alike unheeding all,
And with despairing heart and weary step
Reaches the mighty prophet's mountain home.

* * * * * *

The last faint day-streak gleams on Carmel's brow,
And lights the tearful traveller on her way,
As with the holy man of God she turns
Her sorrowing footsteps backward to her home —
They enter, and once more she stands beside
The silent couch of her unconscious boy.
There, overcome by speechless, mute despair,
Her agony how great! — Cold, deathlike drops
Hang on her snowy brow, and, half-distracted
With o'erwhelming grief, she turns her from the sight
Of the dear object of her fondest love.

* * * * *

Behold the prophet! Lo! the man of God
Is lowly bending o'er the couch of death —
His long, dark mantle floating loosely round
His tall, majestic form; his silver locks
Parted far backward on his noble brow,
And his full, piercing eye upraised to heaven! —
His hands are clasp'd — the feeble fingers
Trembling with emotion, and from his lips
Bursts forth an ardent prayer. He ceased,
And on the body stretch'd his aged form,

Press'd his warm lips upon the marble brow,
And chafed the infant limbs.
'T is done! — behold, the sleeping child awakes,
And sweetly smiles upon the holy man!
And lo! the weeping mother clasps her boy
Again, redeem'd from the embrace of death,
And strains him to her throbbing heart, as though
She fear'd the ruthless tyrant yet once more
Might snatch him from her arms!
While the dread prophet stands aloof from all,
And views the object of his fervent prayer
Restored again to love, and light, and life!

1834.

BELSHAZZAR'S FEAST.

THROUGH proud Belshazzar's lofty halls
  A wavering light is streaming,
And o'er his heaven-defying walls,
  The blaze of torches gleaming.
Hark! the voice of music breaks
  Softly on the midnight air,
Each boisterous shout of laughter speaks
  Of hearts untouch'd by woe or care.

The sounds of joy harmonious floating
  O'er Euphrates' silver tide,
Which flows in ripples, gently passing
  Near many a tower of stately pride.
With mirth, Belshazzar's halls resound,
  Joy spreads each smiling feature o'er,
And laughing hundreds gather round
  The red libations, as they pour

From silver cup, and golden urn,
  Once mantling with the holy wine,
By impious hands in frenzy torn
  From great Jehovah's sacred shrine.
Surrounded by each smiling guest,
  In regal pomp and splendid state,
With all save God's approval blest,
  The warrior king serenely sate.

Their hearts demoniac pleasure found,
  Exulting triumph swell'd their strain,
While Israel's children, captive, bound,
  Were groaning 'neath their weight of pain:
Bright lamps o'erhung the festive scene,
  Diffusing soften'd brilliance round,
While mocking Israel's mighty Lord,
  They dash'd his wine-cups to the ground.

Why does Belshazzar's lip turn pale?
  Why shrinks his form with trembling fear?
Why fades, within his tiger eye,
  The scornful glance, the taunting sneer?
A shadowy cloud o'erhangs the wall,
  A mighty hand each fold reveals!
There's silence in that princely hall,
  And trembling awe each vein congeals.

The mystic fingers darkly move,
  And words unknown in silence trace;
Wide o'er the illumined walls they spread,
  While horror fills each pallid face!
Oh! who those awful words may read,
  Or who their mighty import tell?
What hand perform'd the fearful deed,
  What tongue may break the magic spell!!

Come forth, ye Chaldean seers! come forth,
  Ye men of Egypt's burning soil!
Let the dread words your thoughts employ,
  And be the object of your toil!
Oh, gaze upon the glowing wall!
  Ha! proud magicians, do ye shrink?
Say, does the sight your hearts appal
  As if on death's terrific brink?

Now, strive to win the golden crown,
  The scarlet robe, the badge of power—
And tell if heaven in justice frown,
  If round your king the tempest lower.
But still they shrink with innate fear,
  Still from the awful scene retire;
While trembling lips proclaim their awe,
  And rouse the monarch's fiercest ire.

Who may the characters explain,
  When Chaldea's ancient sages fail?
Must the dread secret thus remain
  Wrapt in its dark mysterious veil?

Come forth, thou man of God, come forth!
  By heaven beloved, by man reviled,
Robed in the mantle of thy faith,
  Come forth, Jehovah's chosen child!
Fear not to read Belshazzar's fate!
  Thy heavenly Father guides thee still!
Though robed in scarlet, throned in state,
  Thy God can mould him at his will.

Oh, mark his firm, majestic mien!
  Oh, mark his broad and lofty brow!
With soften'd courage, calm, serene,
  And flush'd with conscious virtue's glow.

Well might they shrink before the man,
  Whose gaze had reach'd the realms of bliss,
Whose eye had pierced a brighter world,
  Whose spotless soul had soar'd from this.

Oh, hark! his firm and manly voice
  Is heard within that princely hall;
No more the impious crowds rejoice,
  But thrilling silence spreads o'er all.
"Oh king! in wealth, and pride, and power,
  At God's great footstool humbly fall,
That God hath seal'd thy doom this hour,
  'Tis stamp'd on yonder fated wall.

"Thy stubborn knee was never bent,
  Thy earthly heart was humbled never
Before the throne of Israel's God,
  Of life, of breath, of power the giver.
Against the Lord of heaven thy hand
  In bold impiety is raised,
And vessels sacred to his name
  The feasts of idol gods have graced.

He, in whose balance lords of earth
  With justice, mercy, power, are tried,
Hath weigh'd thine errors and thy worth,
  But virtue is o'ercome by pride.
From death thou art no longer free,
  Thy sun of glory shall decline;
The golden crown no more shall bind
  That proud, ambitious brow of thine.

"The Medes and Persians shall possess
  That which so lately was thine own;
God will e'en now our wrongs redress,
  And hurl thee from thy tottering throne."
He ceased,—an awful silence reign'd,
  And chain'd each scarcely throbbing breast.
Where were the passions once so rude?—
  Lull'd by the prophet's voice to rest?

Gaze on Belshazzar's pallid brow,
  And trace the livid horror there;
Big drops o'erhang its surface now,
  And backward starts the clustering hair;
His eyeballs strain'd, and wildly staring
  Upon the spot which bears his doom,
Seem like a frighted lion glaring
  Through the dark forest's lonely gloom.

* * * * *

Morn hath brighten'd o'er Chaldea,
  Morning, lovely, fragrant, bright;
Glory crowns a night of terror,
  Deeds of darkness view her light.

Euphrates' waves are brightly sparkling
  Beneath Aurora's rosy beam,
As though the night had never darken'd
  Above its broad and rapid stream.

The close of evening view'd it smiling,
  Deck'd with barks and forms of light,
The weary moments still beguiling,
  Sporting on its bosom bright.
Where are all its beauties banish'd?
  Why its banks so lone and still?
Have all its pride and glory vanish'd,
  All save desolation chill?

The Mede and Persian have been here,
  Heaven's just vengeance to fulfil;
Proud Belshazzar reigns no more,
  God has wrought his sovereign will.

1834.

TO MY MOTHER ON CHRISTMAS DAY.

When last this morning brightly shone
  Around my youthful head,
Inspiring love and joy and glee,
  Dismissing fear and dread,

I thought not I should see thee here
  Reclining on thy Margaret's breast;
I thought that in a brighter sphere
  Thy weary soul would sweetly rest.

But since the mighty God above
  Has granted this my fervent prayer,
My heart is fill'd with joy and love
  For all his kindness and his care.

Oh, may his guardian wings o'erspread,
  To guard from sorrow, pain, or harm,
My mother's weary aching head,
  And every rising fear disarm.

May sweet reflections soothe thy cares,
  And fill with peace thy beating heart,
And may the feast which love prepares
  A sweet security impart.

When He, who warm'd thy gentle soul,
  And planted every virtue there,
Shall snatch thee hence to realms of bliss,
  And free from earthly sin and care,

Oh, may a daughter's tender hand
  The pillow of affliction smooth,
Teach every grief to lose its pang,
  And every sorrow fondly soothe.

1834.

ON VISITING THE PANORAMA OF GENEVA.

Oh, if a painter's touch can form thee thus,
So bright with all an artist's hand can give,
How passing beautiful those scenes must be,
Which *here* inanimate, *there* sweetly live!

Each verdant shrub, which here inactive bends,
So gently waving o'er the placid stream,
And the sweet brook, which winds so silent now,
Reflecting back the sun's effulgent beam.

Look, where the mighty torrent of the Rhone,
Far, far beyond my wandering eye extends,
And see yon crumbling fort, with moss o'ergrown,
O'er whose high walls the weeping willow bends.

Mark on the right, yon broad expanse of blue,
Lake Leman, placid, beautiful, and fair,
So gently murmuring, as it flows along,
Of peace and happiness implanted there.

And towering far above, the mighty Alps
Rear their tall heads terrific and sublime,
Each snow-capp'd summit mingling with the clouds,
Seems to defy the ravages of time.

It seems as though the glowing canvass moved,
Each figure fill'd with life and joy and love,
As if the dark blue waters at my feet
Would break the chain which binds them there, and move.

Each hill, each rock seem bursting into life,
The painter mock'd reality so well;
It seems as if those shadowy forms would speak,
Could they but break the artist's magic spell.

1834.

THE FUNERAL BELL.

Hark! the loudly pealing bell
Rises on the morning air;
Its tones subdued and sadly swell,
For death, unpitying death is there!—
Hark! again it peals aloud,
Bearing sorrow on its tone;
While from the sad assembled crowd,
Is heard the echoing sob and groan,

Yes, in that solemn note is heard
A voice proclaiming woe and death;
A voice which tells of endless time,
Of sorrow's desolating breath.
To the warm fancy it would say,
In words which strike the heart with fear;

Words for the thoughtless, vain, and gay,
  Words echoed from the sable bier—

"A spirit from the world hath fled,
  A soul from earth departed;
While mourners weep above the dead,
  Despairing—broken-hearted!
Through the vast fields of viewless time
  That conscious soul hath gone;
To answer for each earthly crime,
  At God's eternal throne.

"There at his mighty bar it stands,
  A trembling, guilty thing,
To answer all his Judge demands,
  Or his dread praises sing!
Dust to its kindred dust returns!
  Earth to its mother earth!
Still'd are its passions and its cares,
  And hush'd its voice of mirth.

"Then learn from this how weak and vain
  Is every earthly gift;
How in one instant all may fade,
  And leave thee thus bereft!
When thy fond heart is filled with joy,
  With gay and mirthful feeling,
Bethink thee, that the form of death
  Beside thee may be stealing;
That ere another hour has past,
  That rosy smile may fade,
And the light form that glides so fast,
  In the cold tomb be laid.

"That the young heart within that clay,
  To God's dread bar shall pass away,
And the dim future, dark to thee,
  Shall bear it on its tideless sea,
To light or darkness, joy or woe,
  Just as thy life hath pass'd below."

1834.

VERSES WRITTEN WHEN TWELVE YEARS OF AGE.

LINES ON RECEIVING A BLANK-BOOK FROM MY MOTHER.

Though the new year has open'd in sickness and fear,
Though its dawning has witness'd the sigh and the tear,
Though the load on my heart and the weight on my brain,
And the sadness around me cause sorrow and pain,
Each feeling of woe from my bosom is driven
While I view the sweet volume affection has given,
And gazing delighted on binding and leaf,
I forget every thought which is tinctured with grief.

Though it needed no gift from my mother to prove
The depth of that current of long-cherish'd love,
Which hath flow'd on unceasing, unaltering still,
Through sorrows unable its bright waves to chill,
Yet 'tis strangely delightful, 'tis sweet to possess
Some mementos to cherish and gaze on like this,
Some gift which long hence may impart to the mind
Fresh hues of the image there sweetly enshrined:
Which, when every gay feeling is clouded with night,
May burst on the soul like an angel of light,
And presenting unalter'd the visions of love,
Which had slumber'd awhile the more sweetly to soothe
May illumine the darkness with radiance sublime,
But more bright from repose, and unclouded by time.
Oh, think not, my mother, I ever shall part
From a token thus soothing, and sweet to my heart;
That the dear little volume thus coming from thee,
Shall e'er be less valued, less cherish'd by me.
When the fathomless future its page shall unfold,
When time o'er this head now so youthful has roll'd,
And left me like others, gray, wither'd and old,
Then, then shall this gift of the merry new year,
From the loved one whose spirit no longer is here,
Impart a sweet sadness, and draw the warm tear.
'T will bring to remembrance my own lovely home,
And each feeling, each hope, which is now in its bloom,
As a fair little talisman bound up with joy
'T will be clasp'd to my bosom its fond hopes to buoy,
And the love now within it must cease there to dwell,
When I bid this dear volume a lasting farewell.

1835.

TO FANCY.

Fly on, aerial Fancy! fly
  Back, back through many an age,
To scenes which long have glided by,
  Untold on history's page.

Oh, stretch thy heavenward wings, and soar
  Through clouds mysterious and sublime,
To scenes which earth shall view no more,
  Far down the dark abyss of time.

Lit by thy pure, celestial torch,
  Earth, heaven, and sea have softly glow'd,
Nought in created space which ne'er
  To thine enchanting sway hath bow'd.

Worlds framed and beautified by thee,
  Have glow'd with every rainbow hue,
And o'er each meaner thing thy form
  Hath shed a radiance as it flew.

All potent Fancy! deign to bend
 One glance upon thy suppliant here!
Thy glowing car in kindness send,
 And bear me to thy beauteous sphere.

Believe me, thou hast ever been
 The cherish'd monarch of my heart!
There's not one thought, one hope, one scene,
 In which thy vagaries have no part.

Then deign to look with pitying eye
 Upon thy votary's bended form;
Disperse each cloud from yonder sky,
 And clasp me in thy guardian arm.

1835.

INVOCATION TO SPRING.

Bend down from thy chariot, oh beautiful Spring,
Unfold like a standard thy radiant wing,
And beauty and joy in thy rosy path bring!
We long for thy coming, sweet goddess of love,
We watch for thy smile in the pure sky above,
And we sigh for the hour when the wood birds shall sing,
And nature shall welcome thee, beautiful Spring!
How the lone heart will bound as thy presence draws near,
As if borne from this world to some lovelier sphere!
How the fond soul to meet thee in raptures shall rise,
When thy first blush has tinted the earth and the skies.
Oh, send thy soft breath on the icy-bound stream,
'T will vanish, 't will melt, like the forms in a dream,
Released from its chains, like a child in its glee,
'T will flow in its beauty, all sparkling and free.
It will spring on in joy, like a bird on the wing,
And hail thee with music, oh beautiful Spring!
But tread with thy foot on the snow-cover'd plain,
And verdure and beauty shall smile in thy train.
Only whisper one word with thy seraph-like voice,
And nature to hear the sweet sound shall rejoice!
Oh, Spring! lovely goddess! what form can compare
With thine so resplendent, so glowing, so fair?
What sunbeam so bright as thy own smiling eye,
At whose glance the dark spirits of winter do fly?
A garland of roses is twined round thy brow,
Thy cheek like the pale blush of evening doth glow;
A mantle of green o'er thy soft form is spread,
And the zephyr's light wing gently plays round thy head.
Oh, could I but mount on the eagle's dark wing,
And rest ever beside thee, Spring, beautiful Spring!
Methinks, I behold thee! I hear thy soft voice!
And in fulness of heart I rejoice! I rejoice!

But the cold wind is moaning, the drear snow doth fall,
And naught but the shrieking blast echoes my call.
Oh, heed the frail offering an infant can bring!
Oh, grant my petition, Spring, beautiful Spring!
1835.

FROM THE ONE HUNDRED AND THIRTY-NINTH PSALM.

Where from thy presence shall I flee?
Where seek a hiding-place from thee?
If the pure breath of heaven I share,
Lo! I shall find thy spirit there!
If wandering to the depths of hell,
I trust in secresy to dwell,
Behold! in all thy power and might,
Thou, Lord, shalt pierce the veil of night.
If on the radiant wings of morn
To unknown lands I 'm gently borne;
There, even there thy hand shall lead
Thy voice support my sinking head.
If to my inmost soul I say,
Darkness and night shall shroud my way,
That darkness shall dissolve in light,
And day usurp the throne of night.
No power can dim thy searching eye,
Or bid thy guardian spirit fly.
Thou knowest well each infant thought,
Which passion, pride, or sin has taught;
And doubts and fears, but half express'd,
To thee, Almighty, stand confess'd.
Plain as the waves of yonder sea,
Man's subtlest thoughts are known to thee.
From the small insect tribe, which plays
Within the sun's enlivening rays,
To the broad ocean waves, which rise
In heaving billows to the skies.
Or great or small, each work of thine,
It whispers of a hand divine.
Each breeze which fans the twilight hour,
Speeds onward, guided by thy power;
Each wind which wildly sweeps abroad,
Is teeming with the voice of God.
1835.

STANZAS.

The power of mind, the force of genius,
Oh, what human heart can tell,
Or the deep and stirring thoughts,
Which in the poet's bosom dwell!

The high and holy dreams of heaven,
  Which raise the soul above
This world of care, this sphere of sin,
  To realms of light and love.

Oh who can tell its energy?
  The spirit's power and might,
When genius, with sublimest force,
  Appoints its upward flight,—

And lifts the struggling soul above
  The prison-house of clay,
To roam amid the fancied realms
  Of glory and of day!

And breathes immortal vigour
  To sustain it through this life,
The index of a higher world,
  With power and beauty rife.

Oh, how sublime the very thought,
  That this frail form of mine
Contains a spirit destined soon
  In purer worlds to shine.

To unfold its infant energies,
  In an immortal clime,
And far more glorious become
  Each passing hour of time.

That it contains the heavenly germ
  Of future being now,
Created there to beautify,
  Where clearer waters flow.

And there expand the glowing bud,
  'Mid worlds of light and love,
Through the bright realms of ether,
  In glory still to rove.

LETTER TO A POETICAL CORRESPONDENT,

WRITTEN DURING MY ILLNESS, IN ANSWER TO ONE IN WHICH SHE DESCRIBES PEGASUS AS BLIND, HALT, AND LAME, AND ENDEAVOURS TO CHEER ME WITH THE PROSPECT OF SPEEDY RECOVERY.

Now, my dear Cousin Maggy, behold me again,
Relieved in a measure from sickness and pain;
With a well-sharpen'd phiz, and a cap on my head,
Just bidding farewell to the irksome sick bed,
And endeavouring to tune my enfeebled young lyre
To a theme which was wont its wild notes to inspire.

'Tis long since the muse to my aid has descended,
Or smiling and pleased, her poor votary befriended;
Now tired of entreaties, I'll court her no more,
But alone and unaided her realms I'll explore;
So, dear cousin Maggy, condemn not my muse,
If my verse all its rhyme and its harmony lose,
For, vex'd with refusals so frequent and long,
Without her I've dared to engage in a song;
And shielded and guided by *Clio* no more,
To meet thy Pegasus I tremblingly soar.
While confined by the shackles of sickness and pain,
For many a day on my couch I had lain,
And in seeking for rest, to my weak frame denied,
Was tossing fatigued on each sore, aching side,
There came down a tall spirit of light (as it were,)
From the realms of the sky and the regions of air;
He dispell'd from my bosom its gloom and its dread,
And kindled the torchlight of hope in their stead.
Ah! then, my dear friend, so great was his power,
He could lighten my pain, and soothe solitude's hour;
Ah why then, my cousin, thus brand him with shame,
Ah why then describe him as "sightless and lame?"
All noble and lovely he seem'd to *mine* eye,
And when ceasing to view him I ceased with a sigh!
His wings were expanded, his eyebeam was fire!
And that heart had been old *he* could fail to inspire.
But alas! I should fail, did I strive to portray
But one half of the graces which round him did play,
And held captive my soul with their wildering sway;
So no more I'll contemplate his charms or thine own,
But try to inform you how *we're* getting on.
Dear mother still sits on her old rocking-chair,
Either thinking, or smiling, or silent with care;
Then plying her needle with industry still,
Or scribbling and wearing some tarnish'd goosequill.
Dear Matty is thinking of railroads again,
And longs to get hold of the *rod* and the *chain*.
He talks of embankments, canals, and high-bridges,
Of steam-cars and tunnels, of swamps and of ditches.
While dear little *Kent*, with his well-finger'd book,
Sits gazing around him with complacent look;
But alas! my dear coz, the poor fellow has lost
The frequent amusement he valued the most;
For know, in the midst of our sickness and cares,
The glass in our parlour was carried up stairs,
(Other furniture changed—here was station'd a bed,)
So a mirror much smaller was placed in its stead,
And my hapless young brother is able no more
To admire his own beauty and grace as before;
He looks at the tempter all rueful and sad,
And in vain the attempt to attain it is made,
And with long, disappointed, and sorrowful mien,
He retires from the spot to conceal his chagrin.

Oh! join, my dear cousin, with me, and bewail
That his sources of pleasure thus early should fail.
Old *Leo*, tired out with his frolic and play,
Lies quietly sleeping the rest of the day;
While pussy is purring contentedly near,
Devoid of all care and unconscious of fear.
But enough of this nonsense! I fain would request
That my cousin again may be honour'd and blest
By receiving thy musical Nag as a guest:
His arrival I'll welcome with heartfelt delight,
And gaze on his beauties from morning till night.
Dear uncle and cousins I ne'er can forget,
With sweet little Georgie, his Aunty, and Kate,
Give our love to them all, and yourself must receive
My warm and my lasting affection. Believe,
I shall ever remain as I now am to thee,
Your dear little cousin, and

MARGARET M. D.

Ballston, 1835.

STANZAS.

Though nought but life's sunshine has spread o'er my path,
Though no real distress has e'er clouded my brow:
Though the storms of affliction around me have past,
And shed o'er me nought save the rainbow's bright glow;

Though nursed from the cradle with tenderest care,
Though shelter'd from all that might grieve or distress;
Though life's pathway has blush'd with the fairest of flowers,
And my heavenly Father has ceased not to bless;

Though the chillness of want and the darkness of woe
From my joyous young spirit have rapidly fled:
Though the presence of all whom I cherish and love
Has not fail'd its sweet influence around me to shed;

Still, still there are moments of darkness and grief,
Which steal o'er my soul like the spirit of woe;
I know not their coming, I feel not their cause,
But o'er my rapt spirit they silently flow.

I feel for a while as some terrible blow
Had deprived me of comfort, of friends, and of home;
Then depart they as silent, and leave my freed soul
Again in the bright path of pleasure to roam.

Like clouds in the sky of enjoyment they pass,
And shed o'er my heart a sensation of sadness;
Like clouds do they glide o'er the surface of light,
And leave me again to the spirit of gladness.

1835.

VERSES WRITTEN WHEN THIRTEEN YEARS OF AGE.

VERSIFICATION FROM OSSIAN.

WHERE the stream in its wildness was rushing below,
And the oak in its greatness was bending above,
Fell Cathba the brave by the hand of his foe,
By the hand of Duchomar, his rival in love.

Duchomar repair'd to the cave of the wild,
Where dwelt in her beauty the star of his breast,
Where she wander'd alone, nature's sensitive child,
Knowing little of life but its love and its rest.

"Oh, beautiful daughter of Cormac the proud!
Oh Morna, thou fairest that earth can bestow!
Why dwellest thou here, 'neath the dark, angry cloud?
Why dwellest thou here where the wild waters flow?

"The old oak is murmuring aloud in the blast,
Which ruffles the breast of the far distant sea,
The storm o'er the heavens his thick veil hath cast,
And the sky in its sternness is frowning on thee!

"But thou art like snow on the black, wither'd heath,
Thy ringlets are soft as the mist of the night,
When it winds round the broad hill its delicate wreath,
By the sun at its parting made gorgeously bright."

"Whence comest thou, man of the fierce-rolling eye?"
Said the beautiful maid of the dark flowing hair;
"Oh proud is thy bearing, and haughty, and high,
And thy brow, there is darkness and gloominess there.

"Perchance thou hast heard from our foeman of blood;
Doth Swaran appear on the broad-heaving sea,
Doth he pour on our coast like the deep raging flood?
What tidings from Lochlin, Duchomar, for me?"

"No tidings from Lochlin, oh Morna, I bring,
I come from the chase of the fleet-footed deer;
My arrows have sped like the eagle's swift wing,
And the scatheless have fled from my presence for fear.

"Three deer at my feet in the death-pang have laid,—
Fair daughter of Cormac, one perish'd for thee;
As my soul do I love thee, oh white-handed maid!
And queen of my heart ever more shalt thou be!"

"Duchomar!" the maiden with firmness replied,
"No portion of love do I cherish for thee;
For thy bosom is dark with its passions and pride,
And fickle thy heart as the wide-rolling sea.

"But Cathba! thou only shall Morna adore,
Thine image alone this fond bosom shall fill;
Oh bright are thy locks as the sunbeams of day,
When the mists of the valley are climbing the hill.

"Hast thou seen him, Duchomar, young Cathba the brave?
Hast thou seen the fair chief on his pathway of light?
The daughter of Cormac the mighty is here
To welcome her love when he comes from the fight."

"Then long shalt thou tarry, oh Morna!" he cried,
And fiercely and sullenly gazed on the maid,
"Then long shalt thou tarry, oh Morna! for here
Is the blood of thy chief on Duchomar's dark blade.

"Cold, cold is thy hero, and slain by my hand,
His tomb will I rear upon Cromla's dark hills;
Oh turn on Duchomar thy soft-beaming eye,
For his arm is like lightning, which withers and kills."

"Has he fallen in death, the brave offspring of Torman?"
The maiden exclaim'd in the accents of woe,
"The first in the chase, and the foremost in battle,—
Oh sad is my bosom, and dark was the blow!

"And dark is Duchomar, and deadly his vengeance,
He hath blasted each hope which was bright in the bud;
Fell foe unto Morna, oh lend me thy weapon,
For Cathba I loved, and I still love his blood."

He yielded the sword to her mourning and sighs,—
She plunged the red blade in his fast-heaving side;
And he lay by the stream, as the blasted oak lies,
Till raising his hand he indignantly cried,

"Daughter of blue-shielded Cormac! thy blow
Hath cut off my youth from the fame I love best;
My glory hath fled like a pale wreath of snow,
And Morna! thy weapon is cold in my breast.

"Oh give me to Moina, the maiden of beauty,
Her dreams in the darkness are fraught with my name,
My tomb she will raise in the caves on the mountain,
That hunters may welcome the mark of my fame.

"She will hang o'er my grave like the mists of the morning,
And dwell on my memory with fondness and pride,—
But my bosom is cold, and the lifeblood is ebbing,
Oh Morna, draw forth the cold blade from my side."

Slowly and sadly she came at his bidding,
  And drew forth the sword from his fast-bleeding breast,
But he plunged the red steel in her own lovely bosom,
  And laid her fair form on the damp earth to rest.

Her tresses dishevell'd around her were flowing,
  The blood gurgling fast from the wide-gaping wound,
And the eye that was bright, and the cheek that was glowing,
  In dimness and pallor and silence were bound.

Oh Morna! be thou as the moon, when its light
  Shines forth from her throne on the light fleecy cloud,
To watch o'er the grave of thy lover at night,
  And wrap his cold tomb in thy silvery shroud.

1835.

TO THE MUSE, AFTER MY BROTHER'S DEATH.

Ah, where art thou wandering, sweet spirit of song,
Who once bore my rapt fancy on bright wings slong?
That soaring from earth, with its cares and its pains,
It might bathe in the light of thy seraph-like strains?

Ah, whither art fled in thy beauty and gladness?
  Why leave me in silence thy loss to bewail?
Dost thou shrink from the heart that is tinctured with sadness,
  The eye that is dimm'd, or the cheek that is pale?

Since last waved around me thy pinions of light,
  The chillness of sorrow hath breathed o'er my home,
For one joyful young spirit hath taken its flight,
  One icy-cold form has been borne to the tomb,

Like a flow'ret of summer, he wither'd and died
In the springtime of beauty, of youth, and of pride;
In the freshness of hope he was borne to his tomb,
And the home of his kindred is shadow'd with gloom.

Then return to my bosom, thou wakener of joy,
  Oh touch with thy fingers my drooping young lyre!
Awake it to pleasures time ne'er can destroy,
  And its chords with a heavenly calmness inspire.

1836.

LINES,

ON HEARING SOME PASSAGES READ FROM MRS. HEMANS'S "RECORDS OF WOMAN."

OH, pause not yet, for many an hour
I'd lend a raptured ear,
The thrilling, melting sweetness
Of that seraph strain to hear.

Dispel not yet the soften'd joy
Those gentle tones impart,
While painting in such vivid hues,
The worth of woman's heart.

Priestess of song ! could we but feel
The value of thine own,
How many a soul would bow before
Thy spirit's lofty throne.

How many now elated
With the muse's faintest smile,
Would turn them to thy radiant shrine,
And worship there awhile.

With softest touch thy magic hand
Awaked the sleeping lyre,
To all a woman's tenderness,
And all a poet's fire.

And proudly soar'd thy lofty mind
Each earthly thought above,
And vainly sought thy woman's heart
For something more to love.

1836. [Unfinished.]

AN APPEAL FOR THE BLIND.

THOUGH thousands pass the mourners by,
And scorn the suppliant's bended knee,
"Hope springs exulting" to the eye,
When sorrow turns its glance on thee.

For soft compassion's slumbering ray,
And pity's melting glance is there,
To chase the sufferer's fears away,
And soothe to calmness wild despair.

Oh fan to life the kindling spark,
  Till brightly burns its radiant flame,
For thou art fortune's favour'd child,
  And I would plead in mercy's name.

Scan the dark page of life, and say
  If there thy searching eye can find
A woe more keen, a fate more sad,
  Than that which marks the helpless blind.

Launch'd forth on life's uncertain path,
  Its best and brightest gift denied,
No power to pluck its fragrant flowers,
  Or turn its poisonous thorns aside;

No ray to pierce the gloom within,
  And chase the darkness with its light;
No radiant morning dawn to win
  His spirit from the shades of night.

Nature, whose smile, so pure and fair,
  Casts a bright glow o'er life's dark stream,
Nature, sweet soother of our care,
  Has not a single smile for him.

When pale disease, with blighting hand,
  Crushes each budding hope awhile,
Our eyes can rest in sweet delight
  On love's fond gaze, or friendship's smile.

Not so with *him*—his soul, chain'd down
  By doubt, and loneliness, and care,
Feels but misfortune's chilling frown,
  And broods in darkness and despair.

Favour'd by heaven! oh haste thee on,—
  Thy blest Redeemer points the way,—
Haste o'er the spirit's gloom to pour
  The light of intellectual day.

Thou canst not raise their drooping lids,
  And wake them to the noonday sun;
Thou canst not ope what God hath closed,
  Or cancel aught His hands have done.

But oh! there is a world within,
  More bright, more beautiful than ours;
A world which, nursed by culturing hands,
  Will blush with fairest, sweetest flowers.

And thou canst make that desert mind
  Bloom sweetly as the blushing rose;

Thou canst illume that rayless void,
  Till darkness like the day-beam glows.

Thou canst implant the brilliant gem
  Of thought, in each benighted soul,
Till back from radiance so divine
  The clouds of ignorance shall roll.

Thus shalt thou shed a purer ray
  O'er each beclouded mind within,
Than pours the glorious orb of day
  On this dark world of care and sin.

Prize you a self-approving mind?
  Then lay thine offering here;
The clouded orbits of the blind
  Shall yield a grateful tear.

Would'st thou the blessings of that band
  Should crowd thy path below?
That hearts, enlighten'd by thy hand,
  With gratitude should flow?

And would'st thou seek the matchless love
  To God's own children given,
A conscience calmly resting 'neath
  The fav'ring smiles of Heaven?

Then speed thee on in mercy's cause,
  And teach the blind to see;
"Hope springs exulting" in the eye
  That sorrowing turns to thee.

And warmest blessings on thy head,
  Full many a voice shall call;
And tears upon thy memory shed,
  Like Hermon's dew shall fall!

And when the last dread day has come,
  Which seals thy endless doom;
When the freed soul shall seek its home,
  And triumph o'er the tomb;

When lowly bends each reverend knee,
  And bows each heart in prayer,
A band of spirits, saved by thee,
  Shall plead thy virtues there!

1836.

THE SMILES OF NATURE.

There 's a smile above, and a smile below,
In the clouds that roll, and the waves that flow:
Is the heart unchain'd by sorrow's thrall,
There 's a smile of joy and of peace in all!
There 's a smile on the brow of the waken'd day,
When he gilds the east with his glowing ray,
And a smile on his brow when he sinks to rest,
Like the saint who expires on his Maker's breast.
There are pensive smiles on the evening sky,
Which raise the thoughts to the pure and high,
Which speak to the soul of its glad release,
And tune its quivering chords to peace.
The flow'rets ope with the rising sun,
And wither and die ere his race is run;
Yet a smile is shed o'er their transient bloom,
Adorning the path to their early tomb.
There 's a smile on the brow of the gorgeous spring,
When she spreads o'er the valley her radiant wing;
As she calms the wild winds with her fragrant breath,
And decks the glad earth in her beautiful wreath.
There 's a smile on the rose, though 't will cease to bloom;
There 's a smile on the stream, though the storm may come;
There 's a smile in the sky, though the clouds may roll
Like sin o'er the depths of the human soul!
Thus, all that is lovely is form'd for decay,
But the pure beams of heaven are shed o'er the way.
There are varied smiles on a mortal's brow,
Which speak of the soul from its depths below;
But they too vanish, when brightest they beam,
And bury their light in the world's dark stream.
For the heart of man is the throne of guile,
And sin can shadow each mortal smile;
And the blossoms of light which are planted there,
Are weaken'd by passion, or wither'd by care.
There 's a haughty smile on the conqueror's brow,
As the nations of earth at his footstool bow;
But that smile is chill as the frozen stream
Which glitters pale in the moon's cold beam;
It speaks of ambition, of pride, and of sin,
Which rankle and swell the dark bosom within.
There 's a smile on the brow of aspiring man,
As he pauses the works of his hand to scan,
And gazes far up to that gorgeous height
Which is guarded by danger, and terror, and night;
But 't is cold as the bosom from whence it came,
And is lost in the splendours of grandeur and fame.
There 's a beaming smile upon beauty's brow,
As the young and the gay at her altar bow;
'T is brilliant, 't is dazzling, 't is passing fair,
But the heart in its freshness is wanting there.

There 's a sunny smile on the infant's lip,
As he pauses the cup of enjoyment to sip;
But a moment more shall have hurried by,
And that smile will fade from his clouded eye;
Some childish sorrow, or childish sin,
Shall cast its shade o'er the depths within.
Then where shall we seek for a perfect smile,
If beauty hath sorrow, and youth hath guile?
If the clouds of pride and ambition roll
O'er the inmost depths of the deathless soul?
Oh Nature! the soul is a spark divine,
But I turn from its light for a smile of thine;
The soul in its greatness must ever endure,
But thou, in thy freshness, art holy and pure!
Oh, give me the beams of the summer sky,
Which gladden the bosom and rapture the eye;
Though transient the radiance, though fleeting the smile,
They speak not of sorrow, they breathe not of guile!
But light up the tremulous chords of the soul,
Its virtues to heighten, its sins to control:
For the soft smiles of nature around us are cast,
To light, with their brilliance, the world's weary waste.
To call the lone heart from its sadness away,
And shed o'er its darkness a magical ray!
When oppress'd with the cares and sorrows of life,
The spirit turns back from its turmoil and strife,
When it longs to be happy, and sighs to be free,
Oh nature, 'tis cheer'd by communion with thee.
Though the waters may rise, and the sky be o'ercast;
Though rages the tempest, and whistles the blast;
Though thy brow may be shaded in darkness and fear,
He can read there a lesson to solace and cheer,
As the soft rays of sunshine succeed to thy frown;
As the rainbow encircles thy brows like a crown;
As the tempest rolls off which had reigned there awhile,
And bursts forth in radiance the light of thy smile,
So gently the shadows of sorrow depart,
And hope dawns again on the desolate heart,
And points from thy glories to glories more pure
From thy fast-fading beauties to charms which endure,
And leads the rapt soul from its sinful abode,
To commune for awhile with its Maker and God.
Oh Nature! what art thou?—a mighty lyre,
Whose wings are swept by an angel choir;
Whose music, attuned by a hand divine,
Thrills a chord in each bosom responsive to thine,
And whose gentle strain, as it softly swells,
Soothes many a bosom where sadness dwells;
While the joyous and happy, the youthful and gay,
Pluck the flowers from thy garland and speed on their way.
Oh, give me the beams of the summer sky,
Which gladden the bosom, and rapture the eye,

Though fleeting the radiance, though transient the smile,
They speak not of sorrow, they breathe not of guile,
But light up the tremulous chords of the soul,
Its virtues to heighten, its sins to control.

1835.

ON A ROSE,

RECEIVED FROM MISS SEDGWICK.

AND thou art fading too, my rose,
  Thy healthful bloom is fled,
From thy pale flower the leaves unclose,
  And bows thy pallid head.

I knew how quickly fades away
  Each brighter, lovelier thing,
And did not deem that thou couldst stay,
  Thou fairest rose of spring.

But I have watch'd thy varying hue,
  As fading hour by hour,
And mourn'd that thou must perish too,
  My lovely, cherish'd flower.

Oh, 'tis a mournful thing to see
  How all that's fair must die;
How death will pluck the sweetest bud,
  On his cold breast to lie.

'Tis sad to mark his icy hand
  Destroy our all that's dear,
In silent, shivering awe to stand,
  And know his footstep near.

Yet 'twere unmeet that thou shouldst live,
  When man himself must die;
That death should cull each human form,
  And pass the flow'ret by.

Why do I mourn for thee my rose,
  When graven in my heart,
I read a deeper sorrow there
  Than thou could'st e'er impart.

For one who came from heaven awhile
  To bless the mourners here;
Their joys to hallow with her smile,
  Their sorrows with her tear;

Who join'd to all the charms of earth
  The noblest gifts of heaven;
To whom the Muses, at her birth,
  Their sweetest smiles had given;

Whose eye beam'd forth with fancy's ray,
  And genius pure and high;
Whose very soul had seem'd to bathe
  In streams of melody,—

Was all too like to thee, my rose,
  As fragile and as fair;
For, while her eye most brightly beam'd,
  The mark of death was there.

The cheek which once so sweetly bloom'd,
  Grew pallid with decay;
The burning fire within consumed
  Its tenement of clay.

Death, as if fearing to destroy,
  Paused o'er her couch awhile;
She gave a tear for those she loved,
  Then met him with a smile.

Oh, who may tell what angel bands
  Convey'd that soul away;
And who may tell what tears were shed
  Above that lifeless clay.

They laid her in the silent grave,
  The moist earth for her bed!
And placed the rose and violet
  To blossom o'er her head!

But though unseen by mortal eye,
  She seem'd not to depart,
Her memory linger'd still below
  In every kindred heart;

As if her pure unfetter'd soul
  Return'd to earthly things,
And spread o'er all her cherish'd scenes
  The shadow of her wings.

Still thou art like to her, my rose,
  Though bending in decay;
The tyrant death can never take
  Thy fragrant breath away.

Like thee, my rose, she bloom'd and died,
  Like thee, her life was brief;
And to her name remembrance clung,
  Like perfume to thy leaf.

But when the torch of memory burn'd
  With fainter, feebler flame,
The pen of Sedgwick spread anew
  A lustre round her name.

For this our daily gratitude
  In raptures shall ascend;
For this a sister's blessings
  And a mother's prayer shall blend.

And if the Lord of heaven permits
  His sainted ones to know
The varied scenes of joy and grief
  Which mark the world below;

Then she will bend her angel form,
  With heavenly raptures fired,
And bless the hand which penn'd the tale,
  The genius which inspired.

1837.

THE CHURCH-GOING BELL.

How sweet is the sound of the church-going bell
When it bursts on the ear with its full rich swell,
So slow and so solemn it peals through the air,
It seems as if calling the soul to prepare
To meet in his temple, so holy and pure,
The Saviour, whose presence shall ever endure;
To unburthen the conscience—devoutly to kneel—
To pray for the pardon of sins which we feel;
Before our almighty Preserver to bow,
With a purified soul, and a heart humbled low.

1837. [Unfinished.]

FRAGMENT.

Oh, for a something more than this,
  To fill the void within my breast;
A sweet reality of bliss,
  A something bright, but unexpress'd!

My spirit longs for something higher
  Than life's dull stream can e'er supply;
Something to feed this inward fire,
  This spark, which never more can die.

I'd dwell with all that nature forms
  Of wild or beautiful or gay,
Bow, when she clothes the heaven with storms,
  And join her in her frolic play.

I'd hold companionship with all
  Of pure, of noble, or divine;
With glowing heart adoring fall, !
  And kneel at nature's sylvan shrine.

My soul is like a broken lyre,
  Whose loudest, sweetest chord is gone;
A note, half trembling on the wire,
  A heart that wants an echoing tone.

Where shall I find this shadowy bliss,
  This shapeless phantom of the mind?
This something words can ne'er express,
  So vague, so faint, so undefined?

Language! thou never canst portray
  The fancies floating o'er my soul!
Thou ne'er canst chase the clouds away
  Which o'er my changing visions roll!

1837.

FRAGMENT.

Oh, I have gazed on forms of light,
  Till life seem'd ebbing in a tear—
Till in that fleeting space of sight
  Were merged the feelings of a year.

And I have heard the voice of song,
  Till my full heart gush'd wild and free,
And my rapt soul would float along
  As if on waves of melody.

But while I glow'd at beauty's glance,
  I long'd to feel a deeper thrill:
And while I heard that dying strain,
  I sigh'd for something sweeter still.

I have been happy, and my soul
  Free from each sorrow, care, regret;
Yet ever in those hours of bliss
  I long'd to find them happier yet.

Oft o'er the darkness of my mind
  Some meteor thought has glanced at will;
'T was bright—but ever have I sigh'd
  To find a fancy brighter still.

Why are these restless, vain desires,
  Which always grasp at something more
To feed the spirit's hidden fires,
  Which burn unseen, unnoticed soar?

Well might the heathen sage have known
  That earth must fail the soul to bind;
That life, and life's tame joys, alone,
  Could never chain the ethereal mind.

1837.

WRITTEN WHEN BETWEEN FOURTEEN AND FIFTEEN.

ON RETURNING TO BALLSTON,

AFTER THE DEATH OF A LITTLE BROTHER.

Yes! this is home! the home we loved before,
The dear retreat we hope to leave no more!
Since first we mourn'd thy calm enjoyments fled,
Two weary years with silent steps have sped;
And ah! in that short space what scenes have past!
Death has been with us since we saw thee last!
Yes! robed in gloom he came, the tyrant Death,
To blight our fairest with his chilling breath.
He stole along beneath the smiles of spring,
When youthful hearts to life most fondly cling;
The loveliest flowers were blushing 'neath his tread;
He stole the sweetest of them all, and fled!
In vain, my brother, now we look for thee,
Thy form elastic, and thy step of glee;
In vain we strove our thoughts from thee to win,
Our hearts recoiling feel the void within.
Alas! alas! thou dear and cherish'd one,
How soon on earth thy tranquil course was run!
Like some bright stream that pours its waves to-day,
Glides gently on, and vanishes away!
A brief, brief time has pass'd with giant stride,
And thou hast lived, hast suffer'd, and hast died!
Memory, unmindful of the lapse between,
Paints forth in vivid hues that closing scene;
The more we gaze, we feel its truth the more,
And live in thought those painful moments o'er.
We see his form upon its couch of pain,
We hear his soft and trembling voice again;
Grief forcing from our lips the shuddering groan,
And sweet composure breathing from his own.
The earth was clothed in spring's enlivening hue,
The faded buds were bursting forth anew,
The birds were heard in sweet, melodious strain,
And Nature woke to radiant life again,

While he, too fragile for this world of strife,
Prepared to blossom in a holier life,
The glowing spring of heaven's eternal year
Was usher'd in by all that's loveliest here;
Earth, robed in Nature's fairest, best array,
Led on his fluttering soul to purer day.
The soft winds fann'd him where his couch was laid,
On his hot brow the cooling breezes play'd,
And in his hand (fit type of early death,)
Was clasp'd a faded flower, a wither'd wreath.
Hush'd was each bursting groan, each tumult wild,
Around the death-bed of that darling child;
O'er each sad heart an awful trembling crept;
E'en grief, o'erpower'd, a solemn stillness kept.
His soul, beyond the grasp of care and strife,
Stood on the confines of a deathless life;
His gaze was fix'd upon * * *
The lapse between eternity and time;
His eye was beaming with intenser light,
As broke new glories on his fading sight.
Oh, who may tell that hour of thrilling dread,
That midnight vigil by his dying bed!
When his young spirit left its shrine of clay,
And sped through worlds unknown its pathless way!
Methinks e'en now I see his speaking face,
Death on his brow, and in his bosom peace,
When soft he whisper'd, while the accents fell
Like the soft murmurings of the passing gale,
While his cheek glow'd with death's intensest bloom,
"Mother! dear mother! the last hour has come!"
Yes! thy last hour of pain, thou darling boy,
The opening scene to endless years of joy!
Oh, never more, till memory's sun shall set,
Can I that thrilling scene of death forget!
His earnest gaze, his bright and glowing cheek
Beaming with thoughts his tongue no more could speak,
His soul just hastening to the realms on high,
While all earth's love was kindling in his eye.
Alas! it fades, that deep, unearthly glow,
And the cold drops stand quivering on his brow.
Death has o'ercome! 't is nature's closing strife,
The last, last struggle of departing life!
List to that sigh! the poison'd shaft has sped,
And his young spirit to its home hath fled.
The silver chord is broke, dissolved the tie!
Alas! alas! how all that's fair must die!
Hark to that heavenly strain, so loud, so clear,
Rising so sweet on fancy's listening ear!
Hark! 't is an angel's song, a voice of glee,
A welcome to the soul, unchain'd and free!
On, on it flows in ceaseless tides again,
Till the rapt spirit echoes to the strain,

Till on the wings of song it soars away,
To track its kindred soul through realms of day!
Hark to that lyre, more sweet than all beside;
Mother! 't is hers! oh, weep not that she died!
Hark to that voice, so melting and so clear,
The same, my father, thou wert wont to hear!
And mark that train of infant spirits come
To lead their brother to his glorious home!
All, all are yours! and all shall gather there,
To lead your spirits from this world of care;
Then weep no more; your darling son is blest,
And his young soul has enter'd into rest.

1837.

TWILIGHT.

Twilight! sweet hour of peace,
Now art thou stealing on;
Cease from thy tumult, thought! and fancy, cease!
Day and its cares have gone!
Mysterious hour,
Thy magic power
Steals o'er my heart like music's softest tone.

The golden sunset hues
Are fading in the west;
The gorgeous clouds their brighter radiance lose,
Folded on evening's breast.
So doth each wayward thought,
From fancy's altar caught,
Fade like thy tints, and muse itself to rest.

Cold must that bosom be,
Which never felt thy power,
Which never thrill'd with tender melody
At this bewitching hour;
When nature's gentle art
Enchains the pensive heart;
When the breeze sinks to rest, and shuts the fragrant flower.

It is the hour for pensive thought,
For memory of the past,
For sadden'd joy, for chasten'd hope
Of brighter scenes at last;
The soul should raise
Its hymn of praise,
That calm so sweet on life's dull stream is cast.

Wearied with care, how sweet to hail
Thy shadowy, calm repose,
When all is silent but the whispering gale
Which greets the sleeping rose;
When, as thy shadows blend,
The trembling thoughts ascend,
And borne aloft, the gates of heaven unclose.

Forth from the warm recess
The chain'd affections flow,
And peace, and love, and tranquil happiness
Their mingled joys bestow;
Charmed by the mystic spell,
The purer feelings swell,
The nobler powers revive, expand, and glow.

1837.

ON THE DEPARTURE OF A BROTHER.

Brother! I need no pencill'd form
To bring back glowing thoughts of thee;
Love's pencil, bathed in hues of light,
Shall trace the page of memory.

There they shall live, each look or smile,
Each gentler word, or look, or tone;
Fancy shall view love's work the while,
And add rich colouring of her own.

How throbb'd my heart with sweet delight,
When hope beheld thy near return!
Nor thought that day precedes the night,
And hearts the happiest soonest mourn.

Why knew I not that joy like mine
Was never, never formed to last?
That pleasures only live to die,
And, ere we feel them, ours are past?

Oh! turn not from my strain away,
Nor scorn it, simple though it be!
It is a sister's sorrowing lay,
A token of her love for thee.

Oh! that a prophet's eye were mine,
To read the shrouded future o'er!
Oh! that the glimmering lamp of time
Could cast its mystic rays before!

Then would I trace thy devious way
Along the chequer'd path of life;
Discern each pure, reviving ray,
And mark each changing scene of strife.

Oh! if a sister's partial hand
Could weave the web of fate for thee,
Pleasure should wave her mystic wand,
And all thy life be harmony.

Peace, foolish heart! a wiser Power
Thy hand shall guide, thy footsteps lead;
Each bitter grief, each rapturous hour
By His unerring will decreed.

Farewell, my brother! and believe,
  Through every scene of weal or woe,
A sister's heart with thine shall grieve,
  With thine in rapturous joy shall glow.

Each morn and eve a mother's prayer
  With mine shall seek the courts above:
A mother's blessing rest on thee,
  Embalm'd in all a mother's love.

1837.

LINES

WRITTEN AFTER READING ACCOUNTS OF THE DEATH OF MARTYRS.

Speak not of life, I could not bear
A life of foul disgrace to share!
Wealth, fame, or honour's fleeting breath,
What are they to this glorious death?
Think ye a kingdom back could win
My spirit to this world of sin!
Think ye a few more years of strife
Could draw me from eternal life?—
Dark is the path to Canaan's shore,
But Jesus trod the path before!
He hath illumed the grave for me,—
My Saviour! I will die for thee!
Yes! lead me forth; in faith secure,
The keenest anguish I'll endure!
And while my body feeds the flame,
My soul its bright reward shall claim!
Soon shall these earthly bonds decay,
This trembling frame return to clay,
And earth, enrobed in clouds of night,
Shall fade for ever from my sight.
But who would mourn a home like this,
When gather'd to that home of bliss?
But there is many a tender tie
Would shake my firm resolve to die;
Cords which entwine my longing heart
Affection's death alone can part.
Jesus, forgive each faltering thought,
Which weaker, earlier love hath taught;
Forgive the tears which struggling flow
To view a mother's, sister's woe.
Forgive this grief, though weak it be,
Nor deem my spirit turn'd from thee!
Raise my unworthy soul above
The tempting wiles of earthly love!
Soon shall each torturing pang be o'er,
And tears like these shall flow no more;

And those I love so deeply here
Shall meet me in yon heavenly sphere.
Love! what have I, compared to thine!
Love, pure, ineffable, divine!
Love which could bring a God below
To taste a mortal's cup of woe;
To weep in agony, to sigh,
To bear a nation's scorn—to die!
Oh, love! undying, godlike, free,
All else is swallow'd up in thee.
Soon shall I also soar above,
To dwell with thee, for "*God is love.*"
Yes! pile the blazing fagots high,
Till the bright flames salute the sky!
From each devouring pile you raise,
Shall soar a hymn of love and praise,
And the firm stake you rear for me,
The gate to endless life shall be.
But oh, ye frail, deluded train,
How will ye meet your Lord again!
"Father! their crimes in mercy view!
Forgive, they know not what they do!"

1837.

ON READING COWPER'S POEMS.

Charm'd with thy verse, oh bard, I fain would raise
A feeble tribute teeming with thy praise;
For thee, oh Cowper, touch the trembling string,
And breathe the thoughts the muse inspires to sing;
For thee, whose soul delighted oft to roam
O'er the pure realms of thine eternal home;
Who, scorning folly's smile, or fancy's dream,
Made truth thy guide and piety thy theme;
Who loved to soar where heaven's own glories shine,
And tuned the lyre to harmonies divine!
Whose strains, when pour'd by faith's directing voice,
Made doubt recede, and certainty rejoice;
Whose lofty verse, by sterner justice led,
Made unbelievers, trembling, shrink with dread.
Oh that each bard, from earthborn passions free,
Might tread the path thus nobly mark'd by thee,
And teaching song to plead in virtue's cause,
Might win, like thee, a grateful world's applause!
Knowing from whence thy matchless talents came,
Thou fanned'st to purer life the kindling flame,
And breathing all thy thoughts in numbers sweet,
Laid them adoring at thy Maker's feet.
Thus teaching man that all his nobler lays
Should rise o'erflowing with that Maker's praise;

That his enraptured muse should firmly own
The claims of truth, and faith, and love alone!
That he, who feels within the fire divine,
Should nurse the flame to grace God's holy shrine.
Let those who bask in passion's burning ray,
Who own no rule but fancy's changeful sway,
Who quench their burning thirst in folly's stream,
And waste their genius on each grosser theme,
Let them turn back on life's tumultuous sea,
And humbly gazing, learn this truth from thee;
That virtue's hand the poet's lamp must trim,
And its clear light, unwavering, point to *Him*,
Or all its brilliance shall have glow'd in vain,
And hours misspent shall win him years of pain.

1837.

STANZAS.

Oh, who may tell the joy, the bliss,
  Which o'er the realm of fancy streams;
The varied streams of light and life,
  Which deck the poet's world of dreams?

The ransom'd soul may speed its flight,
  To live and grow in realms above;
May bathe in floods of endless light,
  And live eternal years of love.

But oh, what voice hath e'er reveal'd
  The glories of that blest abode,
Save the faint whisperings of the soul,
  The mystic monitors of God?

Thus may the poet's spirit dance
  And revel in his world of joy,
May form creations at a glance,
  And myriads at a word destroy.

But mortal ear can never hear
  The music of that seraph band;
Nought save the faint, unearthly tones
  Just wafted from that spirit-land.

None but the poet's soul can know
  The wild and wondrous beauty there;
The streams of light, which ever flow,
  The ever music-breathing air.

His spirit seeks this heaven awhile,
  Entranced in glowing dreams of bliss;
Lives in the muses' hallow'd smile,
  And bathes in founts of happiness.

Then, when he sinks to earth again,
His hand awakes the trembling lyre,
He strives to breathe a burning strain,
Kindled at fancy's altar-fire.

But oh, how frail the trembling notes,
Compared * * *
* * * *

1837.

FRAGMENT.

'Twas the song of the evening spirit! it stole,
Like a stream of delight, o'er the listening soul,
And the passions of earth—joy, or sorrow, or pain—
Were absorb'd in the notes of that heavenly strain.
My heart seem'd to pause as the spirit came nigh,
And, array'd in its garment of music pass'd by!
"I am coming, oh earth! I am hasting away,
With my star-spangled crown and my mantle of gray;
I have come from my bower in the regions of light,
To recline on the breast of my parent, Night!
To soften the gloom in her mournful eye,
And guide her steps through the darken'd sky!
I come to the earth in my mystic array;
Rest, rest from the toils and the cares of the day!
I will lull each discordant emotion to sleep,
As I hush the wild waves of the turbulent deep,
And my watch o'er the couch of their slumbers I keep.
The streams murmur 'peace,' as I steal through the sky,
And hush'd are the winds, which swept fitfully by;
The bee nestles down on the breast of the rose,
And the wild birds of summer are seeking repose.
All nature salutes me, so solemn, so fair,
And a glad shout of welcome is borne on the air.
Now, now is the moment, and here is the way
For the spirit to mount from its temple of clay,
And soar on my pinions to regions sublime,
Beyond the broad flight of the giant-wing'd Time"

1837. [Unfinished.]

IMITATION OF A SCOTCH BALLAD.

Sweets of the glowing spring
Float on the air;
Gaily the birdies sing,
Banishin' care.
Softly the burnies flow,
Gently the breezes blow,
I to my Jeanie, oh,
Gaily repair.

Fair as the simmer flower
  Sipp'd by the bee;
Blithe as the weenie birds
  Singin' their glee;
Fresh as the drappin' dew,
Pure as the gowan's hue,
Ever gay an' ever true,
  Is Jeanie to me.

Bright as the gowden beam
  Gildin' the morn;
Sweet as the simmer's wind
  Wavin' the corn;
Sic is my Jeanie, oh,
Stainless as winter snow,
Given to the warld below
  Life to adorn.

Joy to thee, bonnie lass,
  Gently an' braw,
Thou, 'mang the fairest,
  Art fairer than a';
Still mayst thou gladsome be,
Ever from sorrow free,
Blessings upon thine e'e
  Numberless fa'.

Grief may bedim the while
  Joy's glowing flame;
Sorrow may steal the smile
  From its sweet hame;
But the sweet flow'ret love,
Native of heaven above,
In the dark storm shall prove
  Ever the same.

ERE THOU DIDST FORM.

Ere thou didst form this teeming earth,
Or gave these mighty mountains birth;
Ere mortal pressed this yielding sod;
From everlasting thou art God!

Thousands of years, when passed away,
Seem, in thy sight, one fleeting day;
Ages, where man may live and die,
An hour to thy eternity!

Years roll on with a rolling stream,
They fade like shadows in a dream!
Like grass, which springs at morning light,
And withers ere the close of night!

For thou art mighty in thine ire—
Thy wrath consumes like flaming fire;
And, spread before thy searching eye,
Our sins in dreadful order lie.

1837. [Unfinished.]

A FRAGMENT.

I see her seraph form, her flowing hair,
Her brow and cheek so exquisitely fair;
Her smiling lips, her dark eye's radiant beam—
A dream ?—this is not, cannot be a dream!
They tell me 't is some wild and phrensied thought,
Some glowing spark from fancy's altar caught;
Some glowing spirit, fancied and unknown,
Which reigns supreme on Reason's vanquish'd throne.

1837.

FRAGMENT OF THE SPECTRE BRIDEGROOM.

Thus thought I, while in pensive mood,
Beneath a frowning cliff I stood,
And mark'd the autumn sun decline
Above the broad and heaving Rhine!
Oh, 't was a rich and gorgeous sight,
But all too solemn to be bright.
A saddening hue was o'er it cast,
Which seem'd to tell of glories past,
Of summer ripen'd to decay,
Of ancient splendours past away.
The parting monarch's dying glow
Fell on the restless waves below,
As if an angel's hand had dyed
With hues from heaven the sparkling tide.
The fleeting ray an instant beam'd,
O'er hill, and dale, and rock it stream'd,
Till the dark, time-defying cliff,
Seem'd glowing, melting into life,
And the broad scene, so sad and wild,
Beneath its gentle influence smiled,
As care lifts up its sorrowing eye,
When hope has cast a sunbeam by;
Then swiftly fading, glided o'er,
And left it lonely as before.
The distant hills of sombre blue,
Tinged with that rich and varying hue,
Now darker and more mingled grew,
While nearer rose so wild and bold
The rugged cliffs of Odenwald.

The Rhine, enrobed in shadows gray,
  Roll'd on its giant path,
Lashing the rocks which barr'd its way,
Now curling graceful, as in play,
  Now roaring, as in wrath.
The forests murmur'd, bow'd, and slept,
But on the mighty river swept,
As in impatient haste to gain
The gentler waters of the Maine,
Which flow'd along in stately pride,
To mingle with its parent tide.
But where the kindred waters meet,
  A rugged cliff there stood;
It rose above the eddying waves,
With hanging rocks and yawning caves,
  The guardian of the flood;
Fit haunt it seem'd for giant forms
  Of wild, unearthly mould,
The spirits of the winds and storms
  Their mystic rites to hold.
And o'er its rugged brow was spread
  The forest moss and flower,
And, 'mid a grove of solemn firs,
  Arose a ruin'd tower;
The ivied walls and turrets gray
Seem'd vainly struggling with decay,
Still frowning o'er the restless tide,
An emblem of unyielding pride.
All, all was desolate and lone;—
Beside its walls of crumbling stone
A giant beech its arms had thrown,
  And ivy on its threshold grew;
The shouts of mirth, the cries of strife,
The varied sounds of bustling life,
  Its walls no longer knew;
The moaning winds rush'd fitful by,
Blent with the owlet's dismal cry,
And every sad and mournful blast
Seem'd sadly wailing for the past!
Scarce could the wandering eye discern
In that rude pile, so dark and stern,
The remnants of its lofty wall,
The area of its spacious hall,
Or trace in masses rude and steep,
What once was barbacan and keep.

* * * * *

"Roll back, thou tide of time!" and bring
  The faded visions of the past,
And o'er the bard's enchanted string
  Thy veil of shadowy softness cast!
Fancy, unfold thy swiftest wing!
  Thou dreary present, be no more!
And I will tune my heart to sing
  In simple strains the days of yore!

These ruin'd walls again shall rise
  In all their ancient pride and power,
Again the gorgeous banner float
  In triumph from the stately tower!
The moss, the thorn, the poisonous weed
  Shall vanish from the cheerful hearth,
And the rude hall again resound
  With shouts of revelry and mirth!
Again beside that ruin'd gate
  The guard shall pace his weary round,
Again the warder's midnight cry
  Within its massive turrets sound;
Again the bright convivial band
  Shall close around its joyous hearth,
Again the vaulted halls return
  The shouts of revelry and mirth.
Oh, I could tell of thrilling scenes
  Enacted in that lone retreat;
How its paved courts have echoed back
  The clanking tread of armed feet;
How savage chiefs and knights of old,
With forms and souls of iron mould,
Have gather'd round this mountain hold,
  And form'd their councils here,
Then rush'd upon the field below,
  With clashing sword and spear;
And I could tell of princely dames,
  Of powerful lords and highborn peers,
Who dream'd not that their honour'd names
  Could perish in the lapse of years,
Or only live at times to aid
  The wandering minstrel's random song;
An old traditionary tale
  To float on memory's tide along;
And I could sing full many a strain
  Would call the life-blood from the cheek,
What fancy's eye would shrink to see,
  And boldest tongue would fear to speak.
But I will leave to nobler hands
  The framing of those mystic lays,
And only weave a simple tale
  Of later and of gentler days,
When daring souls of daring deeds
  Gave place to peaceful knights and squires,
And warlike gatherings on the field
  To feastings round their evening fires;
When nought remain'd of olden times,
  Of strife and rivalry and blood,
Save where some sterner barons held
  The remnants of an ancient feud.

'T was morning, and the shades of night
Roll'd backward from her brow of light,

As with majestic step she came,
With dewy locks and eyes of flame,
Her wreath of dancing light to twine
On the broad bosom of the Rhine.
The scene beneath her spread was rife
With sights and sounds of bustling life,
Of joyful shouts, and glad halloo,
And quick steps running to and fro.
The castle walls, so dark and gray
Tinged with the morning's cheerful ray,
Seem'd revelling their gloom away,
While from the court came, long and loud,
The shouts of an assembled crowd,
And on the mountain echoes borne,
Peal'd out the huntsman's mellow horn.
The clanking drawbridge fell across
The sparkling waters of the foss,
And servants hurried here and there
With bustling and important air;
Oft from the forest would appear
A group that bore the slaughter'd deer,
And distant shouts would faintly tell
As some new victim bleeding fell.
Light skiffs were floating down the Rhine,
Laden with casks of choicest wine,
And oarsmen bore the precious freight
For entrance to the postern gate.
Oft on the noisy tide along
The minstrel pour'd his careless song,
And all without was bustling glee.

* * * * *

Within, the castle hall was graced
With oaken tables, closely placed,
In preparation for a feast;
The ancient armour on the wall
Was cleansed, and gilt, and burnish'd all;
And helm, and casque, and corslet shone
Like mirrors in the morning sun;
Oh, could the warlike forms which wore
Those garments grim in days of yore,
Come to their mountain home once more,
How would they frown on scene so gay,
And sigh for spirits past away!

Beside the hearthstone of his hall,
The lord and master of them all,
The owner of this proud domain,
Stood, gazing on his menial train.
His ample robes were rich and gay,
His locks were slightly tinged with gray,
His eye, beneath its darker shroud,
Glanced, like a sunbeam from a cloud.

Hope realized and love's warm glow
Seem'd mingling o'er his furrow'd brow,
And smiles of pleasure told in part
The inward gladness of his heart.
But ever and anon there stole
Some softer feeling o'er his soul,
And something like a tear would roll
Unnoticed down his furrow'd cheek,—
The child of thoughts he could not speak.
Why rings the old castle with gladness this morn?
Why echoes the wood with the blithe hunter's horn?
Why standeth their lord with his train at their side,
And his eye beaming lightly with gratified pride?
This day it shall close o'er his doubts and his fears,
It shall witness the realized wishes of years,
And his name shall be join'd, by the dearest of ties,
To the only one worthy so brilliant a prize.
Whose fathers of old were his fathers' allies.
Why stealeth the teardrop so sad to his eye?
Why bursts from his bosom the half-smother'd sigh?
Alas, for that father! this day he must part
From the pride of his household, the joy of his heart;
No more may he gaze on his beautiful child,
Whose step ever bounded, whose lip ever smil'd;
Who cast such a charm o'er his wild mountain life
As the sunbeam may throw o'er the dark frowning cliff.
Now read ye the cause of the joyful array?
'Tis to welcome the lord of this festival day;
For he comes with his glittering train by his side,
To claim of her father his beautiful bride.
* * * * * *
* * * * *
* * * * * *

1837.

ELEGY UPON LEO, AN OLD HOUSE-DOG.

Thou poor old dog! too long affection's tongue
Hath left thy merits and thy death unsung;
Too long the muse hath sought for themes of fame,
And left untold thy well-remember'd name;
And though that name hath lived on memory's leaf,
Has touch'd for thee no thrilllng chords of grief.
Thou dear old dog! thou joy of childish years!
Here let me shed for thee my heartfelt tears;
Here let me turn from life's cold cares aside,
And weep that thou, my faithful friend, hast died.
Oh that no tears less pure might e'er be shed,
Than those which mourn a loved companion dead!
This is a world where faithful hearts are few,
Where love too oft is vain, too oft untrue;
And when some cherish'd form to earth is borne,
O'er fond affection's sever'd chain we mourn;

Thus I for thee, that one more friend hath gone,
Who, though a dog, could love for love alone.
Thou dear old friend! on memory's starlit tide,
Link'd with a sister's name thy name shall glide;
And when for her our tears flow fast and free,
Our hearts shall breathe a ling'ring sigh for thee;
For thee, that sister's dearest, earliest pet,
Whom even when dying she remember'd yet,
Thou wast her playmate in each childish hour,
When her light footsteps sprang from flower to flower;
When not a cloud on life's fair surface lay,
And joys alternate chased the hours away;
When her young heart beat high with infant glee,
And fondly sought to share those joys with thee.
And when youth's star arose on childhood's morn,
And loftier thoughts on time's dark wing were borne;
When hope look'd forward with exulting eye,
And fear, the coward, still crouch'd trembling nigh;
When long had pass'd those hours of infant glee,
Still, still she loved, and still would sport with thee.
1837. [Unfinished.]

MORNING.

How calm, how beautiful a scene is this!
When nature, waking from her silent sleep,
Bursts forth in light, and harmony, and joy!
When earth, and sky, and air are glowing all
With gaiety and life, and pensive shades
Of morning loveliness are cast around!
The purple clouds, so streak'd with crimson light,
Bespeak the coming of majestic day;
Mark how the crimson grows more crimson still,
While ever and anon a golden beam
Seems darting out its radiance!
Herald of day! where is that mighty form
Which clothes you all in splendour, and around
Your colourless, pale forms spreads the bright hues
Of heaven? He cometh from his gorgeous couch,
And gilds the bosom of the glowing east.
1837.

LINES

WRITTEN AFTER SHE BEGAN TO FEAR THAT HER DISEASE WAS PAST REMEDY.

I ONCE thought life was beautiful,
  I once thought life was fair,
Nor deem'd that all its light could fade
  And leave but darkness there.

But now I know it could not last—
  The fairy dream has fled!
Though *thirteen summers* scarce have past
  Above this youthful head.

Yes, life—'twas all a dream—but now
  I see thee as thou art;
I see how slight a thing can shade
  The sunshine of the heart.

I see that all thy brightest hours,
  Unmark'd, have pass'd away;
And now I feel how sweet they were,
  I cannot bid them stay.

In childish love or childish play
  My happiest hours were spent,
While scarce my infant tongue could say
  What joy or pleasure meant.

And now, when my young heart looks up,
  Life's gayest smiles to meet;
Now, when in youth her brightest charms
  Would seem so doubly sweet;

Now fade the dreams which bound my soul
  As with the chains of truth;
Oh that those dreams had stay'd awhile,
  To vanish with my youth!

Oh! once did hope look sweetly down,
  To check each rising sigh;
But disappointment's iron frown
  Has dimm'd her sparkling eye.

And once I loved a brother too,
  Our youngest and our best,
But death's unerring arrow sped,
  And laid him down to rest.

* * * * *
* * * *
* * * * *
* * * *

But now I know those hours of peace
  Were never form'd to last;
That those fair days of guileless joy
  Are past—for ever past!

January, 1837.

TO MY OLD HOME AT PLATTSBURG.

THAT dear old home, where pass'd my childhood's years,
Where fond affection wiped my infant tears;
Where first I learn'd from whence my blessings came,
And lisp'd, in faltering tones, a mother's name;
That cherish'd home, where memory fondly clings,
Where eager fancy spreads her soaring wings;
Around whose scenes my thoughts delight to stray,
And pass the hours in pleasing dreams away.
Oh! shall I ne'er behold thy waves again,
My native lake, my beautiful Champlain?
Shall I no more above thy ripples bend
In sweet communion with my childhood's friend?
Shall I no more behold thy rolling wave,
The patriot's cradle and the warrior's grave?
Thy banks, illumined by the sun's last glow,
Thine islets mirror'd in the waves below?
Back, back, thou present—robed in shadows lie!
And rise the past before my raptured eye!
Fancy shall gild the frowning lapse between,
And memory's hand shall paint the glowing scene;
And I shall view my much-loved home again,
My native village and my sweet Champlain,
With former friends retrace my footsteps o'er,
And muse delighted on thy verdant shore.
Alas! the vision fades, the dream is past;
Dissolved the spell by sportive fancy cast!
Why, why should thus our brightest dreams depart,
And scenes illusive cheat the sorrowing heart?
Where'er through future life my footsteps roam,
I ne'er shall find a spot like thee, my home!
With all my joys the thoughts of thee shall blend,
And join'd with thee shall rise my childhood's friend!

1837.

FAME.

A FRAGMENT.

OH Fame! thou trumpeter of dead men's deeds!
Thou idol of the heart, thou empty flatterer,
That, like the heathen of the Nile, embalmest
Those that thou design'st to love, and ever hiding
Their vices and their follies with a veil
Of soft concealment, doth exalt them high
Above the common crowd, crown'd with thy might,

That future years may copy and admire.
Thou bright, alluring dream! thou dazzling star!
Where shall we find thee! Thou art call'd
Fickle and vain, and worthless of pursuit,
Yet * * * * *

1838.

ON MY MOTHER'S FIFTIETH BIRTHDAY.

Yes, mother, fifty years have fled,
With rapid footsteps o'er thy head;
Have pass'd with all their motley train,
And left thee on thy couch of pain!
How many smiles, and sighs, and tears,
How many hopes, and doubts, and fears,
Have vanish'd with that lapse of years!
Though past, those hours of pain and grief
Have left their trace on memory's leaf;
Have stamp'd their footprints on the heart,
In lines which never can depart;
Their influence on the mind must be
As endless as eternity.
Years, ages, to oblivion roll,
Their memory forms the deathless soul;
They leave their impress as they go,
And shape the mind for joy or woe!
Yes, mother, fifty years have past,
And brought thee to their close at last.
Oh that we all could gaze, like thee,
Back on that dark and tideless sea,
And 'mid its varied records find
A heart at ease with all mankind,
A firm and self-approving mind!
Grief, that had broken hearts less fine,
Hath only served to strengthen thine;
Time, that doth chill the fancy's play,
Hath kindled thine with purer ray;
And stern disease, whose icy dart
Hath power to chill the shrinking heart,
Has left thine warm with love and truth,
As in the halcyon days of youth.
Oh turn not from the meed of praise
A daughter's willing justice pays;
But greet with smiles of love again
This tribute of a daughter's pen.

1838.

THE STORM HATH PASSED BY.

THE storm hath pass'd by, like an angry cloud
Which sweeps o'er the brow of the azure heaven;
The sun and the earth to its sway hath bow'd,
And each radiant beam from the scene been driven.

All hail to the smile of the cloudless sky!
All hail to the sun as he rides on high!
All hail to the heavens' ethereal blue,
And to nature, when deck'd in her own lovely hue!

It hath pass'd! the storm, like a giant form,
Which summons the winds from their tempest cave;
Which opens a grave in each ocean wave,
And wraps the world in its shroud of gloom.

Oh! welcome the smile of the gladden'd earth!
And welcome the voice of the wood-bird's mirth!
And welcome these varying hues which delight
Like dawn at the close of a wearisome night.

The clouds have pass'd, with the shadows they cast,
And hush'd is the sound of the wind-god's power,
And his deep, wild blast, as the tempest pass'd,
Which rang on the ear at the midnight hour.

Oh! welcome the soft, balmy zephyrs of spring!
And welcome the perfumes they silently bring!
And the rosy-tinged cloudlets that gracefully glide
O'er the fair brow of heaven in beauty and pride!

It hath fled in its night, the dark spirit of night,
Which cast such a shade o'er the light of the soul;
It hath fled and died, while the sunset beam
From its surface triumphantly backward shall roll.

Oh! welcome the smiles of a gladden'd heart!
And welcome the joy which those smiles impart!
And welcome the light of that sparkling eye
Which tells that the storm in its dread hath pass'd by!

Ballston, 1838.

EPITAPH ON A YOUNG ROBIN.

DESPITE the curling lip, the smile of scorn,
Thine early fate, oh! hapless bird, we mourn;
Too soon withdrawn thy scanty store of breath,
Too soon thy sprightly carols hush'd in death!
Here let us lay thee on thy mother's breast,
Where no rude steps shall come, no cares molest,
No cruel puss disturb thy silent rest.

Saratoga, 1838.

TO A MOONBEAM.

Ah, whither art straying, thou spirit of light,
  From thy home in the boundless sky?
Why lookest thou down from the empire of night,
  With that silent and sorrowful eye?

Thou art resting here on the autumn leaf,
  Where it fell from its throne of pride;
But oh, what pictures of joy or grief,
  What scenes thou art viewing beside!

Thou art glancing down on the ocean waves,
  As they proudly heave and swell;
Thou art piercing deep in its coral caves,
  Where the green-hair'd sea-nymphs dwell!

Thou art pouring thy beams on Italia's shore,
  As though it were sweet to be there;
Thou art lighting the prince to his stately couch,
  And the monk to his midnight prayer.

Thou art casting a fretwork of silver rays
  Over ruin, and palace, and tower;
Thou art gilding the temples of former days,
  In this holy and beautiful hour.

Thou art silently roaming through forest and glade,
  Where mortal foot never hath trod;
Thou art lighting the grave where the dust is laid,
  While the spirit hath gone to its God!

Thou art looking on those I love! oh, wake
  In their hearts some remembrance of me,
And gaze on them thus, till their bosoms partake
  Of the love I am breathing to thee.

And perchance thou art casting thy mystic spell
  On the beautiful land of the blest,
Where the dear ones of earth have departed to dwell,
  Where the weary have fled to their rest.

Oh yes! with that soft and ethereal beam,
  Thou hast look'd on the mansions of bliss,
And some spirit, perchance, of that glorified world
  Hath breathed thee a message to this.

'T is a mission of love, for no threatening shade
  Can be blent with thy spirit-like hues,
And thy ray thrills the heart, as love only can thrill,
  And while raising it, melts and subdues.

And it whispers compassion; for lo, on thy brow
  Is the sadness of angels enshrined;
And a misty veil, as of purified tears,
  Round thy beautiful form is entwined.

Hail, beam of the blessed! my heart
  Has drunk deep of thy magical power,
And each thought and each feeling seems bathed
  In the light of this exquisite hour!
Sweet ray, I have proved thee so fair
  In this dark world of mourning and sin,
May I hail thee more bright in that pure region, where
  Nor sorrow nor death enter in.

1838.

EVENING.

O'er the broad vault of heaven, so calmly bright,
Twilight has gently drawn her veil of gray,
And tinged with sombre hue the golden clouds,
Fast fading into nothing: o'er the expanse
Are swiftly stealing hues, which mildly blend
And shadow o'er the pure transparence
Of the azure heaven. Now is night array'd
In all her solemn livery, and one by one
Appear the sparkling gems which deck her robe.
Each glittering star shines brighter than its wont,
As though some brilliant festival were held,
Some joyful meeting in the courts above.
Now mark yon group of amber-tinted clouds,
Shrouding the silvery form of Luna;
Their melting tints vanish away, and then
The pale, cold moon springs up unshackled
In her vast domain. Fair empress of the sky!
Chaste queen! thy hallow'd beauty can impart
A soften'd radiance to each sombre cloud
Of melancholy night, and, like a noble mind,
Immersed in seas of darkness, thou canst cast
A portion of thy brilliant, mellow'd softness
Around the deepening gloom. While viewing thee
A sweet and pensive calm o'erspreads my soul,
And, conjured by thy gentle, melting rays,
Unerring memory hastens to my aid;
With her, I view again my own dear home,
My native village, 'neath thy cloudless sky
Serenely sleeping: 't is as fair a picture
Of unsullied peace as ever nature drew.
Thy rays are dancing on the gentle river,
In one unbroken stream of molten silver,
And marking in the glassy Saranac
Thy graceful outline, while the fairy isles
Which on its bosom rest are slumbering
In thy light, while the fair branches, bending
O'er thy wave, turn their green leaves above,
And bathe in one celestial flood of glory.

There, on its banks, I view the dear old home,
That ever loved and blooming theatre,
Where those I most revere have borne their parts,
Amid its changing scenes. Before the threshold
Tower the lofty trees, and each high branch
Is gently rocking in the summer breeze,
And sending forth a low, sweet murmur,
Like the soft breathings of a seraph's harp.
Around its humble porch entwines the vine,
While the sweetbriar and the blushing rose
Now hang their heads in slumber, and the grass
And fragrant clover scent the loaded air.
Oh, my loved home, how gladly would I rove
Amid thy soft retreats, and from decay
Protect thy mouldering mansion, tend thy flowers,
Prune the wild boughs, and there in solitude
Listless remain, unknowing and unknown—
Oh no, not quite alone, for memory,
And hope, and fond delight shall mingle there.

1838. [Unfinished.]

A POETICAL LETTER TO HENRIETTA.

Once more, Henrietta, I open your sheet
To glance at its contents so playful and sweet,
To admire the flow of its easy strain,
And pen you an answer in *nonsense* again.
Perchance you may turn from my page away,
And with scornful lip and expression say,
"I think she might better have spent her time,
Than in stringing such masses of jingling rhyme;"
And perhaps I might,—I admit the blame,
But like others, continue my fault the same.
However, I think such a *deacon* as you
May need the refreshment of nonsense too;
That a creature so sober as you are, my friend,
Her ear to the whisperings of folly may lend.
Never mind—'tis a fancy has cross'd my brain,
Right or wrong, good or evil, I'll finish my strain.
I wish you, my dear Henrietta, could know
How much I am grieved that I now cannot go,
That our dreams of enjoyment have vanish'd in smoke,
And the castles we builded on vapour are broke!
But such are the chances of life,—it is fit
That with stoical fortitude we should submit.
Am I not philosophic?—A fortnight pass'd by
With its fretting and grieving, its tear and its sigh;
Then— a month, peopled well with regretting by me,
And—behold me submissive as mortal can be!
But jesting aside—'tis a very sad thing
To be torn from hope's anchor, where fondly we cling.

I too had been cherishing feelings as vain,
Nursing hopes as delusive, as sweet in my brain;
I had waited in fancy your loved form to see,
With a heart just as happy as happy could be;
Had met you, embraced you, and welcomed you here,
When lo! the bright dream dissolved in a tear!
Like the gay, gorgeous bubble, which floats for awhile,
But departs ere you welcome its hues with a smile.
You were wishing for wings—I enclose you a pair,
Which I hope you will use with all possible care,
For they were not prepared in a mortal mould,
But were form'd by a fairy in purple and gold!
While riding one day by the green-wood side,
This fairy in beautiful garments I spied;
Her mantle with dew-drops was spangled o'er—
She had fairies behind her and fairies before,
And many and gay were the jewels she wore;
But the wings which she raised to her delicate brow
Were the purest of azure and white as the snow!
I bow'd at the foot of the fairy throne,
And begg'd of her beautiful wings like her own.
I sued for the favour in friendship's name;
She assented, and smiling, admitted the claim.
All sparkling and pure as the evening star,
I gather'd the wings from the fairy's bower,
And came home exulting, impatient to send
The gift in its freshness and glow to my friend.
Elated with pride I exposed them to view,
But the touch of a mortal had clouded their hue!
So marvel no more at their dimness — believe
That the very same wings are the wings you receive.
Should my story too wild and too fanciful seem,
Oh, call it no fiction, but name it — a dream.
I am reading "Josephus," a famous old Jew,
Whose name is, I doubt not, familiar to you.
He begins with the world, and proceeds to relate
How the Jews from a nothing grew prosperous and great;
How Jerusalem reign'd as the Queen of the East,
Till her sacred religion was scorn'd and oppress'd;
Then murder, and rapine, and famine ensued,
Till the fields of Judea were streaming with blood.
How I wish you were reading it with me, my friend;
Your presence a charm to each sentence would lend.

Your father's return, you remark, is the time
To send you a budget of love and of rhyme;
The *love* be assured you will always possess,
And you 'll have *rhyme* enough when you once have read this.
So you see what that *love* has induced me to do,
With it *maybe* a *fear* of your scolding too! —

It is evening — the close of a beautiful day,
And the last rays of sunset are fading away;

Till nothing remains but a faint rosy hue,
Just mingling in with a fainter blue.
The shadows of twilight are closing around,
Not a murmur is heard but the cricket's sound,
And pensive thoughts o'er my heart-strings creep
As the "unvoiced" breezes around me sweep.
'T is a tranquil hour, and I lazily lie,
Gazing up at my ease on the delicate sky,
With the sombre light on my dim page playing,
And my pen through its numberless labyrinths straying.
How gentle the spell of this exquisite hour!
How soothing, how sweet its mysterious power!
It steals o'er my heart, like a breeze o'er the lake,
Each half-buried accent of music to wake.
The *kitten* beside me hath fled from its play,
And close in my bosom is nestling away;
And the trembling leaf, and the bending flower,
And the insect millions acknowledge its power.
How the fancy *will* fly from the present, and roam
O'er each corner of earth 'neath heaven's high dome!
Perchance, like myself, you may cloud-gazing be;
Perchance, my sweet friend, you are thinking of me,
And this scene, like a beautiful image of rest,
Has awakened the same delicate chords in *your* breast;
And perchance—how provoking!—that twinkling lamp-night
Hath dissolved with its brilliance my dreams of delight,
Hath deepen'd to blackness the mantle of gray,
And chased all my beautiful visions away.
So it is—they have fled—and again I descend
To converse upon every-day themes with my friend;
But the end of my paper convinces me still
That I soon must release thee, my trusty goosequill;
Though my breast and my head are yet aching to write,
I must bid you, dear Hetty, a loving good night.
If your ears are not tired of the jingling of rhyme,
I will finish my musical letter next time;
In the meanwhile, believe me sincerely to be
Your affectionate scribbler,

MARGARET M. D.

Ballston, 1838.

LINES

ON SEEING SOME FRAGMENTS FROM THE TOMB OF VIRGIL.

HAVE these gray relics, crumbling into dust,
Once rested 'neath Italia's burning sky?
Has this cold remnant of what once was stone,
Reflected back her warm cerulean dye?

Have these white fragments rested o'er the sod
Hallow'd by virgil's ever-sacred clay?
And have they mingled with the grass-grown mound
Which o'er the classic hero's bosom lay?

Perhaps the crumbling stones beside me now
  Fell from the mouldering marble at his head—
The icy tomb which hides his noble brow,
  For ever hallow'd by the mighty dead.

In fancy o'er Italia's fields I roam,
  In fancy view the poet's lowly grave,
Round which, as I in silent sorrow bend,
  The flowering myrtle and the cypress wave.

1838. [Unfinished.]

A SHORT SKETCH

OF THE MOST IMPORTANT IDEAS CONTAINED IN COUSIN'S "INTRODUCTION TO THE HISTORY OF PHILOSOPHY."

According to Cousin, there are three elements of consciousness, three first ideas of the infinite, the finite and their relations succeeding each other in the above order. He believes that as the history of an individual such is the history of mankind in general; that as there are three fundamental ideas there must be three epochs of the world to develope those ideas. As the first idea is that of the infinite, the first age of the world will express this idea in its laws, its arts, its religion, and its philosophy: this will predominate. When fully developed, the idea of the finite will succeed; action, variety, and liberty will take the place of slavery and immobility; man will begin to find *himself*. All the elements of his nature will be brought into action, although still subjected to the predominating principle. When *this* is exhausted, in its turn the idea of the relations between the finite and the infinite will come; man will join these two great principles; every element will assume its proper station without asserting undue authority over the others; man will at once generalize and particularize; and as this is the highest developement of the ideas of humanity, this epoch will be the last. After giving this expansive view of man and his destination, he proceeds to show that different climates and countries are destined for the development of different ideas; that the idea of the infinite must necessarily prevail in a large continent surrounded by vast seas, traversed by inaccessible mountains, and divided by immense deserts, with a burning and enervating climate, where every thing leads to and expresses the idea of the vast, the absolute, the infinite: such a country is Asia. On the contrary, the idea of the finite will occupy a smaller country, intersected by rivers affording every facility of inland communication and commerce, surrounded by small seas, inviting the inhabitants to intercourse with neighbouring nations, and filled with beautiful and diversified scenery, *all* bearing the impress of the finite, urging to action and enterprise, and devoid of that solemn and sombre unity of expression which prevailed in its parent epoch: such a country is Greece. That position of the world destined for the developement of the last and most perfect epoch, must unite the two great external features of the former countries, as it is to assist in expressing the two great ideas in perfect unison with each other. It must combine the sublime with the beautiful, every advantage of internal commerce and high civilization with a manifest appearance of magnitude and duration; it must possess a perfect and minute individuality with a great and striking general character; a vast continent surrounded with vast oceans, containing mighty rivers and inland seas, broad prairies, and long ranges of mountains, together with fertile valleys and streams, and all the minor qualities of a rich and magnificent country, containing facilities for the minutest internal improvements, guided and governed by a lofty and abstract spirit of generalization—thus uniting the relative and the absolute, the finite and the infinite! such a country is America. He then proceeds to speak of war, its causes, and its effects. He considers it not only beneficial but necessary. War is a combat of ideas. Underneath the great and prominent idea of an epoch there exist minor elements in a nation, as in an individual: one people expresses one element, one idea; another seizes upon and developes a second: these truths elevate themselves against each other and combat—hence war. When one of these ideas is exhausted, it is opposed and superseded by a newer and a better one—hence conquest. One idea and one nation make room for another idea and another nation; one epoch is destroyed, and another arises. Mark the benefits of war: had it never existed there had been but one era of the world, and humanity could never have progressed. He then proceeds to justify conquests. He considers that the event proves the right; that when a newer and nobler spirit rises against an exhausted one, that spirit must conquer, and ought to conquer. He does not believe in absolute error; he believes every error is a part of truth, and raised to an undeserved superiority among the elements of humanity.

1838. [Unfinished.]

BRIEF NOTES FROM COUSIN'S PHILOSOPHY,

MADE DURING THE WINTER OF 1838.

HIS first position is this: as soon as man receives consciousness he is surrounded by objects in a world hostile to himself, but by exertion and developement of his power, he has conquered and modified matter, and has, as it were, impressed with his image and rendered it subservient to his will. The first man who overcame any obstacles in the way of his desires created industry, and the first who measured the slightest space around him or united the objects before him, introduced the science of mathematics. All these, mathematics, physics, and political economy, have one object, utility or the useful; but there are other relations in which men stand to each other, besides those of ***hurtful*** or ***useful***, the ***just*** and the ***unjust***. Upon the idea of the useful, man altered the external appearance of nature; upon the idea of justice he created a new society, maintaining their own rights, and respecting the rights of others. But man goes further: besides the hurtful or the useful, the just or the unjust, he has inherent in his nature the idea of the beautiful and its opposite. Impressed with this idea, man seizes, developes, and purifies it in his thought, until he finds that thought superior to the object which presented it. Every thing that is beautiful in nature is also imperfect, and fades when compared with the idea it awakens. Thus, man not only reforms nature and society by industry and the laws of justice, but also remodels those objects which present to him the idea of beauty, and renders them more beautiful than ever. But man is not yet satisfied—he looks beyond the world of industry and arts, and conceives God. The idea of God as separate from the world, but scarcely himself in it, is *natural religion;* but he does not rest there; he creates another world, in which he perceives nothing but its relation to God, the world of * * he expands and elevates the sentiment of religion. Philosophy succeeds. Philosophy is the developement of thought; it may be good or bad, but in itself it is demanded by the mind as much as religion, the sciences, &c. Cousin proves this position by a rapid examination of the wants of man * * * * * * * *

LENORE.

A POEM.

INTRODUCTION.

Why should I sing? The scenes which roused
 The bards of old, arouse no more;
The reign of poesy hath pass'd,
 And all her glowing dreams are o'er!

Why should I sing? A thousand harps
 Have touch'd the self-same chords before,
Of love, and hate, and lofty pride,
 And fields of battle bathed in gore!

Why should *I* seek the burning fount
 From whence their glowing fancies sprung?
My feeble muse can only sing
 What other, nobler bards have sung!

Thus did I breathe my sad complaint,
 As, bending o'er my silent lyre,
I sigh'd for some romantic theme
 Its slumbering music to inspire.

Scarce had I spoke, when o'er my soul
 A low reproving whisper came;
My heart instinctive shrank with awe,
 And conscience tinged my cheek with shame.

"Down with thy vain, repining thoughts,
 Nor dare to breathe those thoughts again,
Or endless sleep shall bind thy lyre,
 And scorn repel thy bursting strain!

"What though a thousand bards have sung
 The charms of earth, of air, or sky!
A thousand minstrels, old and young,
 Pour'd forth their varied melody!

"What though, inspired, they stoop'd to drink
 At Fancy's fountain o'er and o'er!
Say, feeble warbler, dost thou think
 The glowing streamlet flows no more?

"Because a nobler hand has cull'd
 The loveliest of our earthly flowers,
Dost thou believe that all of bloom
 Hath fled those bright, poetic bowers!

"Know then, that long as earth shall roll,
 Revolving 'neath yon azure sky,
Music shall charm each purer soul,
 And Fancy's fount shall never dry!

"Long as the rolling seasons change,
And nature holds her empire here;
Long as the human eye can range
O'er yon pure heaven's expanded sphere;

"Long as the ocean's broad expanse
Lies spread beneath yon broader sky;
Long as the playful moonbeams dance,
Like fairy forms, on billows high;

"So long, unbound by mortal chain,
Shall genius spread her soaring wing;
So long the pure poetic fount,
Uncheck'd, unfetter'd, on shall spring.

"Thou say'st the days of song have past,
The glowing days of wild romance,
When war pour'd out his clarion blast,
And valour bow'd at beauty's glance!

"When every hour that onward sped,
Was fraught with some bewildering tale;
When superstition's shadowy hand
O'er trembling nations cast her veil!

"Thou say'st that life's unvaried stream
In peaceful ripples wears away;
And years produce no fitting theme
To rouse the poet's slumbering lay.

"Not so, while yet the hand of God
Each year adorns his teeming earth;
While dew-drops deck the verdant sod,
And birds, and bees, and flowers have birth;

"While every day unfolds anew
Some charm to meet the searching eye;
While buds of every varying hue
Are bursting 'neath a summer sky.

"'Tis true that war's unsparing hand
Hath ceased to bathe our fields in gore;
That hate hath quench'd his burning brand,
And tyrant princes reign no more.

"But dost thou think that scenes like these
Form all the poetry of life?
Would thy untutor'd muse delight
In scenes of rapine, blood, and strife?

"No—there are boundless fields of thought,
Where roving spirits never soar'd;
Which wildest fancy never sought,
Or boldest intellect explored!

"Then bow not silent o'er thy lyre,
But tune its chords to nature's praise;
At every turn thine eye shall meet
Fit themes to form a poet's lays.

"Go forth, prepared her sweetest smiles
 In all her loveliest scenes to view;
Nor deem, though others there have knelt,
 Thou may'st not weave thy garland too!"

It paused—I felt how true the words,
 How sweet the comfort they convey'd;
I chased my mourning thoughts away—
 I heard—I trusted—I obey'd.

DEDICATION.

TO THE SPIRIT OF MY SISTER LUCRETIA.

Oh thou, so early lost, so long deplored!
 Pure spirit of my sister, be thou near!
And while I touch this hallow'd harp of thine,
 Bend from the skies, sweet sister, bend and hear!

For thee I pour this unaffected lay,
 To thee these simple numbers all belong;
For though thine earthly form hath pass'd away,
 Thy memory still inspires my childish song.

Then take this feeble tribute! 'tis thine own—
 Thy fingers sweep my trembling heartstrings o'er,
Arouse to harmony each buried tone,
 And bid its waken'd music sleep no more!

Long hath thy voice been silent, and thy lyre
 Hung o'er thy grave in death's unbroken rest
But when its last sweet tones were borne away,
 One answering echo linger'd in my breast.

Oh thou pure spirit! if thou hoverest near,
 Accept these lines, unworthy though they be,
Faint echoes from thy fount of song divine,
 By thee inspired, and dedicate to thee!

CANTO FIRST.

'Twas nightfall on the Rhine! the day
In pensive glory stole away,
Flinging his last and brightest glow
Full on the restless waves below,
As if an angel's hand had dyed
With hues from heaven the sparkling tide!
The fleeting ray an instant beam'd,—
O'er hill and vale and rock it stream'd,
Till the dark, time-defying cliff,
Seem'd glowing, melting into life—
Then swiftly fading, glided o'er,
And left it lonelier than before.

The distant hills of sombre blue,
Tinged with that rich and varying hue,
Now darker and more mingled grew;
The Rhine, enrobed in shadows gray,

Roll'd on its giant path,
Lashing the rocks which barr'd its way,
Now curling graceful, as in play,
Now roaring as in wrath!
While trembling in the tinted west,
The fair moon rear'd her silver crest,
And fleecy clouds, as snow-wreaths pale,
Twined on her brow their graceful veil;
And one by one, with tiny flame,
Night's heavenly tapers softly came,
And toward their mistress trembling stole,
Like pleasing memories o'er the soul.

And shade by shade her brilliance grew,
As past away the sunset hue,
Till o'er the heaving Rhine she stood,
Bathing in light its sleeping flood;
Pouring her full and melting ray
Where rock and hill and forest lay,
And where, in clust'ring trees embower'd,
An ancient castle proudly tower'd:
O'er the gray walls her glances play'd,
O'er drawbridge, moat, and tower they stray'd,
As striving with that holy light
To pierce the works of earthly might,
And cast one heavenly beam within
The abode of human toil and sin.

Can sin and sorrow and despair
Be frowning 'neath a sky so fair?
Can nature sleep while tempests roll
Impetuous o'er the tortured soul?

Mark yonder taper, dimly beaming,
From the lone turret faintly streaming
Casting athwart the brow of night
Its wavering and uncertain light!
Beside that torch sit guilt and care
And dark remorse, and coward fear;
And fever'd thought is borrowing there
The haggard visage of despair!
There, with his aged fingers prest
In clasp convulsive to his breast,
Bows, as with secret guilt and pain,
The master of this broad domain.

His ample robes around him stray,
His locks are deeply tinged with gray,
And his dark, low'ring brow is fraught
With marks of avarice and thought.
At every sound which meets his ear,
He starts instinctive as with fear,
And his keen eye roams here and there,
With anxious and expectant air.

His seem'd a mind of timid mould,
Sway'd by some spirit, fierce and bold,

Which lean'd to virtue, but could yield
When vice to avarice appeal'd—
Which gazed on crime with shrinking eye,
But was too cowardly to fly.
He started—heard, with troubled air
A tread upon the turret stair;
Wiped from his brow the gathering dew,
And closer still his mantle drew,
When wide the massive portal flew!

As wondering at this entrance rude,
The aged host in silence stood;
While with a stern unchanging look,
The stranger doff'd his ample cloak,
Unloosed his bonnet's clasping band,
And toward the baron stretch'd his hand.
His host the friendly gesture saw,
But shrank in hatred or in awe—
Then starting, as with eager haste,
The proffer'd hand he warmly prest,
And smiled a welcome to his guest.
The latter mark'd, with flashing glance,
That shrinking fear, this mean pretence,
And then resumed the smile of scorn
His curling lip had lately worn.

Uninjured by the frosts of time,
He seem'd advanced in manhood's prime;
His form was tall, his mien erect,
His locks, though matted by neglect,
Curl'd closely round his swarthy brow
While his dark orbits flashed below.
Nature, with fingers firm and bold,
Had made a form of finest mould,
And painted on his childish face
The outline of each manly grace;
But pride and art, those imps of sin,
Had crept the empty shrine within;
Had taught his heart each serpent wile,
And lent his lip its fiendish smile.

His brow was knit with thought and care,
And dark design was scowling there;
His glance inspired both hate and fear—
Now withering with its biting sneer,
Now flashing like the mid-day sun,
Which scorches all it looks upon.

Boldness and artifice combined
To form the dark, perverted mind,
Within that goodly frame enshrined;
And he, whose steps in early youth
Some kindly hand had led to truth,
With active brain, and heart that burn'd,
From that unpointed pathway turn'd,
Unwarn'd, unguided, plunged within
The blackening gulf of shame and sin.

On his dark face the baron's eye
Gazed anxious and inquiringly,
And when he mark'd his silent guest
Draw forth a casket from the vest
Which folded loosely on his breast,
With half-conceal'd, convulsive gasp,
He stretch'd his eager hand to clasp
The sparkling treasure in his grasp.

But with a smile, more full than speech,
The stranger drew it from his reach;
On the rude bench the casket laid,
Beside his dagger's glittering blade;
Drew near his host, who quaked with dread,
And thus, in low, stern accents said:

"Thou deemest right—that gem doth hold
A something dearer far than gold;
To *thee*, more precious than thy life,
To *me*, the cause of toil and strife!
'T is *that*, which in another's hands,
Would tear thee from these goodly lands,
Send thee and thy fair daughter forth
From all thou thinkest life is worth,
From titles, honours, lands, and hall,
And to young Erstein yield them all,
Which in thine *own* will banish fear,
And make thee lord and master here,
Unchallenged by the rightful heir:
(Then in a low, impressive tone,)
But hold,—that prize is still *mine own!*"

"Villain!"—"Nay, curb that wrath of thine—
Hast thou forgot one word of mine
Could hurl thee from thy high estate,
To beggar'd infamy and hate?
Could I not rend the shrouding veil,
And tell the wondering world the tale;
How when thy kinsman died in Spain,
Thou seized upon his fair domain,
His titles, and his wealth; despite
His heir, the youthful Erstein's right?
Could I not tell, how many a year,
With artful wile and coward fear,
Thou sought'st with vain and mean pretence
These proofs of his inheritance,
That thou might'st thus for aye destroy
The claims of this romantic boy?
Think'st thou I will this power forego,
Another's lands on thee bestow,
The rightful heir for thee despoil,
And gain but hatred, fear and toil?

"Speak not, old man! By heaven! I swear,
Yon casket and its contents there
Were not more safe from grasp of thine,
Though buried in the heaving Rhine,

If thou grant not, unquestion'd, free,
The guerdon I shall claim of thee!"
Ask aught," the baron faltering cried;
"Leave me my gold! take aught beside!"
The stranger knit his swarthy brow,
"Old dotard! yes, thy gold and thou!
Swear by the God whom thou dost fear,
Swear by that gold thou dost revere,
My suit is granted!" and his eye
Flash'd on the baron fearfully.

"Herman, I swear!" he mutter'd low,
And the blood left his cheek and brow;
Scarce said he, ere his fearful guest
The casket's jewell'd lock had press'd,
And from its case of richest mould,
Drawn forth a written parchment fold,
With eager hands, and sparkling eyes,
The aged baron seized the prize,
Tore it in haste, and opening wide
The vine-wreath'd lattice at his side,
With fix'd, exulting gaze, consign'd
Its fragments to the midnight wind.

That scene and act, that form and face,
A painter's hand had loved to trace:
The moon, as if the scene to shroud,
Had sought the bosom of a cloud;
The murmuring waves, the rustling trees,
The fitful sighing of the breeze,
And the hoarse owlet's distant tone,
Blent in one soft and wailing moan,
Disturb'd that midnight calm alone.

His brow with burning drops bedew'd,
The old man at his lattice stood,
And scann'd with sparkling, lingering eye,
Each fragment as it floated by;
And Herman mark'd his host the while
With sneering and contemptuous smile:
At length, with mien of joyous pride,
The baron hasten'd to his side,
And thus in tones of triumph cried:

"*Now* have they perish'd! all that might
Prove to the world young Erstein's right!
His claim is as it ne'er had been,
And these broad lands are mine again!
When first by youthful pride impell'd,
This princely barony I held,
I knew my kinsman lived, and knew
These fatal proofs existed too;
But all my cunning found not *where*.
Thus lived I years, in doubt and care,
In trembling terror, lest my name
Some evil chance should brand with shame;

Or more, lest all my hoarded gold
Should vanish from my loosening hold.

"Blest be the day, good Herman, when
Thou camest from thy mountain den,
And said that thou thyself had known
The secret which I deem'd mine own;
Despair and anguish made me dumb;
I thought the fatal hour had come.
O'erwhelm'd in grief I little knew
Thy heart, so noble and so true,
Nor thought the object of my fears,
Could crown the fruitless search of years!
But knows young Erstein of his claim
To Arnheim's barony and name?
Will he behold his goodly lands
Seized by a stranger's trembling hands?"

"He knows it not; romantic, gay,
To distant lands he roam'd away,
And sought adventure and renown
In nobler countries than his own.
One month return'd from foreign war,
He lives within his lonely tower;
Scouring the forest far and near,
And hunting down the antler'd deer;
But should he search the written past,
And learn this fatal truth at last,
His heart and arm are strong to fight
In brave defending of his right."

"Ay, *should* he so, good Herman!"—Now
A livid paleness robed his brow;
But quick returning crimson spread,
While thus his dark accomplice said:
And canst thou not the path descry?
Why then, good baron, *he must die;*
This barrier in thy way *I hate,*
And dark and wild shall be his fate.
He scorn'd me, and I vow'd to seal
My vengeance on this faithful steel,
And happy shall that moment be
Which bows his lofty crest to me.
But night wears on—I must away—
Thou hast the casket's price to pay."

The old man raised his troubled eye,
As longing, fearing to reply,
Then slowly gasp'd, with effort bold,
"Ay, ay, what wouldst thou, land or gold?"
"Thou hast a beauteous daughter—she
The guerdon of my toil must be!
Her hand must be unite with mine
Before another sun decline
On the broad bosom of the Rhine!"

With smother'd shriek and heaving breast
The father knelt before his guest.
"My child! my own Lenore! *thy bride!*—
Ask aught, ask every thing beside.
The dews which wet the summer flower
Are not more sinless than Lenore!
Through years of guilt and care, my child
Cheer'd my soul's darkness till it smiled!
Now that my locks are turned to gray
Thou *canst* not tear that child away!—
Her gentle purity hath been
A star on life's beclouded scene,
Music her voice, and heaven her eye,—
Oh leave her, leave her, or I die!"

With kindling glances Herman heard
Each smother'd groan, each anguish'd word,
And then replied in tones of scorn,
"Up from thy knees! hast thou not sworn
To grant my suit? dost thou forget
Thine *all* is in my clutches yet?
I swear that she, and only she,
Shall buy my bond of secresy!"

"Forget! why can I not forget?—
Would we had never, never met!
Leave me, for God's sake, leave me now!—
Oh my torn heart, my burning brow!"
"Say thou wilt make thy daughter mine
Before another sun decline,
And I depart to come no more,
Until that joyous bridal hour!"

"Wretch! fiend! I will!"—The accents hung
As loth to leave his faltering tongue;
But ere had ceased that lingering tone,
He turn'd and found himself alone.
The taper's waving glimmer fell
On the rude pavement of the cell,
Where with his trembling fingers prest
Upon his heaving, labouring breast,
With air distracted, yet subdued,
That wretched, erring parent stood.

His eye was fix'd, and bent his ear,
His guest's retiring steps to hear,
Though like a quick and piercing dart,
Each sent a quivering through his heart;
When first that wild vibration ceased,
The floor with rapid steps he paced;
And thoughts of agonizing pain
Flitted like wild-fire through his brain.

How should he give his child, his pride,
To be a branded outlaw's bride?
How could her purity have part
In Herman's cold, perverted heart?—

Then rush'd back memories of youth,
When earth was heaven, and man was truth,
And *her* he loved, too pure for life,
Too gentle for its toil and strife,
She, who, unheeding slander's tongue,
Still to her lord had fondly clung—
Her, he had dared to scorn, deride,
Her, who had suffer'd, wept, and *died!*

While o'er his mind these memories stole,
He groan'd in agony of soul,
"My child! no—never shalt thou be
Heir to thy mother's misery!
These aged eyes had rather weep
O'er thy dark bed of endless sleep."
Then o'er these better feelings came
The ghosts of penury and shame;
He saw his gold another's prey,
His lands, his titles torn away,
Himself the theme of public scorn,
His daughter friendless and forlorn,
And then he whisper'd, "I have sworn!"
But why this picture longer view?
Or why this painful theme pursue?
Oh! rather let us weep that he
Who might allied to angels be
Will sully thus the spark divine,
Imprison'd in its earthly shrine,
And in compassion drop the veil
O'er this sad portion of our tale.
Now let us seek the lonely bower
Where, at this silent midnight hour,
So sweetly sleeps the fair Lenore.
A silver lamp, with flickering beam,
Now dies, now starts with sudden gleam,
Diffusing o'er the vaulted room
Or wavering light, or partial gloom.
Near, on the oaken table, lie
Her crucifix and rosary,
And the small lute, whose golden string
Hath echoed to her evening hymn.

Her head is resting on her hand,
Her hair, escaping from its band,
Falls in rich masses on her neck,
Her fair white brow, and flushing cheek;
The long, dark lashes of her eye
On their fair pillow trembling lie,
Her lips half part, and you can trace
A smile of pleasure on her face.

She dreams—her soul hath pass'd away,
Far from its lovely shrine of clay,
Scenes of enjoyment to explore,
Where waking fancies dare not soar.

She dreams—what soft, subduing thought
Hath her unfetter'd spirit caught?
She whispers "Erstein!"—ah! sweet one,
Thou know'st not what this hour hath done!
What cloud hath dimm'd thy fortune's star,
And *his* thou lovest dearer far!

Dream on! for thou wilt wake to weep,
When morn dispels that balmy sleep,
And in thy pilgrimage of pain
Thou ne'er may'st dream so sweet again.
Hark! 't is the night-breeze, as it twines
Round the tall lattice, wreath'd with vines.
Again! arouse thee, sweet Lenore,
A step is in the corridor.
It pass'd along the echoing floor,
And paused beside the maiden's door,
And from beneath, a brilliant stream
Of wavering light was seen to gleam.
The door unclosed—the torch's fire
Reveal'd its bearer—'t was her sire!
With trembling hand he strove to shade
The beams which through the apartment stray'd,
And o'er the placid sleeper play'd;
Then to her side he softly came,
And moved the shadow from its flame.

She woke—her night-robe closer drew,
A hurried glance around her threw;
Then, with a troubled, anxious gaze,
She scann'd each feature of his face.
"Why come at midnight to thy child,
With cheek so pale, and eye so wild?"
"My daughter, rise!—thou need'st not fear,
But *I* must speak, and *thou* must hear."

Then gave he to her listening ears
A tale of doubts and cares and fears;
Of future wretchedness and pain,
Of threaten'd penury and disdain,
An exile from their native hearth,
And how a generous friend stepp'd forth,
Turn'd from their heads this direful fate,
And freely ransom'd his estate.

And how, in an unguarded hour,
When gratitude alone had power,
He swore by every sacred name
To grant whatever he might claim;
How, while he listen'd in despair,
Did Herman claim his daughter fair;
And he was bound, by all that 's dear,
That solemn promise to revere;
And then, with tears and sighs he said,
"If thou dost love this aged head,

Preserve my wealth, my peace, my life,
And be my kind preserver's wife."

With cheeks and brow as snow-wreath pale,
His daughter heard this fearful tale.
So suddenly that dread blow came,
It struck like palsy on her frame.
Through her veins crept an icy chill,
As if her very heart stood still,
And nought was heard the calm to break,
When her old sire had ceased to speak;
But though her fix'd and glaring eye
No outward object could descry,
Before her spirit's glance, a throng
Of vivid pictures swept along.

She saw the shaded bower, the grove
Where first young Erstein "whisper'd love;"
She saw his dark, reproachful eye
Upraised to hers in agony;
And then a sterner vision came
Of him her fancy dared not name.
She saw his tall and muffled form,
She saw his withering smile of scorn,
She saw—"Lenore!"—her father spoke—
The spell which bound her tongue was broke.
She knelt his bending form beside,
And thus in faltering accents cried:

"My father! canst thou doom so sore
A trial to thine own Lenore?
Is there no spot of refuge still?
Is poverty so great an ill?
To pomp and wealth thy heart is cold—
Yield up to *him* thy hoarded gold!
What carest thou for state or pride,
If *I* am ever by thy side?
Give him thine all, and let us go
Far from this darkest, deadliest foe!
Thou shalt have peace, and I will be
A more than comforter to thee!"

"My child, I cannot change thy lot—
Thou speakest of thou know'st not what!
How wouldst thou hear thy father's name,
Branded with infamy and shame?"

To his dark mantle she had clung,
Now to her feet she swiftly sprung!
A tear had trembled in her eye,
But now she dash'd it firmly by;
Her cheek had blanch'd with fear before,
But now that paleness was no more!
With form erect, and glance of fire,
She gazed upon her cowering sire,
As though her piercing eye could see
His heart's remotest secresy.

A dark and dread suspicion stole
Like burning lava o'er her soul.
"Why is that fear upon his face?
Why should my father dread disgrace?
He, I had thought, no shame could dim,
Why, why should shame descend on him?
What is this mystery, and how
Can I avert this dreaded blow?
I know not, and because mine eye
May not the source of ill descry,
Shall I the power of good forego,
And plunge him into deeper woe?"
Her pure affection answer'd "No!"

If he were noble, as she deem'd,
The path of right most open seem'd,
To chase each shadow from *his* eyes,
E'en at this fearful sacrifice;
If he deserved the meed of shame,
Was not that pathway still the same?
A moment's calm was in her brain,
She dared not pause for thought again,
But springing to her father's side,
She whisper'd, "I will be his bride!"

She heeded not his fond caressing,
She heeded not his parting blessing—
The die was cast!—and there she bent,
Fix'd as a marble monument,
Nought but her quick and gasping breath
Revealing there was life beneath.

Her father left that fatal spot—
She was alone, yet knew it not,
Till his quick footstep as it pass'd,
Dissolved the fearful charm at last,
And sent a wild and burning glow
Through the full arteries of her brow;
Then came affliction's sweet relief,
Weeping, soft child of stern-eyed grief,
That lulls the passions into rest,
And soothes the mourner's tortured breast.

When the first agony was past
Her gushing tears flow'd long and fast,
And with thanksgiving fervent, deep,
She own'd the privilege to weep.

Alas! frail flower! her life had been
One bright, unchanging, tranquil scene;
Loving and loved, as wild bird gay,
Her frolic childhood pass'd away;
And when her stronger mind could feel
More deep emotions o'er it steal,
When her pure heart look'd forth for one,
To rest her pure affections on,
Then did her trusting spirit find
An answering chord in Erstein's mind;

And childhood's laughing glance and tone
Gave place to deeper joys alone.

And only would her cheek grow pale
To hear some wild romantic tale;
And only for imagined woe
Her sympathetic tear would flow—
Her youthful heart had never known
To sigh for sorrows of its own.

The past was all one vision bright,
A storehouse of untold delight,
To which her mind at will might stray;
And bear unnumber'd gems away;
With trusting hope and buoyant glee,
She gazed into futurity,
Nor thought that time's advancing wing
A darker moment e'er could bring.

The dream now faded from her eyes,—
She woke to life's realities!
And feelings pure, aud strong, and deep,
Rose from their long, inactive sleep,
And proudly did the maiden own
A strength within, till then unknown,
That which, secure in virtue, rose
To combat with assailing foes.

Oft would her fearful fancy shrink
Back from the gulf's tremendous brink,
And oft to reason's glance would rise
The madness of the sacrifice.
But o'er her father's aged form
There hung some dark, portentous storm!
A daughter's choice, a daughter's will
Could ward from him that nameless ill!
And thus the hapless maiden sought
To quell each wild, rebellious thought.

And morning came, and soft and still
She dawn'd above the distant hill,
Her wreaths of trembling light to twine
On the blue waters of the Rhine.
The mists which on his bosom lay,
Pass'd like an infant's dream away,
And left the sun's awakening beam
To frolic with his mighty stream.

As though to greet the dawning day,
The rolling billows curl'd in play;
And wild and murmuring tones were borne
Forth on the balmy breeze of morn.
The towering cliffs, so dark and wild,
On its rude shores in masses piled,
Touch'd by her gentle influence, smiled;
And the young flowers the rocks beneath
Woke at the dawn's reviving breath,

And on their leaves, so soft and bright,
Hung tears of worship and delight.

When all is gay with nature's smile,
Forgive me if I pause awhile,
And turn from passion, grief, unrest,
To muse upon her tranquil breast.

Nature! thou ever rollest on,
With winter's blast and summer's sun,
Untouch'd by passion's raging storm,
Rearing on high thy mystic form,
Springing anew to brighter life
Amid the world's enduring strife!
Man lives, and breathes his fleeting day,
Now sinks 'neath sorrow's chilling sway,
Now basks in pleasure's golden ray,
Then, like a snow-curl, melts away.
The piles he rear'd in swelling pride,
To strive with time's o'erwhelming tide,
Proving the weakness of his trust,
Sunk, like their builders, in the dust.

But while the fabrics, rear'd so high,
In ruins on thy bosom lie,
Thou, like some great and mystic page,
Unfoldest still from age to age,
Bearing in every line conceal'd
The wisdom ages could not yield;
Thy flowers shall bloom, thy mountains soar,
Till rolling earth shall be no more;
Thine ocean waves shall sink and rise
Till Time himself exhausted dies;
While on thy mighty bosom spread
The crumbling relics of the dead!

How doth this sweet and solemn hour
Hold o'er the heart its mystic power!
Bidding each wilder tumult cease,
To passion's whirlwind whispering "Peace!"
Calming the frantic flights of joy,
And bright'ning sorrow's downcast eye!

Oh! may it shed its influence o'er
The tortured heart of poor Lenore!
She who was wont at earliest dawn
To chase the wild bird o'er the lawn,
While the young flowers their fragrance cast
As on her fairy footstep past!
Who now, unheeding bird or flower,
Steals forth to seek her favourite bower,
To bid each cherish'd scene farewell,
And calm her heart's convulsive swell.

There, in her childhood's buoyant days,
Oft had she sung her artless lays;

And still, as time roll'd onward, there
At morn and evening would repair,
To rear, in fancy, forms most fair,
Nor dream that she could find them—air!

Once more, within her loved retreat,
She lean'd upon its flowery seat,
And mark'd the clustering vines, which sent
A grateful perfume as they bent;
Above the eastern hills of blue
The sun's broad orb more brilliant grew,
And many a rich and gorgeous ray
Full on the glistening forests lay;
But buried in her lonely bower,
She heeded not the passing hour!

The vines beside her loudly stirr'd
But not a sound her ear had heard;
A step seem'd hast'ning to the spot,
But still the maiden mark'd it not—
And yet more near the intruder came;
A well-known voice pronounced her name:
She started lightly from her seat,
And blush'd—'t was Erstein at her feet!

As the bright sun-hues of the west
Fade from the snow-wreath's pallid crest,
Flitted that blush her pale cheek o'er,
And left it paler than before!
Oh, had you seen his youthful form,
Adorn'd with every manly charm,
And known his heart so bold and warm,
And, like Lenore, that heart had proved,
You would not marvel that she loved.

Bred to a fierce and martial life,
Nurtured for years on fields of strife,
A spirit fiery, bold, and high,
Was pictured in his flashing eye,
And you might think its glance implied
A soul of haughtiness and pride;
But when some gentler feelings stole
O'er the deep waters of that soul,
Then fast that quick and burning ray
Melted in tenderness away,
And lovelier seem'd its gentle beam,
Contrasted with that brilliant gleam.

When first a brave young soldier, come
From clashing sword and pealing drum,
O'er his own land once more to rove,
Then first his soul awaked to love!
And oh, what floods of pure delight
Burst in upon his spirit's sight!
What depths of joy, unknown before,
Oped in the presence of Lenore!

Her gentle influence suppress'd
Each sterner passion in his breast,
And while controlling, quell'd, subdued
Each feeling, haughty, wild, or rude.
From her, unwitting, he could learn
Her father's temper dark and stern ;
And while had glided day by day
In tranquil happiness away,
He dared not break the magic spell
His ardent feelings loved too well,
By laying thoughts and hopes so bold
Before a sire so stern and cold,
Who would have deem'd it daring pride
To claim his daughter as a bride;
He who had nought to aid his claim
But love, his honour, and his name.

Thus he was wont, when morning gray
Cast o'er the hills its earliest ray,
Clad in the huntsman's sylvan gear,
To chase ('t was said) the wild-wood deer;
But ever, when his searching eye
The towers of Arnheim could descry,
He left his faithful steed to wait
Within the thicket's dark retreat,
And bounded lawn and streamlet o'er
To snatch one moment with Lenore.

This, morn with bosom bounding high,
With springing step and sparkling eye,
He came to seek her,—but in vain;
He pass'd her favourite haunts again,
Till winding down a shaded way,
Which o'er the cliff's dark bosom lay,
He turn'd the castle's rearmost tower,
And found this lone, sequester'd bower.

I may not tune my youthful string
That scene of hapless love to sing;
Song cannot well those thoughts reveal
The heart ne'er felt, and cannot feel;
Let fancy then her garland weave,
And fill the trifling void I leave.

Suffice it that with bearing high,
And sad composure in her eye,
And throbbing nerves and bursting heart,
Well did that maiden act her part,
And gave a tale of grief and fear
To Erstein's wondering, listening ear.
Not so the youth,—a burning glow
Was mounting fiercely to his brow,
And grief and anger in his eye,
Were struggling for the mastery.
When Herman's name escaped her tongue,
Quick to his feet he wildly sprung.

"In foreign lands that wretch I met;
Fiend! sordid villain! lives he yet!
Oh! were the scoffer here to meet
From this strong hand his well-earn'd fate,
How few would be the moments given
To make his spirit's peace with heaven!

"But *thou*, Lenore! my steed is nigh,
And I *will* save thee!—Dearest, fly!"
"No! Erstein, no! I'd rather die!
My fate is fix'd, my lot is cast,
Its keenest bitterness is past;
Though her heart break, the poor Lenore
Must think of thee and love no more!

"Oh, leave me! 'tis my prayer, my will;
Make not my task more dreadful still:
Thou knowest more than I would tell,
Erstein, away! farewell, farewell!"
With trembling hand, the cavalier
Dash'd from his eye the starting tear,
Bow'd on her hand his burning head,
And ere her heart could throb, had fled.

END OF CANTO FIRST.

The notes have paused—the song hath died away,
And wonldst thou wake the trembling tones again?
And while the minstrel pours his wandering lay
Bid thy warm heart re-echo to the strain?

Wouldst hear the sequel of this simple tale,
And list attentive to the voice of woe?
Weep with affection, or with fear turn pale,
And smile when riseth joy's triumphant glow?

Then will I touch the quivering harp once more,
While fancy spreads her rainbow-tinted wing,
O'er the dark vale of buried years to soar,
And back to life their faded shadows bring!
And thou must gently glance its errors o'er,
Should the untutor'd bard uncouthly sing.

CANTO SECOND.

Oh, darkly the shadows of evening fell
On forest and mountain, on streamlet and dell,
And the clouds, in masses of sombre hue,
O'er the couch of the morning their draperies threw;
And their shade fell dark on the Rhine below,
Whose billows heaved proudly and slowly, as though
The giant heart of the tempest-god
Was beating strong 'neath its swelling flood.

Its voice came up with a sullen roar
As the waves dash'd fierce on the rock-bound shore,
And the wild-bird scream'd as he skimm'd them o'er,
While the vessel which flew o'er its surface that day.
With her white wings furl'd on its dark bosom lay,

Just kissing the foam with her bending side,
As if owning the power of the lordly tide.

The morning rose meekly, and softly, and fair,
But at evening the frown of the storm-god was there,
And gladness and beauty fled back from his eye,
Like the smile from the spirit when sorrows draw nigh.
Where the sunbeams had wreathed round the mountain's tall crest
Now floated a mantle of darkness and mist,
And the wing of the tempest did fearfully fall
O'er the arches and towers of that time-honour'd hall.

The portal was shut, and the drawbridge was raised,
And no gleam of a torch from the banquet-hall blazed;
But with faces of gloom, and steps measured and slow,
The warders were pacing the gateway below,
Now silently marking the clouds overhead,
Now whispering in accents of sorrow and dread.

The hall was deserted; the court-yard alone
Heard an echoing tread on its pavement of stone,
And parties of menials were gathering there
With faces of mystery, faces of care.
Not a voice was heard but in murmurings low,
Not a torch was seen with its cheerful glow,
Save where a ray was streaming o'er
The ancient chapel's massive door,
And wandering with its glimmer faint
O'er sculptured cherubim and saint.

'Twas an ancient pile, and the creeping vine
Had begun o'er its mouldering arches to twine,
And the long bright grass unmark'd had grown
On the broken pavement of crumbling stone;
And the rude remains of a ruder day,
Shatter'd and torn 'neath its vaulted roof lay.

'Twas a solemn scene, when the ancient pile
Was glittering bright in the morning smile.
  And bold in nerve and in heart was he,
Who would dare to walk in its haunted aisle!
  For oh, it was fearful there to be
  When the night was falling gloomily;
When the tempest shriek'd round its massive wall,
And darkness enrobed it like a pall.

Why then doth light unwonted shine
From the gilded lamps on the ruin'd shrine?
And why o'er the rest of the baron's hall
Is it darkness and silence and dreariness all?
And why with that anxious and sorrowful mien,
Do the menials gaze on the desolate scene?

Alas! those chapel walls this night
Must witness a dark, unholy rite,
And the gale, which shrieks in its fitful start,
Must sing the wail of a broken heart!
And on that sacred altar, where
So soft the suppliant breathed his prayer,
A young and ardent soul must lay
A deeper sacrifice to-day—
Upon its marble bosom fling
The blushing flowers of life's warm spring,

And all the radiant garlands wove
By buoyant hope and guileless love.

Alas, that man's unhallow'd hand
The spirit's sacred veil should rend,
And for his own dark purpose tear
The warm and glowing treasures there;
Then as in mockery dare to twine,
Upon his Maker's holy shrine,
Those pure and fond affections, given
To make this weary earth a heaven.

When last those crumbling walls had heard
Or muffled tread or whisper'd word,
A funeral wail had fill'd the pile,
A train of mourners fill'd the aisle,
And there in solemn pomp interr'd
A distant kinsman of their lord.

Thus still upon the shrouded wall
Hung the black draperies, like a pall,
In long unmoving masses, save
When the chill wind its folds would wave,
And swelling slow the dismal screen
Betray the shatter'd stones between.

Tall torches burn'd the shrine before,
Casting their rays the chapel o'er,
And shedding pale and sickly light
Upon the scowling brow of night!
While, from each lofty arch, the eye
Could mark the thick clouds passing by,
In blackening masses, wildly driven
Athwart the frowning face of heaven.

The vaulted ceiling echoed round
Each clanking tread, or mutter'd sound,
And the blast which crept o'er the pavements bare,
And waved the torches' flickering glare,
Wail'd in a sad and thrilling tone,
Like a departed spirit's moan.

Beside the altar stood its priest,
His wan hands folded on his breast,
The quivering torchlight o'er him playing,
His gray locks round his forehead straying.
And his eye wandering here and there,
With anxious and unsettled air;
And ever, as its glance would fall
On Herman's form, so grim and tall,
He mutter'd, turn'd in shuddering haste,
And sign'd the cross upon his breast.

Well might the priest instinctive turn,
From gazing on a face so stern;
For oh, it told of storms within,
The strife of passion, pride, and sin;
More fearful, more appalling far,
Than the fierce tempest's raging war.

With hurried steps he paced awhile
The grass-grown pavements of the aisle,

And on the open portal nigh
His keen glance fell impatiently,
Till his dark brow yet darker lower'd,
And his hand fiercely grasp'd his sword.

"If he should dare deceive me! then
He'll find the lion in his den!"
Scarce were the startling accents o'er,
When darkening shadows fill'd the door;—
It was the baron and Lenore.

A large dark mantle, closely drawn,
Conceal'd the maiden's fragile form;
But her measured step was firmer far
Than the trembling tread of her aged sire,
And she came with a calm and unfaltering air
To offer up all that was dear to her there.

And when she stood the shrine beside,
A sad and self-devoted bride,
She clasp'd her hands, and raised on high
The thrilling glance of her tearless eye,
And the stern bridegroom shrunk below
That look of fix'd and speechless woe.

But the keen pang pass'd quickly o'er,
And left her tranquil as before:
Her pallid fingers gently press'd
The clasping jewel on her breast,
And the dark mantle falling back,
Reveal'd her bridal robe of *black!*
The massive folds hung drooping there
Around her form, so slight and fair,
As the sad cypress in its gloom
O'er the white marble of the tomb.

In unconfined and native grace
Her long dark tresses veil'd her face,
Contrasting with the cheek and brow
So pallid and so deathlike now,
And casting round her, as they stray'd,
A waving and a dreamlike shade.
Thus stood she, motionless and still,
Like some pale form of Grecian skill,
Placed by the matchless sculptor there,
A breathing image of despair.

One torturing, agonizing day
Had quell'd the heart so light and gay,
And given her mien a bearing high
Of calm and thoughtful dignity.

The baron started as his eye
Fell on her sombre drapery:
"Lenore," he whisper'd, "why to-day
Assume such ominous array?
Couldst thou not find a bridal dress
More fitting such a scene as this?"

She bent her dark and earnest gaze
A moment on her father's face,
As if her senses could not hear
The words which fell upon her ear,
Then said, with quick, convulsive start,
"And wouldst thou gild a bleeding heart?
A broken spirit wouldst thou fold
In sparkling robes of tinsell'd gold?
'T were mockery! this is fittest guise
To deck a living sacrifice."

The baron turn'd in sudden thought
To Herman's towering form, and sought
To melt that heart, more hard than steel,
By one long look of mute appeal,
As half expecting to receive
Some blessed signal of reprieve;
But his knit brow and flushing eye
Reveal'd his dark and stern reply,
And the priest oped the sacred book
With pale and hesitating look.
The thunder's deep and muttering tone
Broke on the listening ear alone;
He paused, bent low his moisten'd brow,
And read with quivering voice and slow.
While yet the feeble accents hung
Unfinish'd on his faltering tongue;
Through the tall arches flashing came
A broad and livid sheet of flame,
Playing with fearful radiance o'er
The upraised features of Lenore,
The shrinking form of her trembling sire,
The bridegroom's face of scowling ire,
And the folded hands, and heaving breast,
And prophet-like mien of the aged priest!

'T was a breathless pause,—but a moment more,
And that fierce, unnatural beam was o'er,
And a stunning crash, as if earth were driven
On thundering wheels to the gates of heaven,
Burst, peal'd, and mutter'd, long and deep,
Then sinking, growl'd itself to sleep,
And all was still;—the priest first broke
Th' oppressive silence as he spoke:
"Both heaven and earth their powers unite
Against this dark, unhallow'd rite!
A voice without, a voice within,
Hath told me that the deed were sin!
Though death and danger bar my way,
I will not—dare not disobey!"

A cloud more dark than the tempest now
Was gathering sternly on Herman's brow:
"Priest! madman! hypocrite! proceed!
Or blows shall mend thy coward creed!"
"For God's sake, peace!" the baron cried,
And closer drew to Herman's side.
One moment, peace! for hark! I hear
Loud cries come nearer and more near!"

"Fool!" 't is the wailing of the blast,
Which sweeps these echoing ruins past!
I brook no dallying! Deal thou fair,
Or by yon heaven, old man, I swear,
Thou shalt have reason to beware!"
Still did the cowering baron stand,
With fixed eye and upraised hand,
As one who bends an earnest ear
Some faint and distant sound to hear.

And while he listen'd, by degrees
That sound came swelling on the breeze.
Now low and hoarse, now shrill and loud,
Like mingled voices of a crowd;
And as more near the tones were heard,
Did Herman fiercely grasp his sword,
As if preparing to chastise
Whate'er should bar his destined prize!
And louder still the clamour rose,
Like mingled sounds of shouts and blows,
And on that tide of tumult came
The baron's and the bridegroom's name.

One moment struck with mute surprise,
Each raised to each his wondering eyes;
But Herman, roused to action first,
Forth from the group infuriate burst;
When, ere the baron reach'd his side,
The low-brow'd portal open'd wide,
And a menial, pale with breathless haste,
Wounded and bleeding, forward press'd:
Fly to the rescue, baron, fly!
Ere all thy faithful followers die!
For armed men the moat have pass'd,
Have gain'd the inner court at last,
And fight and clamour for thy guest!"

A wild and bitter laughter rung
From Herman's lips ere forth he sprung.
"And so my comrades come to trace
Their worthy leader's lurking-place?
'T is well! not yet my race is run,
And dearly shall my life be won!"

The baron and his guest have gone;
The bride and priest are here alone!
How doth that fragile plant sustain
Its courage in this hour of pain?
Perplex'd, bewilder'd, and amazed,
Upon the shifting scene she gazed,
And only felt, with quick delight,
That he whose presence seem'd a blight
To chill each heart with shuddering fear,
That *he* no more was lingering near.

She breathed one deep and thrilling groan,
And sank upon the shatter'd stone!
She had nor power nor will to rise,
But with clasp'd hands, and straining eyes

Fix'd on the portal, did she wait
The coming crisis of her fate.

The wind rush'd in from the open'd door,
And the red torchlight was no more,
And the rude pile was dark, save where
The lightning spread its ghastly glare,
Or from the crowded court-yard came
Some broad and glancing stream of flame.

The wounded man's expiring groan
Seem'd echoed from the roof of stone;
And louder yet the piercing din
Burst on the listening pair within.
The stone-paved court alternate rang
With clashing steel, and shout, and clang;
And waving wildly to and fro,
The torches spread their fiery glow,
Casting o'er every point of sight
A glaring and unearthly light;
While, as the fearful shouts did rise
In blended tumult to the skies,
The spirit of the midnight storm
Rear'd on the clouds his black'ning form,
And with each cry which swell'd the gale
Mingled his wild and shrieking wail.

Now closer drew the assailing band,
With sword to sword, and hand to hand,
And fiercely toward the chapel pressed,
Where stood the baron and his guest.
Herman, with fix'd and cautious eye
Beheld his furious foes draw nigh,
And vow'd in this unequal strife
Not he alone should part with life.

Nearer they came, with shout and cry,
"Down with the traitor! caitiff, die!"
And if a moment more had sped,
The wretch had number'd with the dead;
When, with a voice deep-toned and loud,
A tall form issued from the crowd,
Press'd firmly through the rushing tide,
And springing close to Herman's side,
In calm commanding accents cried:

"And are ye men? Bear back, I say!
Ye throng like tigers on their prey!
Bear back a space, and he or I
In fair and equal fight shall die!"

As waves retire with sullen roar,
From meeting with the rock-bound shore,
The crowd bore back with mutterings low,
In waving columns, long and slow,
And stood, with eager gaze, to wait
The youthful champion's coming fate.

The stranger raised his sword, when nigh
There burst a low and thrilling cry;

He turn'd — a wretch unseen before,
Still linger'd by the chapel door,
And raised in air his gleaming blade
Above the baron's aged head.
One spring—one stroke—with piercing yell,
And long deep groan the miscreant fell;
And the young warrior stood before
His dark-brow'd combatant once more!

Herman, with eager look, intent
Upon his foe his keen eye bent;
And while he thus his form survey'd,
His quivering lip his rage betrayed;
Then forth in furious haste he sprang,
Till the young stranger's armour rang
With his quick strokes' incessant clang.

Regardless to preserve his own,
He sought the stranger's life alone,
With panting breast and flashing eye,
And all a madman's energy;
While calm and firm his foe repaid
Each stroke with true unerring blade.

A few, but fearful moments pass'd,
Till blind with headlong rage at last,
Herman, with desperate fierceness, press'd,
And aim'd a quick blow at his breast;
The youth beheld, sprung lightly round,
Dash'd the rais'd weapon to the ground,
And while the fragments scatter'd wide,
He sheathed his sword in Herman's side!
Then bending o'er his fallen foe,
Whisper'd in accents stern and low,
"Herman! thy miscreant life I spare!
But should we meet again—beware!"
Then gliding through the low-arch'd door,
His manly form was seen no more!

With straining eye and changeless mien
Lenore had marked this fearful scene,
Till her chill'd heart seem'd palsied there,
With terror bordering on despair.
But when the gallant stranger came,
A something whisper'd Erstein's name,
And when beneath the dubious light
She saw him conqueror in the fight,
Her heart seem'd bursting with delight.
Hope, with its trembling radiance, stole
O'er the dark desert of her soul—
Her head droop'd lightly on her breast,
As when an infant sinks to rest;
Her heart gave one convulsive thrill,
Leap'd—flutter'd wildly—and was still.
The courage grief could not destroy
Bow'd to intensity of joy.
The priest, unheeding all beside,
Bent sadly o'er the fainting bride,

With mystic sign and mutter'd prayer,
And all an anxious father's care;
But as he knelt, absorb'd the while,
A quick step echoed through the aisle—
A burst of joy assailed his ear;
He turn'd—the stranger youth was near!

A moment more—his stalwart arm
Had raised the maiden's drooping form,
And turning swift, his eagle eye
Roam'd o'er the walls inquiringly.
The priest observed his doubtful air,
And clearly read his meaning there:
Trembling, he raised the massive pall
Which hung beside the crumbling wall,
And oped a secret door that led
Within a thicket's tangled shade.

The youth bow'd low his plumed head,
And 'neath the ruin'd portal fled!
The priest conceal'd it as before,
And turning, past the draperies o'er,
But breathed a low and smother'd cry,
As, fix'd upon that secret door,
His own met Herman's baleful eye.

It burn'd with hatred's living flame,
And rage convulsed his giant frame,
A curse hung quivering on his tongue;
Each nerve to dark revenge was strung;
And the full arteries of his brow,
Were swelled like livid serpents now.
The boiling blood with sudden start
Had gather'd fiercely at his heart,
And lent his cheeks and lips a hue
Of ghastly and unearthly blue.
But quick the coward tide return'd,
And through his veins like wildfire burn'd
And o'er his features crept the while,
Their sneering and revengeful smile—
When in that crowded court he fell
Beneath that foe he knew too well,
He sought to find a safe retreat
From clashing swords and trampling feet—
And while he lean'd, with whirling brain,
The portal's sculptured arch beside,
Saw with a rage surmounting pain,
The flight of Erstein and his bride.

And where hath he fled with his lovely one, say?
And where are they wending their perilous way?
The lover hath mounted his faithful steed,
He is bounding away with the lightning speed!
One arm is supporting the rescued bride,
One hand is at freedom his bridle to guide,
And his spurs are dash'd in the charger's side.

Beneath them the turf, and above them the sky,
Away and away on their pathway they fly!

The sound of the tumult grew fainter and low,
And faded in distance the torches' red glow,
And in silence unbroken the fugitive sped,
Save when the low thunder was growling o'erhead,
Or the tempest was wailing, now shrill, now deep,
As it crept in the arms of the morning to sleep.

While the black clouds were rolling in masses away,
O'er the hills of the east rose a faint streak of gray;
And as onward they flew, on the dim air was borne
The soft cooling breath of a bright summer's morn!
Their speed as they bounded the forest path o'er
Recall'd the faint throb to the heart of Lenore,
But her senses bewilder'd long laboured in vain
To dispel the wild fancies which thronged on her brain;
And when she awoke to the real at last,
Oh what mingled emotions were stirr'd in her breast,
Till her heart overflowing found soothing relief
In tears of united thanksgiving and grief!
She remember'd the scene in the old ruin'd aisle,
And silently pray'd for the victor the while,
Then she thought of her sire, and she shrank from his side,
And "My father! my father!" she bitterly cried.

"Fear not for your father! yon furious band
Sought nothing but haply his gold at his hand!
It was Herman they sought, and they long'd for the blood
Of that traitor alike to the vile and the good!"

"And whither art bearing me, Erstein, and why?
And where shall Lenore for a resting-place fly?"
"We are hasting away to my rude mountain tower!
'T is a rugged retreat for so fragile a flower;
But my sister shall cherish the blossom with care
Till it blooms again, brighter and sweeter than e'er."
"And how didst thou come in that moment of gloom,
To snatch me away from my terrible doom?"

"Lenore, my beloved! thou rememberest the hour
When I parted from thee in the myrtle-wreath'd bower;
That hour which was fated awhile to destroy
Each hope of the future, each vision of joy;
I mounted my charger, I knew not how,
  And I rode like a madman, I knew not where;
For my brain was hot with a fiery glow,
  And my heart was chill'd with a cold despair;
I abandoned the reins to my faithful steed,
And we bounded away with a maniac speed,
Till exhausted and worn with exertion we stood
On the barren skirts of a lonely wood;
'Twas deep immersed in a mountain dell,
  On the rocky banks of a brawling stream,
Which o'er a dark precipice rapidly fell,
  With dashing and foaming, and murmur and gleam,
I threw myself down by a rock-cover'd cave,
And silently bent o'er the breast of the wave,
And more calm in my veins did the life-current flow,
While the spray dashed cool on my feverish brow.

Of Herman I thought, and my pulses beat higher,
And my bosom throbb'd wild with the "tempest of ire!"
But then o'er my fancy that loved image crept,
And forgive me, Lenore, if in anguish I wept!
While musing thus sadly, I started to hear
The sound of rude voices assailing my ear.
I turn'd,—from the cavern beside me they came,—
And the speaker named Herman's detestable name!
I listen'd—but, dearest, so stainless thou art,
In each word of thy lips, and each thought of thy heart
That could I repeat, I should tell thee in vain
Of a language so loose, so impure and profane!
Then listen, Lenore, as I briefly shall tell
The meaning I gain'd from their words as they fell.
They were robbers—a fearful and ruffian band,
Most sordid of heart, and most bloody of hand,
And Herman had been, for full many a year,
Their chief in each deed of rebellion and fear!
Yes! he whose presumption hath claim'd thee as bride
To that lawless and desperate band was allied;
Meet comrades for one whose degenerate mind
Is stain'd with each crime which can blacken mankind.
Thus a stranger to mercy, a stranger to fear,
He had rush'd on, uncheck'd in his reckless career,
Till, unheeding the pledge which at entrance he gave,
In secret he fled from the robbers' wild cave,
Bearing with him away their iniquitous spoil,
The fruits they had reap'd from unhallowed toil!
Oh long did they labour, but labour'd in vain,
Some trace of their villanous chieftain to gain,
Till a comrade return'd with the tidings at last,
That the Baron of Arnheim received him as guest,
And this eve was to join his perfidious hand
To the fairest flower of his native land.
Then they vow'd revenge, and they fearfully swore
That long ere the shadows of midnight were o'er,
They would give to their leader, false Herman, the meed
He had won by the coward and traitorous deed!
They resolved to assemble at eventide there,
And in arms to the Castle of Arnheim repair,
To recover the gold they had lost, and assuage,
In the blood of their chieftain, their hatred and rage.
Thus said they, Lenore; and now eager I heard
Each ruffian voice, and each half-suppress'd word;
For while o'er my senses their dark import stole,
A light broke in on my desperate soul,
And methought I discovered a path to guide
My steps once more to my dear one's side.
I could join their band at the castle gate;
I could rescue thee from thy dreadful fate,
And while they were in fury revenging their wrong,
  And searching for gold 'neath each time-worn wall,
I could plunge unseen 'mid the motley throng,
  And bear away that which was dearer than all!
Oh, blest be our Lady! who guided me well,
  And supported thy soul on this terrible night!
But Lenore! my beloved! thy cheek is too pale,
  And the tear steals adown it—oh say, was I right?"

She spoke no word, but he read her reply
In the timid glance of her downcast eye,
And the blush which sprung to her varying cheek,
In token of thoughts which she dared not speak!
He saw the glance, and he felt its charm,
And he folded the mantle more close round her form,
And silently spurring his charger again,
They bounded away over forest and plain.

And softly and meekly the morning light
Stole up from the arms of that storm-toss'd night,
And faintly trembled its dawning beam
On each sparkling valley and purling stream.
And danced on the leaves of the forest trees,
As they slowly waved in the sighing breeze,
And with dripping branches bended low,
As if weeping the fate of each fallen bough.

"Lenore!" said Erstein, "Lenore, behold,
How each cloud from the glance of the morning hath roll'd;
How the storm of the midnight has glided away,
And no traces are left of its passage to-day,
Save a pensive hue, which is stealing o'er,
And making all nature more fair than before.

"The whispering gale that is floating past,
Is all that remains of the howling blast,
And the sparkling waves of yon tiny river
Rush onward more swiftly and gaily than ever;
While the emerald turf on the graceful hill
Outrivals in splendour the dew-dripping rill,
And the trees round its base with their broad arms cling,
Like the diamond crown of a giant king.
'T is a beautiful type of our fate, Lenore,
For our storm of misfortune has glided o'er,
And the joyous morning of hope and love
Is dawning our radiant pathway above;
And life shall flow on with its dancing stream,
With murmur and sparkle, with music and gleam,
And the glittering dew-drops alone shall last,
To remind our souls of the storms that have past."

A sunbeam of gladness, a smile from the soul,
O'er the face of Lenore insensibly stole;
They were slowly ascending a verdant hill,
At whose base there rippled a murmuring rill,
And she gazed on the vale they had left, till her sight
Seem'd melting in tears of exquisite delight.

But she suddenly utter'd a smother'd cry,
As a figure advancing arrested her eye;
'T was a horseman, who spurr'd on his foaming steed
With a desperate madman's fiery speed,
While far beyond, on the level green,
A waving line was distinctly seen.

Scarce had the shriek escaped her tongue,
Ere to his feet young Erstein sprung,
And led the wearied steed, which bore
The fragile form of poor Lenore,
Where a dark thicket rose in pride
The leaping, brawling stream beside.

"'T is Herman! and the hour is come
To seal or his or Erstein's doom!
If victor, well! but if I die,
Thine only resource is to fly."

He said, and press'd her hand the while
With fervent grasp and cheering smile:
Then ere had fled that earnest tone,
The trembling maiden was alone.

Meanwhile, with fierce and maniac haste,
The furious Herman forward press'd,
Clear'd the small stream with sudden bound,
And leap'd impetuous to the ground.

Oh, 'twas a dark and fearful sight!
His writhing face was ghastly white;
His horseman's cloak was deeply dyed
With the red life-blood from his side;
His step was hurried and untrue;
His scowling brow was bathed in dew,
And when he pass'd his fingers o'er,
They left its surface stain'd with gore.

Still did his rigid features wear
Their darkly biting, withering sneer,
And in his eye a fiendish glare
Revenge and hate had kindled there.
He wav'd his glancing sword on high,
And cried, "Defend thy life, or die!"
"I fight not," Erstein answered slow,
"A frantic or a bleeding foe!"

A demon's rage fill'd Herman's eye,
Which flash'd around him fearfully.
"Then in thy coward folly die!"
Thus did he yell, and with the word
Plunged at his breast his ponderous sword.
The youth, who mark'd each look with care,
Turn'd—and the weapon smote the air;
Then, ere a second stroke was made,
Swift as the wind unsheath'd his blade;
And springing forth, with gesture light,
Closed firmly in the desperate fight.

How did those sounds of doubt and fear
Ring on the maiden's listening ear!
How did her veins convulsive swell,
As, fast and wild, the stern blows fell!
But passion's rage must yield at length
To calmer reason's vigorous strength,
And Erstein's steel again was dew'd
With the fierce Herman's gushing blood.

Breathing one quick and startling yell,
Upon the trampled sward he fell,
And the dark life-stream gurgling fast,
Blent with the dew-drops on his breast,
And, as the current swifter sped,
Tinged the light sparkling stream with red!
His clench'd hands held, with rigid clasp,
The turf and flowers within their grasp,

And the cold, clammy, deathlike dew
In large drops gather'd on his brow.

Then a dark shade of fell despair
Chased from its glance its frenzied glare,
And yielded to his upraised eye
A look of helpless agony;
It roll'd around from place to place,
And rested last on Erstein's face;
Then shrunk from the moment's encounter again
With a mingled thrill of remorse and pain;
Then he strove to speak, but the accents hung
Unform'd on his quivering, palsied tongue.

Erstein the wounded sufferer gave
A cooling draught from the crystal wave,
And raising his form on the rivulet's brink,
Oh long and deeply did he drink,
Then, as o'ercome with torturing pain,
Sank on the crimson'd turf again.

Convulsions o'er his features past,
And, with a fearful strength, at last
He started—clench'd his blood-stain'd vest,
And groan'd, "This mountain on my breast!"
Erstein bent o'er him—"Herman! now
We stand no longer foe to foe;
Tell me, if to one earthly thing
Thy parting spirit still doth cling;
One deed, which, ere thy race was run,
Thou wouldst have purposed to have done;
One word of penitence to send
An injured or deluded friend;
And here I pledge my promise free,
That act shall be performed for thee!
Aught that may cast a softening ray
Around thy spirit's fearful way,
Or soothe that dark and drear abode
Unbrighten'd by the smiles of God!"

"Of God! *Who* spoke of God?—I own
No God but reckless chance alone;
No *hell* more rife with pain and fear
Than that which burns and tortures *here!*
Though I *could* sink to black despair,
If I met not *his* spirit there!

"Away, away! each look, each word
Pierces my bosom like a sword!
'T is *thou* whom I have injured, thou
Whose arm, in justice, laid me low!
Nay, leave me not, but come more near,
For my breath fails me—bend thine ear!
And ere from life for ever freed,
My soul shall boast one blameless deed!
Child of a rich and ancient line,
Arnheim, its titles, lands, are thine!"

"Thou ravest!"—"List! if there be time
Thine ears shall drink my tale of crime!—
I seem'd thy father's friend, and he
Believed me all fidelity;

He perished in a foreign land,
And, Erstein, by this blood-stain'd hand?
Ay, shudder!—mark me well, and trace
The murderer's impress on my face!
Yes! 'neath a friend's disguise, there stole
A venom'd serpent to his soul!
In youth he dared to taunt me—I
Vow'd for the insult he should die!
"It's very memory pass'd from him;
And when in after years I came,
Conceal'd by friendship's mask and name,
He took me to his bosom, while
Revenge was lurking 'neath my smile.
He died!—start not, but bend thine ear,
For I *must* speak and thou *shalt* hear!
Ay, though it rends my blacken'd heart,
And tears each gaping wound apart!

"He died!—I sought, with keenest hate,
The proofs of this thy fair estate;
I kept the parchments, that I still
Might guide thy fortunes at my will.
I hated—for thy features bore
The smile, the glance thy father's wore.

"Avert that look! the memory brings
A thousand thousand scorpion stings!
Ay, ay! 'tis right, 'tis meet thy steel
This last and deadliest blow should deal!
'Tis right thy *grateful* hand should send
The death-blow to thy father's *friend!*

"But I must on!—I left that shore—
I sought my native land once more:
I join'd the robbers' desperate band;
I found the baron on thy land;
'Twas then I saw, I loved, Lenore!—
Oh heavens! and must I tell thee more?—
I play'd the baron false, and he,
The fool! the idiot! trusted me!

"Here, on my cold and labouring breast—
Raise me—here, here the parchments rest!
But my chill'd limbs grow stiff—the sand
Of life is running fast—the hand
Of death is plunging deep his icy dart—
His grasp is cold—cold—cold upon my heart!"

The youth, with fix'd and wondering eyes,
Bent o'er his form in mute surprise;
When loud, derisive laughter near,
Burst in discordance on his ear.
He rose, and saw before him stand
The dying Herman's ruffian band.

Returning from their midnight broil,
And laden with its varied spoil,
To their wild cave they led in haste
The aged baron and the priest.
But when in distance they beheld
Their leader's flight, so fierce and wild,
They turn'd, pursued, and came to see
His last, expiring agony;

And now, with laugh of scornful hate,
Like fiends, they triumph'd in his fate.
Those tones, with direst vengeance rife,
Recall'd their comrade's flickering life.
With them unnumber'd memories came—
Again he raised his bleeding frame,
Gazed wildly on the furious band,
And shook his clench'd and stiffening hand.
His cheek burn'd with a livid glow,
A black scowl gather'd on his brow,
A fierce revenge his visage fired—
He groan'd, fell backward, and expired.

Silence her breathless mantle threw
A moment o'er that lawless crew,
And awe one instant gain'd the place
Of triumph on each swarthy face.
But as the sun-ray glances past
The rugged cliff's unbending crest,
So did that faint beam disappear,
Lost in a dark demoniac sneer,
The baron and the priest alone
With trembling heard that dying groan,
And mark'd with awe-struck pitying gaze,
His stiffen'd form and ghastly face.

Erstein first broke the silence dread,
And to the outlaw'd chieftain said:
"Thou seekest spoil! dost thou behold
This jewell'd cross, this purse of gold?
These will I gladly give, to gain
Two aged captives of thy train.
High ransom take, and yield to me
The priest's and baron's liberty."

"Yon priest I had design'd to save
The contrite sinners in our cave.
Yon miser lord, to gather in
The gold our midnight frays shall win!
This had I purposed, but in truth
Thy sword hath served us well, brave youth,
By sending to the fiend, who gave,
The spirit of that scowling knave.
Bestow on us that glittering store,
And swear to seek our spoil no more,
Then will we freely yield to thee
The aged captives' liberty."

The pledge was given—the band released
The aged baron and the priest,
And sweeping round a thicket nigh,
Their dark forms vanish'd to the eye.
With heaving breast and clouded brow
The baron wander'd to and fro,
And wrung his hands with gestures wild,
And wept and cried, "my child! My child!"

Swiftly the youthful Erstein fled
To the dark wood's embowering shade,
And soon as swift return'd to lead
The fair Lenore's wearied steed.

With joyful cry and agile bound,
The maiden sprang upon the ground,
And clasp'd her father's neck around.

And o'er and o'er again he press'd
The rescued maiden to his breast,
And gazed upon her features bright
With frantic transports of delight.
"My child! my love! my own Lenore!
Come to thy father's heart once more,
Nor fear that thou again shalt be
A living sacrifice for me!
But who preserved thee? where didst thou
Find refuge on that night, and how?"

Her cheek with crimson blushes warm,
She turn'd her eye on Erstein's form.
"And by what title shall I bless?"—
"Erstein!"—He groan'd—"Alas! alas!
It is the very name, 'tis he
Whom I have heap'd with injury!
A voice, too long a slighted guest,
Once more is whispering in my breast!
And I will listen—will obey;
How shall I all these wrongs repay?"

The youth's dark eye beam'd purest fire,
And his quick pulses bounded higher.
Oh let me, let me call thee sire!"
The baron bent his wondering gaze
Upon the speaker's beaming face;
The youth was at his feet—his brow
Was burning with a crimson glow,
His lips were parted, and his cheek
Flush'd with the thoughts he could not speak,
And his dark eye was raised above,
With mingled glance of hope and love.

He turn'd to Lenore, and her downcast eye,
Her trembling frame, her heaving sigh,
Her cheek, now flush'd, now deadly pale,
In silence told the maiden's tale!

"My children be happy! henceforth to your sire
Shall your peace be his highest, his noblest desire;
He shall see you enjoy, with a rapture tenfold,
Those affections he well nigh had barter'd for gold!
And sorrow's dark pinion shall shadow no more
The loves of brave Erstein and fair Lenore."

1838.

THE END.

www.ingramcontent.com/pod-product-compliance
Lightning Source LLC
LaVergne TN
LVHW050517100826
845148LV00002B/369

* 9 7 8 1 4 2 5 5 2 0 4 3 4 *